365 Easy
Mexican Recipes

365 Easy Mexican Recipes

Marge Poore

A JOHN BOSWELL ASSOCIATES BOOK

HarperCollins*Publishers*

Dear Reader:

We welcome your recommendations for future 365 Ways books. Send your suggestions and a recipe, if you'd like, to Cookbook Editor, HarperCollins Publishers, 10 East 53rd Street, New York, NY 10022. If we choose your title suggestion or your recipe we will acknowledge you in the book and send you a free copy.

Thank you for your support.

Sincerely yours,
The Editor

Series Editor: Susan Wyler
Design: Nigel Rollings
Index: Maro Riofrancos

LIBRARY OF CONGRESS CATALOGING-IN-PUBLICATION DATA
Poore, Marge
    365 easy Mexican recipes / Marge Poore.
        p.   cm.
    "A John Boswell Associates book."
    Includes index.
    ISBN 0-06-016963-X
    1. Cookery, Mexican.   I. Three hundred and sixty-five easy Mexican recipes.
II. Title.
TX716.M4P66   1994
641.5972—dc20
                                                                    93-29183
                                                                         CIP

Contents

Tasty tidbits for nibbling, passing at parties, and sampling for a light lunch. Traditional Mexican and newer Southwestern-style appetite teasers include Baked Beef and Bean Dip, Mushroom Empanadas with Chipotle Chile, Nachos (of course), and Chicken Taquitos.

Quick and easy recipes, such as Cold Avocado Soup, Gazpacho Pacifico, Pinto Bean Soup, Red Devil Tomato Soup with Crisp Tortilla Bits, and Cream of Zucchini and Onion Soup, can start a savory supper or serve as a wholesome meal in a bowl.

Choose first courses, side salads, and light luncheon dishes from an assortment of recipes that includes Avocado and Papaya Salad, Ceviche, Cantaloupe and Shrimp with Citrus Vinaigrette, Chicken Taco Salad, Jicama and Orange Salad, and Spicy Crab Cakes with Chipotle Mayonnaise.

Add zest to almost any food you cook with these bright ideas for serving up flavor: Red Chile Sauce, Green Enchilada Sauce, Black Bean Salsa, Mango Lime Salsa, Quick Mole, and Fresh Pineapple Salsa, to name just a few.

Fresh and sparkling Mexican seafood shines with wholesome, sprightly taste. Sample traditional recipes— Clams Mexicana, Skillet Shrimp in Garlic Sauce, and Red Snapper Veracruzana—as well as some new preparations —Fish Fillets with Toasted Garlic and Papaya Sauce and Salmon Fillet with Fresh Tomatillo Sauce.

Chicken, turkey, game hens, and duck get a zesty lift from Mexican cooking. You'll find them featured in

Chicken Fajitas, Arroz con Pollo, Maverick Turkey Chili, Turkey Cutlets with Melon Salsa, Barbecued Game Hens, and more.

Ranchero Steak with Potatoes, Ropa Vieja, Chile Verde, Drunken Pork Chops with Hominy, Grilled Butterflied Leg of Lamb, and Pork Stew with Fried Plantains, Sweet Potato, and Pineapple are a sampling of these exciting main-course meats.

Standard accompaniments to almost any Mexican meal include recipes like Refried Black Beans, Pinto Bean Casserole, Ranch Beans with Bacon, Green Rice Puebla Style, and Fiesta Rice Salad.

Here you'll find all your familiar favorites—Party-Time Beef Tacos, Swiss Enchiladas, Speedy Microwave Bean Burritos, Chicken Tamale Pie—and some tasty innovative combinations—Shrimp-Filled Chimichangas, Crab Enchiladas with Tomatillo Sauce, and Vegetarian Enchiladas.

Explore a wide variety of vegetables in exciting new ways in dishes like Chayotes with Tomato and Cheese Topping, Baked Corn Casserole, Chiles Rellenos with Cheese, Golden Plantains, and Cauliflower with Carrots and Jalapeños.

They are also exceptionally tasty when prepared in breakfast and brunch dishes like Huevos Rancheros, Baked Eggs with Black Beans and Tomato Sauce, Scrambled Eggs with Chorizo, and Sunrise Chilaquiles.

Breads, muffins, biscuits, and cookies featured here include savory Jalapeño Corn Bread, Quick-Rise Bolillos, and Blue Corn Muffins as well as tempting sweets, such as Mexican Almond Cookies, Coyote Gingerbread Cookies, and Chocolate Meringues, to enjoy with a cup of hot chocolate or espresso.

365 Easy
Mexican Recipes

Introduction to Mexican Cooking

Authors, chefs, and travelers have been spreading the word that Mexico has a remarkable ancient cuisine, which combines its unique native ingredients with European products that arrived after the discovery of the New World. In pre-Columbian times, Mexico's cuisine flourished using products the rest of the world had yet to see: corn, beans, tomatoes, chocolate, chiles, sweet potatoes, squash, pineapple, vanilla, coffee, turkey, and much more. The indigenous foods tasted by the explorers for the first time were transported to Spain and other European destinations, and eventually caused culinary transformations worldwide. Of course, ships traveled both ways, and Mexico's cuisine was also greatly enriched by the products from European markets that spilled onto its shores, especially pigs, cattle, chickens, rice, and new varieties of fruits and vegetables.

The merging of this bounty of ingredients has produced an exciting, colorful, flavorful, richly seasoned, and sometimes spicy cuisine, which is still not very well known outside its borders. Many people still think of Mexican food as tacos, enchiladas, rice, and beans, all heaped together on one plate, buried in a hot sauce and covered with melted cheese. True Mexican plates are more artful and carefully presented. Sauces are varied in color, flavor, level of heat, and they are used with some restraint. Cheese is either absent or added with thought as to its contribution to the flavor and visual impact of the plate. Fresh salsas and beans are usually served separately.

Mexican snacks play a very important part in Mexico's eating habits. They are normally eaten as street snacks, or a quick bite, rather than a whole meal. These tacos, burritos, nachos, and the like are the foods that have become so popular in fast-food chains in this country, but they make up only a small part of the total cuisine.

Happily, word continues to spread about the variety and depth of the Mexican kitchen, and we are steadily being exposed to a wider assortment of authentic Mexican food. With the current interest in healthier diets, there is more interest in the lighter side of Mexican cooking as well.

Mexico is a huge nation, and it produces a vast number of fruits and vegetables and raises poultry and livestock; its exceptionally long coastlines offer an abundance of fresh fish and seafood. These products all find their way into the various regional foods that contribute to the uniqueness of Mexican cuisine. The original native products of corn, beans, tomatoes, and chiles, along with a few herbs and spices, weave a common thread throughout the cuisine and are largely responsible for its distinctive taste.

In *365 Easy Mexican Recipes*, I've brought together recipes from all over the country, offering samplings of regional foods, from the popular and well-known tacos and enchiladas, to lesser known specialties, such as chiles en nogada and manchamanteles, seldom offered in restaurants here. There are also recipes for newer style dishes based upon and inspired by Mexican cooking and ingredients, which we often loosely refer to as Southwestern.

Thought has been given to the availability of products and seasonings needed to achieve the flavors of real Mexican cooking. Most of the ingredients called for in this book are available in supermarkets or in Mexican specialty markets. New products are becoming more widely distributed all the time. For added convenience, a mail-order list follows the ingredients glossary. Mail-order is especially helpful to find dried chiles, Mexican chocolate, and certain special salsas your local supermarkets may not stock.

To make cooking easier, recipes are streamlined and simplified and preparation time is shortened by taking advantage of seasonal fresh produce, convenient packaged items, and canned and frozen foods. Every effort has been made to create recipes that are not too long or involved, yet still capture the tantalizing flavor of authentic Mexican cooking.

Today's trend toward healthy eating habits has also been taken into account. Vegetable oil and olive oil are used for sautéing and frying, butter and vegetable shortening for pastries and cakes. Although good-quality pork lard makes refried beans, tamales, and some other dishes taste wonderful, most Americans prefer not to use it, so you will not find lard called for in this book.

When planning a Mexican menu, balance your work time by mixing simple, quickly prepared dishes with one or two more time-consuming preparations, and look for recipes that can be done in advance. Beans and soups, for example, almost always taste better cooked a day ahead. Most desserts can be prepared ahead. Fresh salsas, salads, and cooked fish, on the other hand, are best made close to time of serving for optimum flavor and texture.

The real aim of this book is to inspire you to cook Mexican dishes you may never have experienced, by making the recipes easy enough, and yet with true Mexican taste and flair, in the hope that you'll gain a greater appreciation for this fine, festive cuisine. If you are tempted to travel and go beyond the popular Mexican resorts to experience native cuisine on its own turf, you'll have an adventure of the kind I regularly enjoy. It takes an intrepid spirit and curiosity to find wonderful regional foods, even in Mexico, but when you do, it's very rewarding.

In the meantime, cook something Mexican. Be adventurous in your own kitchen, and with 365 recipes to choose from, you'll please a lot of hungry diners.

GLOSSARY OF COMMONLY USED MEXICAN INGREDIENTS

Most of the recipes in this book use ingredients that are readily available in the United States. Some of the following items may not be familiar, but they are important to the unique flavor of Mexican cuisine. Most are stocked in supermarkets; a few require searching out in specialty markets. This listing describes the items, how they are used, and where to buy them.

AVOCADOS: Avocados are native to Mexico; through agricultural development, many new varieties now exist. For creamy texture and rich flavor, the Hass is clearly tops. When ripe, the rough and pebbly skin is almost black. It should feel solid yet yield to slight pressure, like a ripe peach. Never squeeze, since ripe avocados bruise easily and should be handled gently. To ripen avocados at home, purchase blemish-free green avocados that feel hard and put them in a paper bag at room temperature; let stand for 2 to 3 days.

CHAYOTE: This pale green vegetable with its pearlike shape is related to squash. It is indigenous to Mexico and is also known as mirliton and vegetable pear. The flavor is delicate, with a moist texture. Chayotes are used in the same way as summer squash, as well as made into a dessert by stuffing with a sweetened mixture of raisins, nuts, and spices. When buying them, look for unblemished pale green solid chayotes. To cook, cut in half and boil in salted water until crisp-tender, then peel and proceed as recipe instructs. The flat, tender seed in the center is considered quite a delicacy; it is usually consumed in the kitchen and never reaches the table. It is best not to peel chayotes raw, because the juice causes a skin irritation in some people, and peeling is much easier after cooking.

CHILES: See page 7.

CILANTRO: The herb cilantro, also called fresh coriander and Chinese parsley, is used to flavor and garnish. It has a fresh, clean taste and is one of the most distinctive flavors in Mexican foods. It is especially important in fresh spicy salsas. Cilantro is available in most supermarkets and in Hispanic and Asian markets. When purchasing, avoid limp or discolored cilantro. The leaves should look fresh and bright green. To store, rinse very well, shake off excess water, wrap in paper towels, and place in a plastic bag in the refrigerator. The herb will keep for about 5 days. Chop cilantro shortly before using because its flavor dissipates quickly.

CREMA: Mexican *crema* is thick and a bit acidy, like French crème fraîche. It is used to garnish enchiladas, tacos, chilaquiles, some snacks, and certain salads. You can make your own crema at home (see page 82) or you can substitute plain sour cream diluted with milk; use 3 to 4 tablespoons milk per cup of sour cream.

JICAMA: A large root vegetable shaped like a turnip, with tough light brown skin and white interior flesh. It is always peeled before eating and is crisp and sweet to the taste, somewhat like a fresh water chestnut. In Mexico, jicamas are very popular eaten raw, as a snack, with a squeeze of lime juice and a dash of chili powder. Occasionally they are cooked in soups or stews. A somewhat new style of cooking cuts jicama into julienne strips and sautés them in oil or butter. They become slightly limp cooked this way and are very tasty.

LARD: In much of Mexico, lard is still the chosen fat for cooking, and good-quality lard does give a delicious authentic flavor to many dishes. But current health considerations regarding fat intake in our diets have changed many cooking habits, so lard is not used in this book. Butter and vegetable shortening are used in some pastry recipes, and vegetable oil or olive oil is used in cooking.

MASA: This fresh dough is made from dried corn that is specially processed with slaked lime, which causes the kernels to swell and the skins to split, after which it is ground. It is used to make corn tortillas, tamales, and other dishes. The fresh dough can be purchased from a tortilla factory if there is one in your vicinity. Otherwise, use masa harina, which is masa that has been dehydrated into a flour, packaged, and sold with other dry flours in the baking section of markets. It is widely available and easy to use. By reconstituting it with water to make masa dough, it can be turned into corn tortillas, tamales, and other masa dishes. Store dry masa harina in a well-sealed container and keep in a cool dark cupboard. Masa harina is not the same as cornmeal, and they are not interchangeable, except possibly to use as a substitute thickener in some stews, but the flavor is different.

MOLE: Moles are complex sauces containing chiles, herbs, spices, nuts, seeds, fruits, and often chocolate, all ground together to make a paste, then blended with broth or other wet ingredients to cook and serve with meats and poultry. There are many kinds of these complex sauces known as moles, which descended from Aztec cooking. They come in many hues—black, brown, red, green, and yellow. The most famous is Mole Poblano, from the city of Puebla. The story goes that it was invented some 200 years ago by the nuns in the Convent of Santa Rosa for a very important visit by a Spanish viceroy. Their inspired dish included just about everything they had in the kitchen, even a touch of chocolate, and according to all reports, it was a huge success. Today it is commonly served in restaurants and made at home, especially for Christmas. The addition of chocolate intrigues diners as much today as it did long ago. Mole Coloradito is another favorite mole from Oaxaca, which is often called the region of the seven moles. Its recipe appears in this book. Shortcut mole is possible, too, using a prepared mole paste, available in 8-ounce jars in many supermarkets. Use the recipe for Quick Mole (page 88), or follow the instructions on the jar of mole paste.

NOPALES: The thick paddles, or leaves, of the prickly-pear cactus are called *nopales*. When cut into small pieces they are called *nopalitos*. They are used in salads, stews, and egg dishes. Nopales have a bland flavor somewhat like green beans. They are available in this country packed in 11- and 15-ounce jars. Look for those packed in water and salt only, rather than those containing onions, peppers, and vinegar. They have better color, texture, and flavor. For a first taste trial, cactus salad or cactus bits with scrambled eggs are liked very much by most people. It may seem strange to eat cactus, but most of us find them to be very good, and they are reputed to be very good for your health.

OIL: Most of the recipes in this book call for vegetable oil in cooking and in salad dressings. I recommend corn oil, safflower oil, or other light oils. Occasionally olive oil is specified, and a light-tasting good-quality olive oil is best. There is no need for rich extra-virgin olive oil, which often has too much flavor of its own for Mexican cooking.

PEPITAS: Pumpkin seeds, both roasted and salted or raw and unsalted, are used a great deal in Mexican snacking and cooking. Raw hulled unsalted pumpkin seeds are green in color. To use, they are pan-toasted and finely ground for cooked sauces, or used whole to toss into salads. Raw pepitas are available in health food stores and Mexican markets. Since pepitas turn rancid rather quickly, they should be kept in the freezer. Toasting them in a dry skillet brings out the nutty taste, which is very distinctive in the traditional cooked green sauce called *pipian*.

PLANTAINS: Plantains are large cooking bananas. They are used in both savory and sweet dishes, but are not eaten raw. When ripe, they darken in color to almost black and yield to slight pressure. Avoid those that show any sign of mold. If possible, purchase unripe ones about 1 week ahead and let stand at room temperature out of direct sunlight. Plantains are widely available in Latin American, Asian, and many supermarkets. A common way to use them is to slice into rounds, or lengthwise into quarters or halves, and fry in lard, oil, or butter; serve with rice, black beans, or stew dishes. When cooked this way they turn golden brown and are delicious. Regular bananas, barely yellow and still firm, can be substituted.

QUESO FRESCO: Queso fresco is a perishable white crumbly Mexican cheese, made from cow's milk. It is sprinkled over enchiladas, refried beans, tostadas, and salads. It is hard to find outside Mexico, so I usually substitute mild fresh goat cheese, feta mixed with dry cottage cheese to lessen the salty taste, or Italian ricotta.

TOMATILLOS: Tomatillos look like small green tomatoes covered in a papery husk; however, they are not tomatoes, but are related to the gooseberry. They are an important ingredient in Mexican cooked green sauces and fresh green salsas. Tomatillos have become very popular, and now they can be found fresh in many supermarkets. They are also available in cans in the Mexican section of markets. To use the fresh ones, remove the husks, rinse, and cook in boiling water until the bright green fades and they become slightly tender, 8 to 10 minutes. Then they are ready to puree with other ingredients to make sauces. Both fresh and canned tomatillos are used in the recipes in this book. Tomatillos are almost always cooked, but nowadays they are occasionally added raw to salads and salsas, where they add a tart, unusual taste some people enjoy.

VINEGAR: The vinegars used in Mexico are

generally lighter and less acidic than ours. I find unseasoned rice vinegar to be excellent in Mexican cooking, and it is specified in many recipes in this book. It is available in the Asian section of most supermarkets.

Chiles, Fresh and Dried

Chiles give life, flavor, color, texture, and heat to Mexican cuisine. The generic Mexican word *chiles* is used for the great variety of capsicum peppers, which range from mild to extremely hot and are used both fresh and dried in cooking. For simplicity in this book, I have referred to the fresh as peppers and the dried as chiles. The fresh peppers and dried chiles used in this book can be found in many supermarkets, Latin American markets, and specialty produce shops. Mail-order sources for dried chiles and chile powders can be found on page 9.

Authentically prepared Mexican dishes use a large number of fresh and dried peppers to impart the desired flavor and heat to the food. The fresh ones are generally used in their green form, but are sometimes sold in the ripe red stage. Canned and pickled varieties are important, too. Dried chiles are red to reddish-brown and black. They are sold in bulk and packaged. They are also used in canned prepared sauces, salsas, prepared mole pastes, and ground chili powders. The heat level varies greatly from pepper to pepper and chile to chile. The veins carry the heat and the seeds become hot, too, so sensitive folks may want to cut away the veins and be sure to shake out seeds. If you love hot food, leave some of them in. The following listing describes the fresh hot peppers and dried chiles that are used in this book.

FRESH HOT PEPPERS

Anaheim or California: This variety is light green, long and slender, mild to quite hot, and is usually roasted and peeled. It is used for Chiles Rellenos, sauces, and vegetable dishes. It is canned and marketed as whole green chiles and diced green chiles.

Guero: This is a pale yellow, waxy, small, tapered hot pepper, and a milder variety also known as banana and Hungarian Wax, about 4 inches long. It is used in sauces and salads and is sometimes pickled.

Jalapeño: The jalapeño is probably the best known and most used small hot fresh pepper of all. It is about 2½ inches long, dark green and plump, with a rounded to tapered bottom. It is commonly used raw in fresh salsas and sauces. The canned pickled form is called "jalapeños en escabeche."

New Mexico: This green 6- to 8-inch-long pepper resembles the Anaheim, but is hotter. It is used in the same ways as the Anaheim pepper.

Poblano: Poblanos are dark green and shiny, with broad shoulders, tapering to a rounded or pointy tip. The best ones have meaty flesh and are about 4 inches long, making them ideal to roast, peel, and stuff, for rellenos. They range from fairly mild to hot. They are also used a great deal as a garnish by roasting, peeling, and cutting into thin strips called *rajas.* Poblanos are justly popular, for they have wonderful color and flavor.

Serrano: This bright green, small fresh pepper is slim and very hot. It is mainly used raw in fresh salsas and cooked sauces. It can be used interchangeably with fresh jalapeños.

Canned: Look for whole or diced green chiles in 4-ounce and 7-ounce cans. They are very useful when fresh peppers are not available. Several recipes in this book use the canned variety.

DRIED CHILES

Ancho: The ancho chile is the dried form of a poblano. It is brick-red to almost black, with a wrinkled skin, wide shoulders, and tapered to the tip, 3 to 4 inches long and 2 inches wide at stem end. Anchos are often toasted to enhance their flavor, then reconstituted in boiling water and pureed in sauces. Anchos are mild to hot with a rich dried fruit flavor.

California: This shiny dried chile with a smooth red skin is 4 to 5 inches long, and mild to fairly hot. It is used in cooked sauces and ground into chili powders.

Chipotle: The chipotle is a dried smoked jalapeño and it is very hot. It is often canned in a sauce called *adobo.* There is also a bottled chipotle salsa that is a bit milder. The wonderful smoky hot taste of chipotle chiles has become very popular, and they are currently being added to many sauces, stirred into mayonnaise, and discreetly dropped into soups.

Guajillo: This is a long, narrow, medium-size dark red chile pod, used mainly in cooked sauces. It is medium hot to hot. It may be difficult to find.

New Mexico: The New Mexico has a shiny smooth red skin and looks like the dried California chile, but is hotter. It is used in cooked sauces and ground into chili powders.

Chile Powders: The common and familiar chili powders are a seasoned blend of the milder varieties of dry red chiles ground with cumin, oregano, garlic, and other spices. Chili powders are useful and convenient. They are used in chili beans, stews, and tamale pies. A few recipes in this book call for prepared chili powders.

Pure Ground Chili: Unseasoned chili powders are labeled pure ancho, pasilla, California, and New Mexico. They do not contain preservatives. The advantage of pure ground chiles is that cooks can control the amount of other herbs and spices to be added to their dishes. For storage, place in heavy-duty plastic bags and freeze 6 months to 1 year for best flavor retention.

MAIL-ORDER SOURCES

The companies listed have catalogs, and they carry a large assortment of dried chiles, herbs, spices, salsas, seasonings, and other useful items for Mexican cooking.

Coyote Cocina
1364 Rufina Circle #1, Santa Fe, NM 87501
toll-free (800) 866-HOWL, or fax (505) 473-3100

Don Alfonso Foods
P.O. Box 201988, Austin, TX 78720
toll-free (800) 456-6100

Nancy's Specialty Market
($2.00 for catalog) P.O. Box 1302, Dept. PD31, Stamford, CT 06904
toll-free (800) 462-6291

Pendery's
304 East Belknap, Fort Worth, TX 76201
toll-free (800) 533-1870

Chapter 1

Fiesta Appetizers and Snacks

Festive, taste-tempting appetizers and snacks, called *antojitos*, which means "little whims," are probably the most popular category of Mexican food in this country. These delightful *antojitos* can be baked, steamed, or fried. They can be hot, at room temperature, or cold. They can be quite traditional, or they can be invented on the spot, using bits of leftovers or imaginative combinations accenting the Mexican flavors. We see them everywhere—in fast-food operations, typical Mexican-American and new Southwestern restaurants, at sports events and movie houses. Whether they are authentic or innovative, these tasty, easy-to-make foods are among our favorites for casual entertaining and at-home quick snacks. Many can be expanded to become part of a complete meal.

This chapter has good things to serve for many occasions. Sometimes one simple appetizer, such as Guacamole Dome with Tortilla Wedges, Chile con Queso, or Texas Caviar will suffice. For something fancier, there are finger snacks with company manners to pass on a tray or place on a party buffet, such as Spicy Stuffed Mushrooms with Chipotle or Chili-Baked Shrimp. (Look also in Chapter 9, "Totally Tortillas," for more party food ideas.)

Most of all, Mexican snacks and appetizers are eagerly eaten by almost everyone of any age. These are the fun foods to enjoy with family and friends. Most have been lightened and simplified for today's life-style.

1 ARTICHOKE AND CHILE DIP
Prep: 10 minutes   Cook: 20 minutes   Serves: 6

This creamy Mexican-flavored hot appetizer dip to serve with tortilla chips has long been a California favorite.

1 (7-ounce) can diced green
   chiles
1 (14-ounce) can artichoke
   hearts, drained, rinsed,
   and finely chopped
3 to 4 pickled jalapeño
   peppers, seeded and
   minced

1 cup mayonnaise
1 cup shredded Monterey Jack
   cheese (about 4 ounces)
⅓ cup grated Parmesan cheese

1. Preheat oven to 400°F. Butter a shallow 9-inch ovenproof casserole or pie plate. In a medium bowl, mix all ingredients together. Spread mixture evenly in prepared baking dish.

2. Bake 20 minutes, or until bubbling. Serve hot, directly from baking dish, with crisp tortilla chips or thin slices of sourdough bread.

2 MELTED CHEESE WITH CHORIZO
Prep: 5 minutes   Cook: 9 to 12 minutes   Serves: 6

Queso fundito, as it's often called, is popular all over Mexico. Cheese is melted in shallow earthenware plates and commonly eaten with flour tortillas in a do-it-yourself manner. Salsa Fresca Mexicana (page 84) should accompany this appetizer, which is great with margaritas or beer.

½ pound chorizo or other spicy
   sausage, removed from
   casing

¾ pound Monterey Jack
   cheese, shredded
12 (7-inch) flour tortillas

1. Preheat oven to 375°F. In a medium skillet, cook chorizo over medium heat, breaking it up into small bits, about 5 minutes, or until well done. Drain off excess fat and reserve off heat.

2. Butter an 8-inch heatproof earthenware plate or gratin dish and warm in oven 3 to 4 minutes. With a potholder, remove from oven and spread cheese evenly in hot dish. Bake 6 to 8 minutes, or until cheese is melted and bubbling.

3. While cheese bakes, warm tortillas in microwave, wrapped in damp paper towels, or directly over gas flame of stove, one by one, until soft. Wrap in napkin and place in basket. Reheat reserved cooked chorizo over medium heat until it sizzles, about 2 minutes.

4. Remove cheese from oven, scatter hot chorizo over the surface, and serve at once with warm tortillas. Diners scoop up a bit of cheese onto a tortilla, roll it up, and eat it with their hands.

3 BAKED BEEF AND BEAN DIP

Prep: 15 minutes   Cook: 33 minutes   Serves: 8

This lively combo can be assembled ahead and heated just before serving.

1 tablespoon vegetable oil
1 medium onion, minced
1 pound ground beef
½ teaspoon salt
⅛ teaspoon pepper
1 (16-ounce) can refried beans
½ cup thick and chunky red salsa

8 ounces Cheddar cheese, shredded (about 2 cups)
4 scallions, chopped
1 (4-ounce) can chopped black olives
Tortilla chips

1. Preheat oven to 350°F. In a large skillet, heat oil over medium heat. Add onion and cook until softened and translucent, about 3 minutes. Add beef and cook, breaking up lumps, until it is browned, about 5 minutes. Season with salt and pepper.

2. Spread beans over bottom of a greased 8-inch square glass baking dish or 1½-quart shallow ceramic casserole. Layer on meat mixture, salsa, and cheese.

3. Bake 25 minutes, or until heated through and cheese is melted. Top with scallions and chopped olives. Serve with tortilla chips for dipping.

4 CAULIFLOWER WITH AVOCADO DIP

Prep: 10 minutes   Cook: 30 seconds   Serves: 8 to 10

In this light appetizer, crunchy cauliflower is quickly cooked, cooled, and arranged on a platter with seasoned avocado dipping sauce.

1 medium head of cauliflower, about 2 pounds
½ teaspoon salt
1 tablespoon unseasoned rice vinegar

1 tablespoon vegetable oil
1 large ripe avocado
2 tablespoons bottled green salsa
1 tablespoon lime juice
1 tablespoon minced parsley

1. Trim cauliflower and cut into 1-inch florets. In a large saucepan of boiling water, cook cauliflorets about 30 seconds, until crisp. Drain and rinse under running water until cool. Drain again.

2. In a medium bowl, toss cauliflower with salt, vinegar, and oil.

3. Cut avocado in half and remove pit. With a large spoon, scoop avocado from skin and place in a small bowl; mash with a fork. Stir in green salsa and lime juice.

4. To serve, place bowl in center of a large round platter and arrange cauliflower around dip. Sprinkle with parsley and serve at room temperature. (If made ahead, cover and refrigerate cauliflower and dip separately.)

5 GUACAMOLE DOME WITH TORTILLA WEDGES

Prep: 20 minutes   Cook: 16 minutes   Serves: 6

At dinner one evening in San Miguel de Allende, one of Mexico's historic colonial cities, I was delighted with this guacamole presentation. It has become my favorite way to serve guacamole and chips at a small dinner party. It looks whimsical and pretty at the same time.

1 cup corn oil	⅓ cup chopped cilantro
8 corn tortillas, each cut into 12 slim wedges	⅓ cup fresh lime juice
3 large ripe avocados	½ teaspoon salt
½ medium white onion, finely chopped	1 medium tomato, seeded and cut into ¼-inch dice
3 serrano peppers, finely chopped	1 large cucumber, peeled and sliced

1. In a large heavy skillet, preferably cast iron, heat oil over medium heat to 375°F. Fry tortilla wedges, in batches about 12 at a time, for 2 minutes, or until lightly browned and crisp. With a slotted spoon, transfer to paper towels to drain. Repeat until all have been fried.

2. Cut avocados in half and remove pits. Scoop out avocado with a large spoon into a medium bowl and mash with a fork. Add onion, serrano peppers, cilantro, lime juice, and salt. Mix well. Gently stir in tomato, taking care not to muddy colors.

3. On a large oval or round platter, mound guacamole, centered, in a rounded dome shape on the platter. Place cucumber slices around the outer edge in an overlapping pattern. Arrange tortilla wedges, points up, all over the dome, in uniform lines, pincushion fashion. Serve at once with remaining chips in a basket alongside.

6 OLIVE AND GREEN CHILE DIP

Prep: 8 minutes   Cook: none   Chill: 1 hour   Makes: about 2 cups

Harry and Ellen Hills of Sacramento, California, entertain often, and their guests appreciate the quick treats that Harry whips up. Use as a chip dip or spread on crackers.

1 (4-ounce) can chopped black olives	2 scallions, finely chopped
1 (4-ounce) can diced green chiles	1 garlic clove, minced
	1 tablespoon cider vinegar
2 large tomatoes, seeded and finely chopped	3 tablespoons olive oil
	⅛ teaspoon cayenne
	¼ teaspoon salt

In a medium bowl, mix all ingredients together. Cover and refrigerate 1 to 4 hours before serving.

7 CHEESY BEAN DIP

Prep: 5 minutes   Cook: 6 to 8 minutes   Makes: 2 cups

Here's a mild bean dip for those who prefer the gentle touch of chili powder rather than fiery hot chile peppers.

1 (16-ounce) can pinto beans, drained
1 small tomato, peeled, seeded, and chopped
3 scallions, finely chopped

1 cup shredded sharp Cheddar cheese
2 tablespoons chili powder Corn tortilla chips, as accompaniment

1. In a food processor or blender, puree beans and tomato until smooth. Transfer to a medium saucepan or chafing dish.

2. Add scallions, cheese, and chili powder. Cook over low heat, stirring, until cheese is melted and dip is heated through, 6 to 8 minutes. Serve hot, with crisp tortilla chips for dipping.

8 TEXAS CAVIAR

*Prep: 20 minutes   Cook: none   Chill: 2 hours
Makes: about 3½ cups*

A casual party dish folks keep hankering for. This is my version of a very popular Texas-style dipping sauce for tortilla chips. Try putting it on hamburgers or serving it with grilled steaks or chicken. This is a dish you can take to a potluck, and the only thing you'll take home is an empty dish. Serve with a basket of crisp corn tortilla chips.

1 (15-ounce) can black-eyed peas, drained and rinsed
1 (4-ounce) can chopped black olives
½ green medium bell pepper, finely chopped
¼ red medium bell pepper, finely chopped
4 scallions (white and 2 inches of green), finely chopped

2 garlic cloves, minced
¼ cup minced pickled jalapeño peppers
1 teaspoon ground cumin
2 tablespoons chopped fresh cilantro
1 tablespoon cider vinegar
¼ teaspoon salt
2 tablespoons olive oil

In a large bowl, combine all ingredients. Stir to mix well. Cover and refrigerate about 2 hours, until ready to serve.

9   PARTY BEAN DIP WITH GREEN CHILES
Prep: 10 minutes   Cook: 3 minutes   Makes: about 3 cups

2 tablespoons vegetable oil
1 small onion, finely chopped
2 garlic cloves, minced
1 (16-ounce) can refried beans
¾ cup chopped peeled
    tomatoes, fresh or canned

1 (4-ounce) can chopped green
    chiles
2 tablespoons prepared red
    salsa, hot or medium
    Crisp tortilla chips, for
    dipping

1. In a medium skillet, heat oil over medium heat. Add onion and garlic and cook, stirring, until onion begins to brown, about 3 minutes.

2. In a food processor or blender, place onion mixture, refried beans, tomatoes, chopped chiles, and salsa. Blend to a coarse puree.

3. Transfer to a small nonreactive saucepan or chafing dish and heat through, stirring often. Serve hot with crisp tortilla chips, or cover and refrigerate until ready to serve.

NOTE: *Bean dip can be reheated in a microwave or in a saucepan over boiling water to avoid scorching.*

10   SEAFOOD SALPICON
*Prep: 20 minutes   Cook: 7 to 12 minutes   Chill: 1 hour
Serves: 6 to 8*

A salpicon is made of ingredients cut into small pieces and mixed with fresh lime juice and a light olive oil. Serve as an appetizer with crisp tortilla chips for dipping or a basket of soft, warm tortillas.

½ pound medium shrimp,
    shelled and deveined
½ pound sea scallops
3 Anaheim or poblano
    peppers
3 tablespoons finely chopped
    white onion

¼ cup fresh lime juice
1 tablespoon olive oil
2 tablespoons chopped fresh
    cilantro
½ teaspoon salt
⅛ teaspoon pepper

1. In a medium saucepan, bring about 1 quart water to a boil over medium-high heat. Add shrimp and cook 1 minute, or until pink. With a slotted spoon, remove shrimp from water, drain, and cool under running water. In same pan of boiling water, cook scallops until just opaque throughout, 45 to 60 seconds. Do not overcook. Drain and let cool. Cut scallops into ¼-inch dice. Cut shrimp into ¼-inch pieces. Place in a medium bowl, cover, and refrigerate.

2. Preheat oven broiler. Place Anaheim or poblano peppers on a baking sheet and broil as close to heat as possible, turning, until charred all over, about 10 minutes. Or roast peppers directly over a gas flame, turning, about 5 minutes. Place peppers in a paper bag and let steam 10 minutes. Peel off blackened skin and rinse peppers under cold running water. Cut open and discard stems and seeds. Cut peppers into ¼-inch dice. Put diced peppers in bowl with seafood.

3. Add chopped onion, lime juice, olive oil, cilantro, salt, and pepper. Toss to mix. Cover and refrigerate until cold, about 1 hour.

11 CHILE CON QUESO
Prep: 10 minutes   Cook: 7 to 10 minutes   Serves: 4 to 6

Melted cheese dip with green chiles comes in numerous variations. The trick is to keep the cheese from separating. Careful attention and a bit of flour added to the mixture does the job. This recipe is quite mild. For extra heat, add minced fresh or pickled jalapeño peppers to your taste.

1 tablespoon vegetable oil
3 tablespoons minced onion
1 tablespoon flour
1 cup drained canned tomatoes, finely chopped
1 (4-ounce) can diced green chiles
½ cup whipping cream

3 ounces cream cheese, room temperature, cut into small pieces
8 ounces jalapeño Monterey Jack cheese, shredded (about 2 cups)
Tortilla chips, for dipping

1. In a heavy medium saucepan, heat oil over medium heat. Add onion and cook, stirring, until golden brown, 3 to 4 minutes. Add flour and cook, stirring, 1 minute. Add tomatoes and green chiles. Cook, stirring until thickened, 1 to 2 minutes. Add cream and cook, stirring, until mixture begins to boil, about 1 minute.

2. Reduce heat to low and gradually add cream cheese, stirring until cheese is melted, 1 to 2 minutes. Gradually add Monterey Jack cheese, stirring, until melted. Do not allow mixture to boil or cheese might separate. Serve at once with tortilla chips for dipping.

   NOTE: *To keep cheese mixture warm or to reheat, place over a pan of hot—but not boiling—water.*

12   GUAYMAS SHRIMP BUTTER

Prep: 10 minutes   Cook: none   Chill: 2 hours   Serves: 6

Here is a creamy shrimp spread that's wonderful on crisp tortilla chips or crackers. If there's no time for fresh shrimp, rinsed and drained canned ones will do.

½ pound medium shrimp,
    shelled and deveined
3 ounces light cream cheese, at
    room temperature
2 tablespoons butter, softened
1 small garlic clove, minced

1 jalapeño pepper, seeded and
    minced
2 tablespoons fresh lime juice
¼ teaspoon salt
    Tortilla chips

1. In a medium saucepan of boiling water, cook shrimp over high heat until pink and curled and opaque throughout, 2 to 3 minutes. Drain, rinse under cold running water to cool, and drain well.

2. Chop shrimp into small bits. In a medium bowl, combine chopped shrimp with cream cheese, butter, garlic, jalapeño pepper, lime juice, and salt. Mix well. Cover and refrigerate about 2 hours or overnight. Serve as a spread with crisp tortilla chips or crackers.

13   ZESTY CHIP DIP

Prep: 20 minutes   Cook: none   Serves: 10 to 12

Carole Lattimore of Defiance, Missouri, keeps her guests warm with this high-spirited dip, no matter what the weather. The ingredients can be pantry available year-round.

1 (10-ounce) can bean dip
1 (10-ounce) jar picante sauce
3 cups guacamole, homemade
    or prepared
1 cup sour cream
½ cup mayonnaise
1 (2-ounce) package taco
    seasoning mix

4 scallions, finely chopped
3 medium tomatoes, finely
    chopped
1 (4-ounce) can chopped black
    olives
8 ounces Cheddar cheese,
    shredded (about 2 cups)
    Tortilla chips, for dipping

1. In a medium bowl, mix bean dip and picante sauce. Spread over bottom of an 8 x 11-inch glass dish. Carefully spread guacamole over bean mixture. In a small bowl, mix sour cream, mayonnaise, and taco seasoning mix. Spread over guacamole.

2. In another small bowl, mix scallions, tomatoes, and olives. Carefully spread over sour cream mixture. Top with shredded cheese. Serve with tortilla chips.

14   TEXAS FIESTA COMPUESTA
Prep: 20 minutes   Cook: none   Serves: 8 to 10

This *compuesta*, or composed, party dish is made with convenient super-market ingredients. It's always greeted with enthusiasm. It's a fine choice to take along, for it maintains its composure quite well. Serve at room temperature along with crisp tortilla chips.

1 (16-ounce) can refried beans
1 (7-ounce) can diced green
   chiles
1 cup thick and chunky
   prepared red salsa
2 cups guacamole (page 85), or
   use prepared

1 cup shredded Cheddar
   cheese (about 4 ounces)
1 cup sour cream, thinned
   with 2 tablespoons milk
1 (4-ounce) can sliced black
   olives
   Tortilla chips, for dipping

Spread beans evenly over bottom of a 1½-quart casserole about 2 inches deep. Layer chiles, salsa, guacamole, cheese, and sour cream. Scatter olives on top. (If beans are hard to spread, heat briefly to make them easier to work with.) Serve with tortilla chips for dipping.

15   CRISP TORTILLA CHIPS
Prep: 5 minutes   Cook: 8 minutes   Makes: 48

It's easy to prepare your own tostaditas or totopos, as these crisp chips are called. Homemade are better than commercial chips for nachos, and they're terrific for dipping. This recipe provides a perfect way to use leftover tortillas that are a bit stale.

12 corn tortillas
 1 cup vegetable oil

Salt (optional)

1. Stack 2 or 3 tortillas on a cutting surface and, with a large sharp knife, cut into quarters. Repeat until all are quartered.

2. In a heavy medium skillet, heat oil over medium-high heat until a tortilla wedge sizzles when dipped in. Fry tortilla wedges in batches about 2 minutes, or until crisp and lightly browned. Remove with a slotted spoon and drain on paper towels.

3. Sprinkle each batch lightly with salt, if desired, as soon as they are removed from oil. Serve from a napkin-lined basket, or store in an airtight container if made ahead.

NOTE: *Leftover oil can be strained, stored in a jar, and reused.*

16   OVEN-TOASTED CORN TORTILLA CHIPS

Prep: 5 minutes   Cook: 8 to 10 minutes per batch
Makes: 48 to 96

Oven toasting gives tortilla chips a drier finish and taste than frying. The results are excellent and provide a great option for people who wish to cut down on fats.

12 corn tortillas	**Salt (optional)**
1½ teaspoons vegetable oil	

1. Preheat oven to 325°F. Lay a tortilla on a flat surface. Brush one side with about ⅛ teaspoon vegetable oil. Repeat with remaining tortillas and oil. Cut tortillas into quarters, sixths, or eighths, depending on how large you want chips. Arrange as many wedges in a single layer as will fit on a large baking sheet.

2. Bake in middle of oven 8 to 10 minutes, or until chips are lightly browned and crisp. Watch carefully during last 2 minutes to avoid burning, which can happen fast. Remove chips from oven and let cool on paper towels. Sprinkle lightly with salt to taste while hot. Repeat baking until all wedges have been toasted.

3. Serve from a napkin-lined basket, or store in an airtight container if made ahead.

17   ARTICHOKE BOTTOMS WITH HAM

Prep: 15 minutes   Cook: 3 minutes   Makes: about 20

Artichokes are surprisingly popular in cosmopolitan Mexico City. This easy do-ahead appetizer owes its special punch to the spicy jalapeño cheese in the filling. Allow 2 to 3 per person as an appetizer. They always make a hit.

2 (7-ounce) jars marinated artichoke bottoms, drained, with 2 tablespoons oil from jars reserved	**1 tablespoon minced onion**
	1 tablespoon minced parsley
	3 drops of Tabasco
	½ cup finely shredded jalapeño Jack cheese
½ cup finely chopped smoked ham (about 2½ ounces)	**2 tablespoons bread crumbs**

1. Drain artichokes but don't rinse. Place on a baking sheet.

2. In a medium bowl, mix reserved oil from jars with ham, onion, parsley, Tabasco, cheese, and bread crumbs. Fill artichoke cavities with 1 rounded teaspoon of ham mixture.

3. Just before serving, run under a preheated broiler about 4 inches from heat for 3 minutes, or until lightly browned on top. Serve hot or at room temperature.

18 OPEN-FACE BEAN AND CHEESE SANDWICHES

Prep: 10 minutes   Cook: 7 to 8 minutes   Serves: 6

Open-face Mexican sandwiches are known as *molletes*. They are made with oval-shaped rolls called *bolillos*. Split, filled with beans, topped with cheese, and baked, they are served hot for breakfast or anytime as a delicious and easy snack. Use French rolls, or try making the recipe for Quick-Rise Bolillos on page 220.

1 (16-ounce) can refried beans
6 small torpedo-shaped French rolls, cut lengthwise in half

3 tablespoons butter, softened
1 cup shredded Cheddar cheese (about 4 ounces)
6 teaspoons bottled salsa

1. Preheat oven to 400°F. Heat refried beans in a glass or ceramic bowl in a microwave oven, or in a small saucepan over medium heat, stirring, until hot, 2 to 3 minutes. Cut rolls in half lengthwise and pinch out a bit of the crumb inside to make a hollow. Butter each half and fill with 2 tablespoons refried beans. Top each with 1 heaping tablespoon shredded cheese.

2. Place sandwiches on a large baking sheet and bake in preheated oven about 5 minutes, or until cheese is melted and shiny. Top each sandwich with 1 teaspoon salsa and serve hot.

NOTE: *Each baked sandwich can be cut into thirds and served as an appetizer.*

19 APPETIZER CORN FRITTERS

Prep: 15 minutes   Cook: 6 minutes   Makes: 24

These little pancakes cook up quickly and are wonderful to pass at a party.

1 tablespoon olive oil
½ medium onion, minced
1 cup canned whole kernel Mexicorn, drained
1 jalapeño pepper, seeded and minced
½ teaspoon ground cumin

¼ cup shredded Cheddar cheese
½ cup flour
½ teaspoon baking powder
¼ cup milk
1 extra-large egg, separated Vegetable oil, for frying

1. In a small skillet, heat olive oil over medium heat. Add onion and cook, stirring, until softened and translucent, about 2 minutes. Transfer to a medium bowl and mix in corn, jalapeño, and cumin. Let corn mixture cool briefly, then stir in cheese, flour, baking powder, milk, and egg yolk. Batter will be thick.

2. In a medium bowl, beat egg white to soft peaks. Fold into corn mixture. In a small skillet, heat 1 inch of oil to 375°F. Drop batter by teaspoonfuls into hot oil. Fry in batches, turning once, until golden brown, about 1 minute. Drain on paper towels and serve.

20   JICAMA, ORANGE, AND CUCUMBER STICKS

Prep: 20 minutes   Cook: none   Serves: 6

This jicama, orange, and cucumber snack is a typical nibble to serve with drinks. Fingers or toothpicks are used to pick up the pieces.

1 medium jicama (about 1 pound)	½ teaspoon salt
3 oranges	1 teaspoon chili powder
2 medium cucumbers	1 lime, cut into wedges
4 leaves of romaine lettuce, shredded	

1. Peel jicama and cut into finger-shaped pieces about 2½ inches long. Cut ends off oranges and cut away skin and white pith. Cut into segments. Peel cucumbers and cut into finger-shaped pieces about 2½ inches long.

2. On a serving platter, spread shredded romaine and arrange jicama, oranges, and cucumbers in an attractive pattern. Sprinkle salt and chili powder over platter. Garnish with lime wedges for diners to squeeze on as desired.

21   ARIZONA CHEESE CRISP

Prep: 5 minutes   Cook: 7 minutes   Serves: 4

An open-face flour tortilla, oven toasted, with melted cheese topping is informal party food, easy enough for children to make themselves for a quick snack.

1 tablespoon butter or margarine, softened	4 ounces Monterey Jack cheese, shredded
2 large (10-inch) flour tortillas	4 pickled jalapeño peppers, seeded and cut into ⅛-inch strips
4 ounces Cheddar cheese, shredded (about 1 cup)	

1. Preheat oven to 425°F. Spread butter on one side of each tortilla. Place on a large baking sheet and bake about 5 minutes, or until lightly browned and crisp around edges.

2. Remove from oven. Immediately sprinkle Cheddar cheese and Monterey Jack generously over each tortilla. Return to oven and bake until cheese is melted and bubbly, about 2 minutes.

3. Scatter strips of pickled jalapeño peppers over melted cheese. Cut into wedges and serve immediately.

22   JALAPENOS RELLENOS WITH TUNA
Prep: 15 minutes   Cook: none   Serves: 8

Pickled jalapeños, cut in half and filled with tuna, are a popular party snack, especially for those who really like it hot.

1 **(16-ounce) jar whole pickled**
   jalapeño peppers
1 **(6⅛-ounce) can water-**
   packed tuna

3 **tablespoons mayonnaise**
1 **tablespoon finely chopped**
   parsley

1. Drain and rinse pickled jalapeños. Slit lengthwise down center, leaving stem intact on one half. Scrape out seeds and veins. Place peppers on paper towels and reserve.

2. Drain tuna well. In a medium bowl, break up tuna with a fork. Add mayonnaise and parsley and blend well. With a teaspoon, fill each jalapeño half with a mound of tuna mixture. Arrange on a serving plate, cover, and refrigerate until ready to serve.

23   BAKED CHILE-CHEESE APPETIZERS
Prep: 7 minutes   Chill: 2 hours   Bake: 10 to 12 minutes
Makes: about 48

Serve these spicy, cookie-shaped savories with drinks, salads, soups, or first courses.

1 **cup flour**
½ **cup yellow cornmeal**
1 **teaspoon baking powder**
¼ **teaspoon salt**
⅛ **teaspoon cayenne**
4 **tablespoons butter, softened**

2 **cups shredded sharp**
   Cheddar cheese
1 **(4-ounce) can diced green**
   chiles
¼ **cup dry roasted, salted**
   sunflower seeds

1. In a medium bowl, combine flour, cornmeal, baking powder, salt, and cayenne. In a food processor, combine butter and cheese; process until blended, about 10 seconds. Add chiles and flour mixture. Process to form a stiff dough, about 15 seconds. Transfer to a medium bowl and work in sunflower seeds. Cover and refrigerate about 2 hours, or until dough is firm.

2. Preheat oven to 375°F. With hands, roll dough into walnut-size balls. Place on a large baking sheet about 2 inches apart. Bake 10 to 12 minutes, or until lightly browned. Transfer to a rack. Serve warm or at room temperature. If made ahead, store in an airtight container, or place in heavy-duty plastic bags and freeze up to 3 months.

24 JALAPEÑOS RELLENOS WITH CHEESE
Prep: 15 minutes   Cook: 6 to 8 minutes   Serves: 8

These stuffed hot chiles are for the fire-eaters! The melted cheese filling tempers the heat somewhat, but pickled jalapeños are quite spicy.

1 (13-ounce) can pickled
  jalapeño peppers
1 (3-ounce) package cream
  cheese, at room
  temperature

½ cup shredded Cheddar
  cheese
1 (2-ounce) jar pimiento strips

1. Preheat oven to 375°F. Drain and rinse jalapeño peppers. Slit lengthwise down center, leaving stem intact on one half. Scrape out seeds and veins. Reserve peppers.

2. In a medium bowl, beat cream cheese until soft and fluffy. Beat in Cheddar cheese. With a teaspoon, fill each jalapeño half with a mound of cheese mixture. Top with a strip of pimiento. Arrange cheese side up on a baking sheet.

3. Bake in preheated oven 6 to 8 minutes, or until cheese is melted. Serve warm.

NOTE: *Peppers can be filled ahead, covered with plastic wrap, and refrigerated 4 to 6 hours until ready to bake and serve.*

25 SINCRONIZADAS
Prep: 10 minutes   Cook: 8 minutes   Serves: 4

This Mexican version of a grilled ham and cheese sandwich is made with tortillas. Serve as a quick snack, or cut into wedges for a terrific appetizer.

8 (7-inch) flour tortillas
4 tablespoons unsalted butter,
  melted
¼ pound thinly sliced ham
1½ cups shredded Cheddar or
  Monterey Jack cheese
  (about 6 ounces)

1 cup finely shredded lettuce,
  loosely packed
1 cup fresh Mexican or bottled
  red salsa
2 ripe avocados, peeled and
  cut into ½-inch cubes

1. Brush tortillas on 1 side with melted butter. Place 1 tortilla, buttered side down, on a flat surface. Cover with 2 slices ham to within ½ inch of tortilla edge. Cut ham to fit, as needed. Cover ham with about one quarter of cheese. Top with another tortilla, buttered side up. Place on a tray and repeat with remaining tortillas.

2. In a medium skillet, toast *sincronizadas* one at a time over medium heat, turning once with a wide spatula, until cheese is melted and tortillas are golden brown, about 1 minute on each side. Transfer to plates. Top each with lettuce, salsa, and avocado. Serve at once.

26 MUSHROOM EMPANADAS WITH CHIPOTLE CHILE

Prep: 20 minutes   Cook: 13 to 15 minutes   Makes: about 48

Among the canned and bottled sauces in the Mexican section of most markets you can find 7-ounce cans of chipotle chiles in a red sauce called adobo sauce, or a bottled chipotle salsa. Both preparations work very well to give the spicy smoky taste so distinctive of the chipotle chile, which is dried smoked jalapeño and is widely used in Mexican and Southwestern American cooking. Empanadas are popular in all Latin American cooking, and this version is easy and delicious. Pass some at your next party.

6 ounces cream cheese, at room temperature	2 tablespoons olive oil
1 stick (4 ounces) soft butter	1 tablespoon mashed canned chipotle chile or bottled chipotle salsa
1½ cups flour	
½ medium onion, chopped	½ teaspoon dried oregano
½ pound fresh mushrooms, quartered	¼ teaspoon salt

1. In a food processor, place cream cheese and butter. Process about 20 seconds, or until blended and fluffy. Add flour and process until dough forms and holds together, about 20 seconds. Remove dough from processor bowl and shape into a disk. Wrap in plastic wrap and refrigerate for at least 20 minutes.

2. In food processor, combine onion and mushrooms. Process until finely chopped. In a large skillet, heat oil over medium-high heat. Add onion and mushrooms and cook, stirring frequently, until all moisture has evaporated, about 3 minutes. Remove from heat and stir in chipotle, oregano, and salt. Transfer to a small bowl and let cool.

3. Preheat oven to 450°F. Remove dough from refrigerator and divide in half. Roll out half on a lightly floured board to ⅛-inch thickness. Cut into 3-inch rounds. Gather scraps, roll, and cut until all dough is used. Repeat with remaining dough. Put about ½ teaspoon filling on each round. Fold in half. Seal edges by pressing with a fork. Vent tops with fork tines. Arrange empanadas on ungreased baking sheets.

4. Bake in middle of oven for 10 to 12 minutes, or until golden brown. Transfer to a platter. Serve hot. (Baked empanadas can be frozen and reheated for 20 minutes at 325°F.)

NOTE: *For a shiny finish, brush empanadas with 1 egg beaten with 1 teaspoon water before baking.*

27   SPICY STUFFED MUSHROOMS WITH CHIPOTLE

Prep: 20 minutes   Cook: 6 to 8 minutes   Serves: 6

Chipotle chiles lend a distinctive smoky-hot taste to many Mexican foods. Look for 7-ounce cans of chipotle chiles in adobe sauce, or bottled chipotle salsa. Use sparingly. Chipotles are very hot!

24 **medium mushrooms**	6 **whole pecans, finely**
3 **tablespoons olive oil**	**chopped**
¼ **medium onion, minced**	1 **tablespoon minced parsley**
½ **cup minced red bell pepper**	¼ **cup fine bread crumbs**
1 **tablespoon mashed canned**	½ **teaspoon salt**
chipotle chile or bottled	½ **cup shredded Monterey Jack**
chipotle salsa	**cheese**

1. Wipe mushrooms clean. Remove stems, finely chop, and reserve. Rub about 1 tablespoon olive oil over mushroom caps and place cavity side up on an oiled baking sheet.

2. In a large skillet, heat remaining oil over medium-high heat. Add onion, bell pepper, and reserved chopped mushroom stems. Cook, stirring, until onion is softened, about 3 minutes. Remove pan from heat. Stir in mashed chipotle, pecans, parsley, bread crumbs, salt, and cheese. Mix well.

3. Place 1 mounded tablespoon measure of mushroom mixture in each mushroom cap. Cover and refrigerate until shortly before serving. This recipe can be made to this point 1 day ahead.

4. Preheat broiler. Broil mushrooms about 4 inches from heat until hot and bubbly, 3 to 5 minutes. Serve warm as an appetizer or atop tossed greens as part of a salad.

28   NACHOS

Prep: 15 minutes   Cook: 1 minute   Makes: 36

Nachos are crisp fried tortilla triangles or circles, sometimes called *totopos,* which are generally topped with beans and cheese, then quickly run under the broiler to melt the cheese. Often toppings are more elaborate, and there are many variations. This is a common and very simple one.

1 **cup refried beans**	1 **cup shredded Monterey Jack**
36 **round corn tortilla chips**	**or Cheddar cheese (about**
(tostaditos) (about a	**4 ounces)**
9-ounce bag)	½ **cup prepared hot red salsa**

Preheat broiler. Spread refried beans over tortilla rounds. Top with a mound of cheese. Arrange in a single layer on a large baking sheet. Broil about 4 inches from heat until cheese is melted, about 1 minute. Top each with a small dollop of hot salsa and serve at once.

29 STACKED NACHOS
Prep: 20 minutes   Cook: 6 minutes   Makes: 24

Nachos don't have to come hot from the oven with melted cheese. This version uses room temperature ingredients arranged on a platter. Let your guests build their own. The results are very tasty no matter how they stack it. Of course, you can buy crisp tortilla chips in bags in the supermarket. If you do so, skip to step 2.

½ cup vegetable oil
6 corn tortillas, cut into quarters
24 thin slices of Monterey Jack cheese, cut 2 x 2 inches
24 thin slices of jicama, cut 2 x 2 inches

1 (7-ounce) can whole green chiles, cut into strips ½ inch wide and 2 inches long
½ cup cilantro leaves, lightly packed

1. In a medium skillet, heat oil over medium-high heat. Add tortilla wedges and fry 4 at a time, about 1 minute per batch, or until crisp and lightly browned. Drain on paper towels and place in a napkin-lined basket.

2. Arrange cheese slices, jicama slices, green chile strips, and a mound of cilantro leaves on a serving platter. Place a basket of tortilla chips alongside. Diners serve themselves by stacking ingredients on the chips.

30 NACHOS LAS PALOMAS
Prep: 15 minutes   Cook: 2 to 3 minutes   Serves: 6 to 8

These were inspired by a terrific platter of nachos served at Las Palomas Restaurant in Puerto Vallarta. This is finger food to enjoy with cold beer and margaritas.

50 to 60 corn tortilla chips, round or triangular
1 (16-ounce) can spicy refried beans
½ cup shredded Monterey Jack cheese
½ cup shredded Cheddar cheese

4 scallions, finely chopped
1 large avocado, peeled and cut into ¼-inch dice
6 pickled jalapeño peppers, cut into thin strips
1 cup sour cream
½ cup bottled red salsa

1. On a baking sheet, arrange tortilla chips in a single layer. Spread each chip with about 1 heaping teaspoon refried beans. Push tortillas together into a large round; overlapping is fine.

2. Preheat oven broiler. Scatter cheeses and scallions over entire surface of tortillas.

3. Broil about 4 inches from heat 2 to 3 minutes, or until cheese begins to bubble. Remove from oven. Slide nachos onto a platter. Scatter avocado and jalapeño strips over top. Dollop with sour cream and drizzle with salsa. Serve at once.

31   CHILI-BAKED SHRIMP

Prep: 10 minutes   Marinate: 1 hour   Cook: 3 to 5 minutes
Serves: 6

Convenient oven-baked shrimp can be served hot or at room temperature for a spicy appetizer, with nuts, chips, and cold beer.

1 tablespoon New Mexico or
   pasilla chili powder
½ teaspoon dried oregano
¼ teaspoon ground cumin
¼ teaspoon ground cinnamon
⅛ teaspoon ground allspice
¼ teaspoon salt

2 garlic cloves, crushed
   through a press
1 tablespoon fresh lime juice
1 tablespoon vegetable oil
1 pound large shrimp (16 to
   20), shelled, deveined,
   tails intact

1. In a medium bowl, combine all ingredients except shrimp. Mix well. Add shrimp and toss to coat completely. Cover and marinate in refrigerator at least 1 hour or up to 6 hours.

2. Preheat oven to 500°F. Remove shrimp from refrigerator and place on a lightly greased baking sheet in a single layer. Let stand at room temperature about 15 minutes before cooking.

3. Bake 3 to 5 minutes, until shrimp are pink, curled, and opaque throughout. Serve hot or at room temperature.

32   TOSTADITAS WITH SHRIMP

Prep: 25 minutes   Cook: 3 minutes   Chill: 1 hour   Makes: 12

2 tablespoons olive oil
¼ cup minced onion
⅓ pound medium shrimp,
   shelled, deveined, and
   cut into ¼-inch pieces
¼ teaspoon dried oregano
2 tablespoons thick and
   chunky bottled spicy red
   salsa

1 ripe avocado
1 tablespoon fresh lime juice
¼ teaspoon salt
12 round corn tortilla chips
   (tostaditas)

1. In a medium saucepan, heat olive oil over medium heat. Add onion and cook, stirring, until softened, about 2 minutes. Add shrimp and oregano. Cook, stirring, until shrimp is pink, about 1 minute. Remove from heat and stir in salsa. Transfer to a small bowl, cover, and refrigerate until cold, about 1 hour.

2. Just before serving, peel avocado. Place in a small bowl and mash. Mix in lime juice and salt.

3. On each tostadita, spread about 1 teaspoon mashed avocado. Top with about 1 teaspoon cold shrimp salsa and serve at once.

33   CHILI-BEEF TORTAS
Prep: 10 minutes   Cook: 10 to 12 minutes   Serves: 4

Almost like our old friend, the Sloppy Joe, these juicy Mexican sandwiches rate several *olés*. Guacamole is a must on the side.

½ pound lean ground beef	½ cup prepared red salsa
½ medium onion, chopped	2 tablespoons ketchup
½ medium green bell pepper, finely chopped	4 (5- to 6-inch) crusty French rolls, halved lengthwise
1 tablespoon chili powder	4 slices Cheddar cheese, about
¼ teaspoon salt	2 x 4 inches

1. In a medium skillet over medium heat, cook ground beef, stirring and breaking it up into bits as it cooks, until no longer pink, about 5 minutes. Add onion, bell pepper, chili powder, salt, salsa, and ketchup. Cook until onion begins to soften, 3 to 5 minutes. Remove from heat.

2. Preheat oven broiler. Remove some of the soft inside from bottom half of each roll and fill each cavity with one fourth of meat mixture. Place on a baking sheet. Put 1 slice cheese on each roll top and place on same baking sheet. Broil about 4 inches from heat until meat mixture is hot and cheese is melted, about 2 minutes. Put melted cheese roll halves on meat-filled halves and serve at once.

34   CHICKEN TORTAS
Prep: 15 minutes   Cook: none   Serves: 4

Tortas are Mexican sandwiches made with the wonderful native rolls called *bolillos*. French rolls from the bakery can also be used to create these delicious sandwiches. Turkey can be substituted for the chicken. It's a great way to use leftovers.

4 (5-inch) torpedo-shaped French rolls	½ large ripe avocado, mashed
4 teaspoons butter, softened	¼ cup mayonnaise
1 cup refried beans, warm or at room temperature	1 tablespoon chipotle salsa (optional)
1 cup shredded cooked chicken or turkey	1 large tomato, halved and thinly sliced
	1 cup shredded lettuce

1. Cut rolls lengthwise in half. Pull out part of soft white center to create a depression for filling. Spread 1 teaspoon butter on bottom half of each roll. Spread on 2 tablespoons refried beans. Add chicken or turkey.

2. In a medium bowl, combine avocado, mayonnaise, and chipotle salsa. Stir to mix well. Spread 1 tablespoon over chicken. Add tomato slices and lettuce. Cover with top half of roll. Repeat with remaining rolls to make 4 tortas.

35   CHICKEN TAQUITOS
Prep: 20 minutes   Cook: 22 to 25 minutes   Makes: 24

Taquitos de pollo, literally "little chicken tacos," are a favorite snack or light meal all over Mexico. They are commonly served with a topping of guacamole and sour cream. For a snack, put guacamole and sour cream in separate bowls for dipping.

1¼ pounds skinless, boneless chicken breasts	3 ounces cream cheese, at room temperature
5 tablespoons vegetable oil	½ teaspoon salt
1 medium onion, finely chopped	⅛ teaspoon pepper
½ teaspoon dried oregano	12 corn tortillas

1. Place chicken breasts in a medium saucepan of lightly salted water. Bring to a boil over medium-high heat, reduce heat to low, and simmer until chicken is white throughout but still moist, 12 to 15 minutes. Let chicken cool in liquid until cool enough to handle; shred into thin strips.

2. In a medium skillet, heat 1 tablespoon of oil over medium-high heat. Add onion and oregano and cook, stirring, until limp, about 2 minutes. Remove from heat and stir in cream cheese. Place in bowl with shredded chicken. Add salt and pepper. Mix thoroughly.

3. In a medium skillet, heat 2 tablespoons of oil over medium-high heat. Using tongs, soften tortillas 1 at a time by dipping in hot oil for about 2 seconds on each side, or until very limp. Add additional oil, if needed, to finish softening tortillas. Drain between layers of paper towels. Stack and keep covered with a clean kitchen towel.

4. To fill, place 1 soft tortilla on a plate, spoon about 2 tablespoons chicken mixture in a strip across lower third of tortilla, and roll up tightly. Secure with a toothpick and lay seam side down on another plate. Repeat with remaining tortillas and filling. Taquitos can be held, covered and refrigerated, up to 6 hours before frying. Cover with plastic wrap to keep from drying out.

5. In a medium skillet, heat remaining 2 tablespoons oil over medium-high heat. Fry taquitos 2 at a time, seam side down, turning, until lightly browned on both sides, about 2 minutes. Drain on paper towels. Repeat until all are cooked. With a sharp knife, cut each taquito in half and arrange on a plate.

36   ZUCCHINI-TORTILLA APPETIZER
Prep: 10 minutes   Cook: 10 to 15 minutes   Makes: about 60

This colorful fresh vegetable mixture, enclosed in a flour tortilla, makes a delicious and easy finger snack for parties, or any other time. The large 10-inch burrito-size flour tortilla or the smaller 7-inch may be used for the recipe. A food processor is ideal for preparing the chopped and shredded ingredients.

2 jalapeño peppers, seeded and coarsely chopped
3 scallions, coarsely chopped
1 small carrot, peeled and coarsely chopped
¼ cup parsley sprigs, loosely packed
¾ pound zucchini

¼ cup vegetable oil
½ cup shredded Monterey Jack cheese, preferably aged
½ teaspoon salt
⅛ teaspoon pepper
6 (10-inch) flour tortillas or 10 (7-inch) flour tortillas

1. In a food processor fitted with steel blade, place jalapeño peppers, scallions, carrot, and parsley. Process to chop to a fine mixture. Remove steel blade from processor, leaving vegetables in bowl. Insert shredding blade. Cut zucchini in chunks to fit feed tube and shred. Remove vegetable mixture to a medium bowl and toss to mix.

2. In a large skillet, heat 2 tablespoons of oil over medium-high heat. Add vegetables and cook quickly, stirring, until zucchini is bright green at edges and barely tender, 1 to 2 minutes. Remove pan from heat. Stir in cheese, salt, and pepper.

3. To assemble, soften tortillas in a microwave wrapped in paper towels about 1 minute or in an oven wrapped in aluminum foil about 7 minutes, just until pliable. Place 1 tortilla on a flat surface and place 2 heaping tablespoons vegetable mixture on one half. Fold over to create a half-moon shape. Cover with a clean kitchen towel to keep soft. Repeat with remaining tortillas.

4. In a large skillet, heat remaining 2 tablespoons oil over medium heat and cook turnovers, 2 at a time, about 2 minutes on each side, or until lightly browned and crisp. Drain on paper towels and keep warm in a 200°F. oven while preparing remaining turnovers. Cut into wedges and serve while warm and crisp.

Chapter 2

Soups Mexican Style

When you think of planning a Mexican meal, don't forget the soup. Soups are never neglected in Mexico, and they are a very important part of a complete menu. Before the Spanish arrived and European customs influenced the cuisine, soups were not a separate part of the meal, but one of the main dishes. With such a heritage, Mexican cooking, both ancient and more modern, has created a wide variety of delicious soups.

This chapter has some recipes that are light and perfect to start the meal, such as Valley of Mexico White Onion Soup, Yucatán Lime Soup, Black Bean Soup, and Cold Avocado Soup. For more robust soups that make a satisfying meal in a bowl, try Pozole, Poblano Pepper and Corn Soup, Potato, Onion, and Green Chile Soup, or Red Lentil Soup.

So that you can enjoy these great soups often and with little effort, most of the following recipes call for quick, convenient canned broths. Reduced-sodium chicken broth, which I think has better flavor than the regular kind, is a real boon to busy people who wish to restrict the use of salt, and it is called for in many of the soups in this chapter. For those who like to start from scratch when time allows, I've also included recipes for several basic soup stocks.

37 MEAT STOCK

Prep: 10 minutes   Cook: 3½ to 4 hours   Makes: 2 quarts

Beef or pork stock is useful for soups and adding to some sauces.

3 **pounds beef and/or pork bones**	2 **bay leaves**
1 **medium onion, sliced**	1 **teaspoon dried oregano**
1 **medium carrot, sliced**	½ **teaspoon dried marjoram**
1 **celery rib, sliced**	½ **teaspoon dried thyme leaves**
6 **garlic cloves, peeled**	8 **peppercorns, cracked**
	2 **parsley sprigs**

1. Place bones in a stockpot and add 4 quarts of cold water. Bring to a boil over medium heat, skimming often. Add all remaining ingredients, reduce heat to medium-low, partially cover, and cook 3½ to 4 hours, or until liquid has reduced by about half.

2. Strain stock, discarding solids. Let cool, then skim all fat from top. Cover and refrigerate up to 5 days, or freeze up to 2 months.

38   CHICKEN STOCK
Prep: 10 minutes   Cook: 1½ to 2 hours   Makes: 2 quarts

When shredded chicken is called for, use this cooking method, and remove chicken pieces after 45 minutes; cool chicken and remove meat from bones, then shred. For richer stock, return bones to pot and continue to cook 45 minutes to 1 hour longer, as directed in this recipe.

1 **(3-pound) chicken, cut into serving pieces**	4 **garlic cloves, peeled**
1 **medium onion, sliced**	2 **bay leaves**
1 **medium carrot, sliced**	1 **teaspoon dried oregano**
1 **celery rib, sliced**	8 **peppercorns, cracked**
	1 **parsley sprig**

1. Rinse chicken inside and out under cold running water. Place in a stockpot or large flameproof casserole and add 2½ quarts of water. Bring to a boil over medium heat, skimming often. Add all remaining ingredients, reduce heat to medium-low, partially cover, and cook 1½ to 2 hours, or until liquid has reduced by about half.

2. Strain stock, discarding solids. Let cool, then skim all fat from top. Cover and refrigerate up to 3 days, or freeze for up to 2 months.

39   CALDO TLALPENO
Prep: 20 minutes   Cook: 18 to 21 minutes   Serves: 6

Dorothy and Frank Davis, frequent Mexico travelers from Orinda, California, discovered this light and lively chicken and vegetable soup in San Luis Potosí north of Mexico City.

1 **cup Mexican-style stewed tomatoes, with juices**	1 **whole canned chipotle chile pepper**
3 **skinless, boneless chicken breast halves (about 1 pound)**	¼ **pound thickly sliced smoked ham, preferably Black Forest, cut into 1 x ¼-inch strips**
6 **cups homemade chicken stock or 3 (14½-ounce) cans reduced-sodium chicken broth**	¼ **teaspoon salt**
	Dash of pepper
2 **small red potatoes, peeled and cut into ½-inch dice**	1 **small avocado, peeled and sliced**
2 **medium carrots, peeled and sliced ¼ inch thick**	1 **lime, cut into 6 wedges**

1. In a blender or food processor, puree stewed tomatoes until smooth. Set tomato puree aside.

2. In large saucepan over medium heat, cook chicken breasts in chicken broth until white throughout, but still tender and juicy, 7 to 8 minutes. Remove chicken and cut into bite-size pieces.

3. Add potatoes, carrots, pureed tomatoes, chipotle pepper, and ham to the chicken broth. Cook over medium heat, partially covered, until vegetables are barely tender, 8 to 10 minutes. Remove chipotle pepper and discard.

4. Add reserved chicken pieces to soup and season with salt and pepper. Cook, uncovered, until completely heated through, about 3 minutes. Ladle soup into 6 bowls. Garnish each bowl with avocado slices. Serve with lime wedges to squeeze into soup.

40   COLD AVOCADO SOUP

Prep: 10 minutes   Cook: none   Chill: 2 hours   Serves: 2 to 3

An elegant chilled soup to serve in hot weather before a spicy meal.

1   large ripe avocado, peeled
    and mashed
1   (14½-ounce) can reduced-
    sodium chicken broth
3   tablespoons fresh lime juice
¼   teaspoon salt

⅛   teaspoon pepper
¼   cup sour cream or plain
    yogurt
¾   tablespoon chopped cilantro
2   teaspoons dry sherry
    (optional)

In a blender or food processor, place all ingredients except sherry and puree until smooth. Transfer to a bowl, cover, and refrigerate about 2 hours, or until cold. Serve in chilled soup cups. Each diner may add optional sherry at the table.

41   BLACK BEAN SOUP

Prep: 10 minutes   Cook: 13 to 17 minutes   Serves: 4

Not enough time to cook dry beans? Never mind. Prepare this popular Mexican soup using canned black beans, and "soup's on" in just minutes.

2   tablespoons vegetable oil
1   medium onion, chopped
2   garlic cloves, chopped
1   teaspoon dried oregano
1   teaspoon ground cumin
1   (15-ounce) can tomatoes
¼   cup prepared red salsa

2   (16-ounce) cans black beans,
    drained but not rinsed
1   (14½-ounce) can chicken
    broth
1   lime, quartered
    Cilantro sprigs, for garnish

1. In a large saucepan, heat oil over medium-high heat. Add onion, garlic, oregano, and cumin. Cook, stirring often, until onions begin to brown, 3 to 5 minutes. Add tomatoes, salsa, black beans, and chicken broth. Bring to a boil and cook, stirring, 5 minutes.

2. In 2 batches, puree soup in a blender or food processor. Return soup to pan and cook over medium-low heat, stirring often, until heated through, 5 to 7 minutes. Serve with lime wedges and garnish with cilantro.

42   SONORAN CHEESE SOUP

Prep: 20 minutes   Cook: 27 minutes   Serves: 4

1 tablespoon butter
1 tablespoon vegetable oil
6 scallions, chopped
3 garlic cloves, minced
2 medium red potatoes,
    peeled and cut into
    ¼-inch dice
2 medium tomatoes, peeled,
    seeded, and chopped

1 (14½-ounce) can reduced-
    sodium chicken broth
1 cup heavy cream
½ teaspoon salt
⅛ teaspoon pepper
4 ounces Monterey Jack
    cheese, cut into ½-inch
    dice

1. In a large saucepan or flameproof casserole, melt butter in oil over medium heat. Add scallions and garlic and cook, stirring, until softened, about 2 minutes. Add potatoes and tomatoes and cook, stirring often, until tomato juices evaporate, about 5 minutes.

2. Add chicken broth, cream, salt, and pepper. Bring to a boil, reduce heat to medium-low, cover, and simmer 20 minutes, or until potatoes are very tender. Divide cheese cubes among 4 soup bowls. Ladle hot soup over cheese and serve at once.

43   CAULIFLOWER SOUP

Prep: 15 minutes   Cook: 22 to 27 minutes   Serves: 6

Mexico's soup kitchen offers a great variety. Many European vegetables are as popular as indigenous varieties. This smooth and mild cauliflower soup is typical of the sort to begin a meal or as a restorative at the end of a busy day.

3 tablespoons butter
1 medium onion, chopped
1 medium head of
    cauliflower, about 1½
    pounds, trimmed and
    coarsely chopped

1 cup chicken broth
1 cup milk
1 teaspoon salt
¼ teaspoon pepper
⅛ teaspoon ground allspice
2 scallions, chopped

1. In a large saucepan or flameproof casserole, melt butter over medium heat. Add onion and cook until softened, about 3 minutes. Add cauliflower and cook, stirring, 2 minutes. Add chicken broth, milk, salt, pepper, and allspice. Bring to a boil, then reduce heat to medium-low, cover, and simmer, stirring often, until vegetables are very soft, 15 to 20 minutes. Add scallions. Cook 2 minutes.

2. In a food processor or blender, puree soup until smooth. Reheat and serve hot. If made ahead, cover and refrigerate.

44 CHICKEN, VEGETABLES, AND GARBANZO BEAN SOUP

Prep: 25 minutes   Cook: 32 minutes   Serves: 6

This is another version of *caldo tlalpeño*, from the region around Mexico City. The hot and smoky taste of chipotle chiles is essential to the flavor of the soup. Canned chipotles, or bottled chipotle sauce, are available in Hispanic markets and many supermarkets.

6 cups homemade chicken stock or 3 (14½-ounce) cans reduced-sodium broth
2 chicken breast halves on the bone (about 1 pound)
1 teaspoon dried oregano
½ teaspoon dried thyme leaves
2 medium tomatoes, peeled, seeded, and chopped
2 tablespoons vegetable oil
1 medium onion, quartered and sliced
3 garlic cloves, minced

2 medium carrots, peeled and thinly sliced
1 (15-ounce) can garbanzo beans, drained and rinsed
½ teaspoon salt
1 sprig of epazote (optional)
2 canned chipotle peppers, seeded and mashed, or 1 tablespoon bottled chipotle sauce
Diced avocado, lime wedges, and chopped cilantro, as accompaniment

1. In a large saucepan, bring broth and chicken breasts to boil over medium heat, uncovered. Reduce heat to low and simmer 3 minutes, skimming several times. Add oregano, thyme, and tomatoes. Cover and cook 12 minutes.

2. Remove chicken to a plate. Strain broth through a sieve into a bowl, pressing down on solids to remove as much liquid as possible. Set broth aside. As soon as chicken is cool enough to handle, tear meat into shreds, discarding skin and bones.

3. In a clean large saucepan or soup pot, heat oil over medium heat. Add onion, garlic, and carrots and cook, stirring frequently, until onion is beginning to brown, about 5 minutes. Add reserved broth, garbanzo beans, salt, and epazote. Cook, partially covered, 10 minutes, or until carrots are tender.

4. Add chipotles and shredded chicken. Cook until heated through, about 2 minutes. Serve soup garnished with avocado, lime, and cilantro.

45 CORN SOUP WITH SWEET RED PEPPER SAUCE

Prep: 25 minutes   Cook: 35 minutes   Serves: 4

A fabulous soup to make when summer corn is at its peak. The red pepper garnish looks striking. A plastic squirt container is the easiest thing to use to make this kind of design.

3 tablespoons unsalted butter
½ medium onion, chopped
2 shallots, chopped
½ medium carrot, chopped
  Corn kernels from 4 large
  ears (about 3 cups)
1 jalapeño pepper, seeded and
  minced

1 (14½-ounce) can reduced-
  sodium chicken broth
¾ cup milk
½ teaspoon salt
  Dash of cayenne
  Sweet Red Pepper Sauce
  (recipe follows)

1. In a large saucepan or flameproof casserole, melt butter over medium heat. Add onion, shallots, and carrot, cover, and cook 5 minutes, stirring occasionally. Add corn, jalapeño pepper, and chicken broth. Bring to a boil. Reduce heat to low, cover, and simmer 20 minutes, stirring frequently and scraping bottom of pan to keep soup from sticking.

2. In a food processor or blender, puree soup until smooth. Rinse saucepan and place wire strainer over pan. Strain soup into pan, 1 cup at a time, using back of wooden spoon to push mixture through strainer. Discard corn pulp. Add milk, salt, and cayenne. Cook soup over medium-low heat, stirring, until hot, about 10 minutes.

3. Ladle soup into bowls. Pipe red pepper sauce or drizzle from a spoon to make squiggles on each serving.

46 SWEET RED PEPPER SAUCE

Prep: 5 minutes   Cook: 8 to 10 minutes   Makes: about ½ cup

1 large red bell pepper,
  seeded and chopped
1 tablespoon paprika

½ teaspoon ground cumin
½ teaspoon salt

1. In a small saucepan, combine pepper, paprika, cumin, salt, and ½ cup of water. Bring to a boil, reduce heat to medium, and cook, partially covered, until pepper is very soft, 8 to 10 minutes. Transfer to a blender or food processor and puree until smooth.

2. Strain puree back into saucepan, using a wooden spoon to push contents through. Discard pulp. Sauce should be about as thick as heavy cream. Thin with a little water, if necessary. Reheat, or cover and refrigerate up to 3 days.

47   HALF-HOUR SOUP
Prep: 10 minutes   Cook: 28 minutes   Serves: 4

A nourishing soup for busy cooks, known in Mexico as *sopa de media hora*.

2 tablespoons vegetable oil
1 medium onion, chopped
4 medium zucchini, cut into
    rounds ½ inch thick
2 medium carrots, cut into
    rounds ½ inch thick
2 medium tomatoes, peeled,
    seeded, and chopped

½ teaspoon salt
2 (14½-ounce) cans reduced-
    sodium chicken broth
1 bay leaf
1 teaspoon dried oregano
1 tablespoon chopped parsley
1 large avocado, cut into
    8 slices

1. In a large saucepan or flameproof casserole, heat oil over medium heat. Add onion and cook, stirring frequently, until translucent, about 3 minutes.

2. Add zucchini, carrots, tomatoes, and salt. Cook until tomato juices have evaporated, about 5 minutes. Add chicken broth, bay leaf, oregano, and parsley. Bring to a boil, reduce heat to low, cover, and cook 20 minutes, or until vegetables are tender.

3. To serve, remove and discard bay leaf. Place 2 avocado slices in each of 4 bowls. Ladle soup into bowls.

48   TWO-MELON SOUP
Prep: 8 minutes   Cook: none   Chill: 3 hours   Serves: 6 to 8

A striking cold soup presented by showing off the beautiful hues of both melons.

1 ripe cantaloupe, about
    2½ pounds
2 tablespoons lemon juice
1 ripe honeydew melon,
    about 2½ pounds

2 tablespoons lime juice
2 teaspoons chopped fresh
    mint plus mint sprigs

1. Peel and seed cantaloupe; chop coarsely. Place in a food processor or blender, add lemon juice, and puree until smooth. Transfer to a large bowl, cover, and refrigerate until very cold, about 3 hours.

2. Meanwhile, peel and seed honeydew melon; chop coarsely. Place in a food processor or blender, add lime juice and chopped mint, and puree until smooth. Transfer to a separate bowl, cover, and refrigerate about 3 hours.

3. To serve, pour each mixture into separate measuring cups. Simultaneously, pour melon purees into chilled glass bowls, each from an opposite side. Colors will stay separated. Garnish each bowl with a sprig of mint.

49   VALLEY OF MEXICO WHITE ONION SOUP
Prep: 15 minutes   Cook: 20 minutes   Serves: 6

Bellinghausen Restaurant in Mexico City serves a delicious soup made with white onions. Fresh cilantro, lime, and cheese are added at the table. This is my adaptation of their recipe.

3 **tablespoons unsalted butter**	1 **fresh lime, cut into wedges**
3 **large white onions, cut into thin slices**	1 **cup finely diced Monterey Jack cheese (about 4 ounces)**
1 **teaspoon salt**	
¼ **teaspoon freshly ground pepper**	3 **tablespoons chopped cilantro**
6 **cups Chicken Stock (page 34) or 3 (14½-ounce) cans reduced-sodium broth**	

1. In a large saucepan, melt butter over medium-low heat. Add onions and cook, uncovered, stirring occasionally, until onions are very tender and fragrant, about 15 minutes. Do not brown. Stir in salt, pepper, and chicken stock. Raise heat to medium, bring soup to a boil, and cook about 5 minutes to blend flavors.

2. Serve hot, with lime wedges, cheese cubes, and fresh cilantro for each diner to add at table.

50   COASTAL FISH SOUP WITH CILANTRO AND TOMATOES
Prep: 20 minutes   Cook: 40 to 46 minutes   Serves: 4

Any firm white fish qualifies for this popular seafood soup, but it must be meticulously fresh to ensure fine flavor.

3 **tablespoons olive oil**	⅔ **cup dry white wine**
1 **large onion, chopped**	4 **cups Fish Stock (recipe follows) or 2 (14½-ounce) cans reduced-sodium chicken broth**
2 **celery ribs, with leaves, chopped**	
3 **garlic cloves, minced**	
½ **green bell pepper, cut into ¼-inch dice**	1 **pound firm white fish fillets, such as cod, snapper, or halibut**
1 **teaspoon dried oregano**	
2 **bay leaves**	¼ **cup chopped cilantro**
2 **small potatoes, peeled and cut into ½-inch dice**	1 **tablespoon lime juice**
2 **medium tomatoes, peeled and diced**	¾ **teaspoon salt**
Pinch of crushed hot red pepper	⅛ **teaspoon pepper**

1. In a large saucepan or soup pot, heat oil over medium heat. Add onion, celery, garlic, and bell pepper and cook, stirring frequently, until vegetables begin to soften, 3 to 5 minutes.

2. Add oregano, bay leaves, potatoes, tomatoes, hot pepper, wine, and fish stock. Bring to a boil. Reduce heat to medium-low, partially cover, and simmer until potato is barely tender, 6 to 8 minutes.

3. Meanwhile, remove any small bones from fish fillets and cut fish into 1-inch pieces. Add fish and cilantro to soup. Cover and cook 5 to 7 minutes, or until fish is opaque throughout. Remove and discard bay leaves. Stir in lime juice. Season with salt and pepper. Serve hot.

51 FISH STOCK
Prep: 10 minutes   Cook: 26 minutes   Makes: 2 quarts

Fish stock is easy to make. The important part is locating the best fish market for fish heads and carcasses. Choose mild-flavored white fish for stock; avoid salmon, bluefish, and mackerel.

2 **pounds fish heads (gills removed) and bones**	3 **garlic cloves, sliced**
2 **tablespoons vegetable oil**	2 **medium tomatoes, sliced**
1 **celery rib, chopped**	2 **bay leaves**
1 **medium onion, chopped**	½ **teaspoon dried marjoram**
1 **medium carrot, chopped**	1 **parsley sprig**
	6 **peppercorns, cracked**

1. Rinse fish parts and place in a large saucepan or flameproof casserole. Add vegetable oil and toss to coat. Place over medium heat, cover, and cook 3 minutes.

2. Add celery, onion, carrot, and garlic. Cook, uncovered, stirring, until onion is softened and translucent, about 3 minutes.

3. Add tomatoes, bay leaves, marjoram, parsley, peppercorns, and 2½ quarts water. Bring to a boil, reduce heat to medium-low, and simmer, partially covered, 20 minutes. Strain through cheesecloth or a fine-mesh sieve. Discard solids. Let cool, then skim off any fat. Cover and refrigerate up to 3 days, or freeze for up to 1 month.

52 MEXICAN GAZPACHO
Prep: 15 minutes   Cook: none   Chill: 2 hours   Serves: 6

Enjoy this refreshing cold soup when summer tomatoes are at their peak. The addition of a fresh jalapeño pepper and spicy vegetable juice tingles the tongue just a little.

3 pounds ripe tomatoes, peeled, seeded, and chopped
1 medium cucumber, peeled, seeded, and chopped
1 celery rib, chopped
½ large red bell pepper, seeded and chopped
½ medium red onion, chopped
1 garlic clove, chopped
1 jalapeño pepper, chopped

3 tablespoons red wine vinegar
¼ cup extra-virgin olive oil
1 (12-ounce) can spicy vegetable juice, such as V-8 or Snappy Tom
½ teaspoon salt
3 tablespoons chopped cilantro
1 cup crisp croutons
2 limes, quartered

1. In batches if necessary, combine tomatoes, cucumber, celery, bell pepper, onion, garlic, jalapeno, vinegar, olive oil, vegetable juice, and salt in a blender or food processor and puree until smooth. Transfer to a large bowl. Cover and refrigerate until very cold, about 2 hours.

2. Serve soup in shallow soup plates. Garnish each serving with cilantro and croutons. Pass lime wedges at table.

53 GAZPACHO PACIFICO
Prep: 20 minutes   Cook: 2 minutes   Chill: 2 hours   Serves: 4 to 6

Shrimp, which are plentiful along Mexico's Pacific coast, are added here to the usual cold salad soup. It is a marvelous summer soup.

½ pound medium shrimp, shelled and deveined
3 large ripe tomatoes, peeled, seeded, and quartered
2 tablespoons chopped onion
1 celery rib, chopped
1 medium cucumber, peeled, seeded, and chopped
½ medium red or green bell pepper, seeded and chopped
1 (12-ounce) can spicy vegetable juice, such as V-8 or Snappy Tom

½ cup canned chicken broth
2 tablespoons red wine vinegar
¼ cup extra-virgin olive oil
½ teaspoon salt
1 large avocado, peeled and cut into ½-inch dice
2 tablespoons chopped cilantro
2 limes, quartered

1. In a medium saucepan of boiling lightly salted water, cook shrimp until pink and loosely curled, about 2 minutes; drain. Cut cooked shrimp into thirds. Place in a small bowl. Cover and refrigerate until ready to serve soup.

2. In a blender or food processor, combine tomatoes, onion, celery, cucumber, bell pepper, vegetable juice, chicken broth, vinegar, olive oil, and salt. Puree until smooth. Pour into a large bowl, cover, and refrigerate until very cold, about 2 hours.

3. Just before serving, stir shrimp into soup. Ladle into shallow soup plates and garnish with avocado and cilantro. Pass lime wedges to squeeze juice into soup.

54 GARBANZO BEAN SOUP
Prep: 5 minutes   Cook: 21 to 24 minutes   Serves: 4

In the Oaxaca region of Mexico, garbanzo beans—otherwise known as chick-peas—find their way into a number of dishes, among them this flavorful soup. My version shortens the cooking time substantially by using canned beans.

2 tablespoons unsalted butter	1 (14½-ounce) can reduced-sodium chicken broth
1 medium onion, chopped	
1 medium carrot, chopped	1 tablespoon chopped fresh mint, or 1 teaspoon dried
2 garlic cloves, chopped	
½ teaspoon ground cumin	½ cup sour cream
½ teaspoon salt	1 tablespoon chopped cilantro or parsley
⅛ teaspoon pepper	
2 (15-ounce) cans garbanzo beans, rinsed and drained	

1. In a large saucepan, melt butter over medium heat. Add onion, carrot, and garlic and cook, stirring often, until onion is golden, about 5 minutes. Add cumin, salt, and pepper. Cook, stirring, 1 minute. Add drained garbanzo beans and chicken broth. Cover and simmer 10 minutes.

2. In a food processor or blender, puree soup with chopped mint until smooth. Return soup to pan. Rinse processor bowl with ½ cup water and add to soup. Reheat soup slowly over low heat, stirring frequently, until completely heated through, 5 to 8 minutes.

3. Serve hot, with a dollop of sour cream and a sprinkling of cilantro on each serving.

55 RED LENTIL SOUP
Prep: 20 minutes   Cook: 24 to 29 minutes   Serves: 4 to 6

Lentils are widely available in Mexican markets and find their way into home cooking. Red lentils make a delicious, delicately colored soup. If they are not in your supermarket, look for them in a health food store. Cilantro or parsley leaves would add attractive contrast as a garnish.

1 cup red lentils
2 tablespoons vegetable oil
1 large onion, chopped
2 garlic cloves, chopped
1 teaspoon ground cumin
1 medium carrot, chopped
1 (14½-ounce) can reduced-
    sodium chicken broth

1 (14½-ounce) can ready-cut
    tomatoes, with their
    juices
⅛ teaspoon crushed hot red
    pepper
½ teaspoon salt

1. Pick over lentils to remove any grit. Place in a wire strainer. Rinse well in 3 changes of water, or until water remains clear. Drain and reserve.

2. In a large saucepan, heat oil over medium heat. Add onion and garlic and cook, stirring, about 3 minutes, until onion is softened. Add cumin and cook 1 minute longer. Add carrot, broth, tomatoes, hot red pepper, salt, lentils, and 1 cup water. Bring to a boil, reduce heat to medium-low, cover, and simmer 15 to 20 minutes, or until lentils are tender.

3. In 2 batches, puree soup in a blender or food processor. Return soup to pan and cook over medium heat, stirring, until heated through, 5 minutes. Serve hot.

56 MEATBALL SOUP
Prep: 25 minutes   Cook: 25 minutes   Serves: 6

In this classic soup known as *sopa de albondigas,* meatballs are poached in the soup broth, rather than being browned first. This dish is not spicy, but hot salsa and fresh lime wedges should accompany it at the table.

½ pound lean ground beef
½ pound lean ground pork
2 tablespoons minced onion
2 garlic cloves, minced
2 tablespoons bread crumbs
1 teaspoon ground cumin
2 tablespoons finely chopped
    fresh mint, or 2 teaspoons
    dried
¼ teaspoon salt

⅛ teaspoon freshly ground
    black pepper
1 egg
2 (14½-ounce) cans reduced-
    sodium chicken broth
1 (14½-ounce) can beef broth
¾ cup tomato puree
½ teaspoon dried oregano
1 medium carrot, thinly sliced
1 celery rib, thinly sliced

1. In a large bowl, combine ground beef, ground pork, onion, garlic, bread crumbs, cumin, mint, salt, pepper, and egg. Mix thoroughly. Form meatballs about 1 inch in diameter. Reserve on a plate.

2. In a large saucepan, combine chicken broth, beef broth, and tomato puree. Bring to a boil over medium-high heat. Reduce heat to medium-low and gently drop meatballs into simmering broth. Partially cover and cook 10 minutes.

3. Skim surface of soup. Add oregano, carrot, and celery. Cover and cook about 15 minutes, or until vegetables are tender. Serve hot.

57 MENUDO
Prep: 30 minutes   Cook: 2 hours 55 minutes   Serves: 4 to 6

In Mexico, this soup has a reputation as a restorative following a vigorous night of partying. It tastes wonderful whatever your condition. Tripe may be partially cooked one day ahead, and the rest is easygoing.

1 pound beef honeycomb tripe, rinsed in warm water, drained, and cut into ½-inch squares
1½ tablespoons ancho or pasilla chili powder
1¼ teaspoons salt
1 teaspoon dried oregano
10 small garlic cloves, chopped
¾ pound meaty country-style pork ribs

1 (14-ounce) can white hominy, rinsed and drained
½ medium onion, chopped
⅛ teaspoon crushed hot red pepper
2 scallions, chopped
1 tablespoon chopped cilantro or parsley
1 lime, quartered

1. Place tripe in a medium saucepan. Add water to cover. Bring to a boil, reduce heat to medium, and cook 10 minutes. Drain into a colander and rinse under cold running water. Return tripe to pan. Add 8 cups water, chili powder, salt, oregano, and garlic. Bring to a boil, reduce heat to medium-low, and cook, partially covered, 1 hour. (Soup may be cooked to this point, cooled, covered, and refrigerated overnight. Reheat before proceeding.)

2. Add pork ribs to simmering soup. Cook over medium-low heat, partially covered, until pork is very tender, about 1½ hours. Remove ribs to a plate. As soon as they are cool enough to handle, shred meat, discarding excess fat and bones.

3. Return shredded pork to pan. Add hominy, chopped onion, and hot pepper. Partially cover and cook over medium heat 15 minutes to blend flavors. Season with additional salt to taste. Serve hot, topped with scallions and cilantro. Pass lime wedges to squeeze into soup.

58   POBLANO PEPPER AND CORN SOUP
Prep: 25 minutes   Cook: 31 to 36 minutes   Serves: 4

There are many versions of this satisfying soup, which is called *sopa poblano* in Mexico. If poblano peppers are not available, Anaheim peppers can be substituted.

3 poblano peppers
2 tablespoons vegetable oil
½ pound lean boneless pork, cut into ½-inch pieces
1 medium onion, chopped
¼ teaspoon salt
⅛ teaspoon pepper
1 teaspoon dried oregano

1 cup corn kernels, fresh or frozen
1 medium zucchini, cut into ½-inch dice
1 cup tomato puree
2 (14½-ounce) cans reduced-sodium chicken broth
1 lime, cut into wedges

1. Place peppers on a baking sheet and broil as close to heat as possible, turning, until charred all over, about 10 minutes. Or roast peppers directly over a gas flame, turning, until charred, about 5 minutes. Place peppers in a paper bag and let steam 10 minutes. Peel off blackened skin, rinsing under cold running water. Cut peppers open, discard stems and seeds. Cut peeled peppers into thin strips about 2 inches long.

2. In a large saucepan or flameproof casserole, heat oil over medium heat. Add meat and cook, stirring, until no longer pink, 3 to 5 minutes. Add onion, salt, pepper, and oregano. Cook, stirring, until onion is translucent, about 3 minutes.

3. Add poblano pepper strips, corn, zucchini, tomato puree, and chicken broth. Bring to a boil, reduce heat to medium-low, partially cover, and cook until vegetables are tender, 15 to 18 minutes. Serve hot. Pass lime wedges to squeeze into soup.

59   PINTO BEAN SOUP
Prep: 12 minutes   Cook: 25 minutes   Serves: 6

Here's a very tasty bean soup made simply and quickly with canned beans. A tossed salad and some crusty bread are all that's needed for a substantial lunch or light supper.

2 tablespoons vegetable oil
1 medium onion, chopped
2 teaspoons ground cumin
1 teaspoon dried oregano
½ teaspoon dried thyme leaves
2 (15-ounce) cans pinto beans, drained but not rinsed

1 (14-ounce) can ready-cut tomatoes
1 (14½-ounce) can beef broth
½ cup thick and chunky bottled red salsa
6 tablespoons sour cream
3 scallions, finely chopped

1. In a large, nonreactive saucepan or flameproof casserole, heat oil over medium-high heat. Add onion and cook, stirring frequently, until pale golden brown, 4 to 5 minutes. Add cumin, oregano, and thyme and cook, stirring, 1 minute.

2. Transfer mixture to a food processor. Add beans, tomatoes, beef broth, and salsa. Puree until smooth. Return soup to pan and simmer over low heat, stirring frequently, 20 minutes.

3. Divide soup among 6 bowls. Top each serving with 1 tablespoon sour cream. Garnish with chopped scallions and serve hot.

---

60 POZOLE

Prep: 20 minutes   Cook: 55 to 65 minutes   Serves: 6

Traditional Mexican *pozoles* are substantial meal-in-a-bowl soups, chock-full of pork, chicken, and hominy. Authentic versions are usually made with a pig's head and feet, but this streamlined version uses pork stew meat instead. The soup is topped with salad vegetables and a generous squeeze of lime is a must here.

1½ pounds boneless pork shoulder, cut into 1-inch pieces
2 (14½-ounce) cans reduced-sodium chicken broth
12 garlic cloves, peeled
1 large white onion, chopped
1½ teaspoons dried oregano
1 teaspoon salt
¼ teaspoon freshly ground pepper
6 chicken thighs (about 2½ pounds), skinned

1 (30-ounce) can white hominy, drained and rinsed
½ iceberg lettuce, shredded
8 radishes, thinly sliced
4 scallions, finely chopped
1 cup thick and chunky red salsa
1 large avocado, cut into ½-inch dice
3 limes, quartered

1. In a large saucepan or flameproof casserole, combine pork, chicken broth, garlic, onion, oregano, salt, pepper, and 2 cups of water. Bring to a boil over medium-high heat. Reduce heat to medium-low, cover, and cook 15 minutes.

2. Add chicken and cook until chicken is tender, 30 to 40 minutes. Remove thighs to a plate and pull meat from bones. Discard bones and return chicken meat to soup.

3. Add hominy and simmer over low heat 10 minutes to blend flavors.

4. To serve, place lettuce, radishes, scallions, salsa, avocado, and limes in separate small bowls. Divide hot soup among 6 large bowls. Pass garnishes for each diner to add at table.

61 POTATO, ONION, AND GREEN CHILE SOUP

Prep: 20 minutes   Cook: 28 to 30 minutes   Serves: 4

This soup can be mild or spicy by adjusting the amount of serrano peppers added with the final seasoning. Serve with quesadillas or crusty bread.

2 tablespoons butter	1 (5-ounce) can evaporated
1 tablespoon vegetable oil	milk
1 medium onion, coarsely	1¼ teaspoons salt
chopped	1 teaspoon ground cumin
2 shallots, sliced	4 scallions, thinly sliced
2 medium russet potatoes	1 to 2 serrano peppers, seeded
(about 1½ pounds),	and minced
peeled and thinly sliced	1½ tablespoons finely chopped
1 (7-ounce) can diced green	parsley
chiles	

1. In a large saucepan, melt butter in oil over medium-high heat. Add onion and shallots and cook, stirring frequently, until edges begin to brown, 3 to 5 minutes. Add potatoes, diced chiles, milk, salt, cumin, and 2 cups of water. Bring to a boil. Partially cover, reduce heat to medium-low, and simmer until potatoes are very tender, about 20 minutes. Soup may appear curdled, but it will blend smooth.

2. Puree soup, in batches if necessary, in a food processor or blender. If soup is too thick, thin with a little water or milk to achieve consistency of heavy cream. Return soup to pan. Add scallions, serrano peppers, and parsley. Bring to a boil, reduce heat to medium-low, and simmer 5 minutes. Serve hot or cold.

62 VERMICELLI SOUP

Prep: 25 minutes   Cook: 16 to 17 minutes   Serves: 4 to 6

Thin strands of vermicelli or angel-hair pasta, called *fideos* in Spanish, are used to make this popular soup called *sopa de fideo*.

3 tablespoons vegetable oil	6 cups Chicken Stock (page
3 ounces vermicelli, broken	34) or 3 (14½-ounce) cans
into 4-inch lengths	reduced-sodium chicken
½ medium onion, chopped	broth
2 garlic cloves, minced	3 scallions, chopped
½ teaspoon dried oregano	4 ounces Monterey Jack
½ teaspoon salt	cheese, cut into ½-inch
1 medium carrot, thinly sliced	cubes
2 medium tomatoes, peeled	2 tablespoons chopped
and finely chopped	cilantro

1. In a large saucepan, heat oil over medium heat. Add vermicelli and cook, stirring constantly, until it browns lightly, about 1 minute. With a slotted spoon, immediately remove vermicelli from pan and drain on paper towels.

2. In the oil, cook onion, garlic, oregano, salt, and carrot, stirring occasionally, until onion is softened and translucent, about 2 minutes. Add tomatoes and cook, stirring frequently, until juices have evaporated, 3 to 4 minutes. Add chicken stock and return vermicelli to pan. Cook until vermicelli is just tender, about 10 minutes. Stir in scallions. Remove from heat.

3. Divide cheese cubes among 4 to 6 soup bowls. Ladle hot soup into bowls and garnish with chopped cilantro.

63 YUCATAN LIME SOUP
Prep: 20 minutes   Cook: 28 to 30 minutes   Serves: 4

This is the Yucatán version of tortilla soup. For a very appealing presentation, serve in glass bowls.

4 corn tortillas	1 celery rib, thinly sliced
½ cup vegetable oil	1 small carrot, thinly sliced
1 whole skinless chicken breast, on the bone (1 to 1¼ pounds)	1 large tomato, peeled and chopped
	1 teaspoon salt
2 (14½-ounce) cans reduced-sodium chicken broth	2 scallions, finely chopped
	Juice of 3 limes, about ⅓ cup
1 bay leaf	1 large avocado, cut into 8 slices
4 garlic cloves, chopped	
2 parsley sprigs	2 tablespoons chopped cilantro
1 medium onion, chopped	

1. Cut tortillas into thin strips, about ⅜ inch wide. In a medium skillet, heat oil to 370°F. Fry tortilla strips, about 12 pieces at a time, stirring to keep them from sticking together, until lightly browned and crisp, about 30 seconds per batch. Remove with a slotted spoon and drain on paper towels. Reserve cooking oil.

2. In a medium saucepan, place chicken breast, chicken broth, bay leaf, garlic, and parsley. Bring to a boil over medium-high heat. Reduce heat to medium-low and cook until chicken is white throughout but still juicy, about 15 minutes. Let chicken cool in liquid about 20 minutes, then remove chicken breast and tear meat into ¼-inch shreds, discarding skin and bones. Strain chicken stock through a fine-mesh sieve into a medium bowl. Skim fat off top.

3. In a large saucepan, heat 1 tablespoon reserved oil over medium heat. Add onion, celery, carrot, tomato, and salt. Cook, stirring, until vegetables are softened, juices are rendered, and mixture is nearly dry, 6 to 8 minutes. Add reserved chicken broth, shredded chicken, and scallions. Cook until completely heated through, about 5 minutes. Stir in lime juice.

4. To serve, divide tortilla strips among 4 soup plates. Ladle hot soup over crisp tortilla strips. Add 2 slices of avocado to each bowl and sprinkle cilantro on top.

64 SPINACH AND GARBANZO BEAN SOUP
Prep: 25 minutes   Cook: 40 minutes   Serves: 4

4 bacon slices, chopped
1 medium onion, chopped
4 garlic cloves, minced
1 teaspoon ground cumin
⅛ teaspoon ground allspice
1 (14-ounce) can Italian peeled
  tomatoes, chopped, with
  juices
1 (14½-ounce) can reduced-
  sodium chicken broth

1 (15-ounce) can garbanzo
  beans, rinsed and drained
1 bunch of fresh spinach
  (about 1 pound), washed,
  drained, and chopped
4 scallions, chopped
1 tablespoon Worcestershire
  sauce
¼ teaspoon pepper

1. In a large nonreactive saucepan or flameproof casserole, cook bacon, onion, and garlic over medium heat, stirring occasionally, until bacon renders its fat and onion begins to brown, about 5 minutes.

2. Add cumin and allspice and cook, stirring, 1 minute. Add tomatoes and chicken broth. Cook, uncovered, 5 minutes.

3. Add garbanzo beans, spinach, scallions, Worcestershire, and pepper. Bring to a boil, reduce heat to low, cover, and cook, stirring occasionally, 30 minutes. Serve hot.

65 CREAM OF ZUCCHINI AND ONION SOUP
Prep: 10 minutes   Cook: 23 minutes   Serves: 4

This marvelous soup, which is a snap to make, features the versatile and abundant zucchini. It deserves your nicest soup bowls and is just right for a special dinner. It reminds me of many a Mexican soup I've been served.

3 tablespoons butter
1 medium onion, chopped
4 medium zucchini, sliced
  (about 1¼ pounds)
¼ teaspoon pepper
1 teaspoon salt

4 scallions, chopped
¼ cup chicken broth
1 (5-ounce) can evaporated
  milk
2 tablespoons chopped
  cilantro

1. In a large saucepan, melt butter over medium heat. Add onion and cook, stirring, until softened but not browned, about 3 minutes. Add zucchini, pepper, salt, and 1 cup of water. Cover and cook over medium heat until zucchini are very soft, about 15 minutes.

2. Add scallions, chicken broth, and milk. Cook, uncovered, 5 minutes. In a blender or food processor, puree soup until smooth. Serve hot or cold, garnished with cilantro.

66 TORTILLA SOUP

Prep: 45 minutes to 1 hour   Cook: 1 hour   Serves: 6

Sopa de tortilla may be the best known of all Mexico's soups. There are many versions, and it's an adventure to order tortilla soup in restaurants to taste different interpretations. In this recipe, the onion, garlic, and tomatoes are roasted to deepen the flavor.

1½ teaspoons dried oregano	6 cups Chicken Stock (page
½ cup vegetable oil	34) or 3 (14½-ounce) cans
6 corn tortillas, halved and cut	reduced-sodium chicken
crosswise into thin strips	broth
1 medium onion, halved	½ teaspoon salt
4 garlic cloves	Diced avocado, chopped
1½ tablespoons olive oil	cilantro, lime wedges,
4 medium tomatoes, cored	and Crisp Ancho Chile
	Strips (page 78)

1. Preheat oven to 375°F. In a small dry skillet, cook oregano over medium heat, shaking pan often, until fragrant, 1 to 2 minutes. Transfer to a small bowl.

2. In a medium skillet, heat vegetable oil over medium heat until hot but not smoking. Add tortilla strips, a few at a time, and fry until golden brown, about 45 seconds per batch. With tongs or a slotted spoon, remove tortilla strips and drain on paper towels.

3. Rub onion and garlic with ½ tablespoon olive oil and place in a small baking dish. Cover tightly with aluminum foil and roast about 30 minutes, or until soft. At the same time, place tomatoes in another small baking dish and roast, uncovered, about 45 minutes, or until very soft and skins are wrinkled. Remove skins from onion, garlic, and tomatoes. Place in a blender or food processor. Add toasted oregano and puree until smooth.

4. In a large nonreactive saucepan, heat remaining 1 tablespoon olive oil over medium heat. Add roasted tomato puree and cook, stirring frequently, until thickened, about 4 minutes. Add chicken stock and salt. Bring to a boil. Reduce heat to low, cover, and simmer 10 minutes to blend flavors.

5. Divide crisp tortilla strips among 6 soup bowls. Ladle hot soup into bowls and garnish each serving with a little diced avocado and chopped cilantro. Pass lime wedges and ancho strips to add at table.

67 GOLDEN SQUASH SOUP
Prep: 10 minutes   Cook: 21 to 26 minutes   Serves: 4

This gleaming golden soup is very low in fat and deeply satisfying.

1 butternut squash, about
   2 pounds
2 tablespoons olive oil
1 small onion, chopped
2 garlic cloves, chopped
1 medium carrot, peeled and
   thinly sliced
½ teaspoon ground cumin
½ teaspoon salt

⅛ teaspoon pepper
1 fresh jalapeño pepper,
   seeded and minced
1 (14½-ounce) can reduced-
   sodium chicken broth
   Nonfat plain yogurt or sour
   cream and chopped
   cilantro

1. Cut squash in half; scoop out seeds. Peel squash and cut into 1-inch pieces. In a large saucepan or flameproof casserole, heat oil over medium heat. Add onion and garlic and cook, stirring often, until they begin to brown, about 5 minutes. Add carrot, cumin, salt, and pepper. Cook, tossing, 1 minute.

2. Add squash, jalapeño pepper, and chicken broth. Bring to a boil, reduce heat to medium-low, cover, and cook 15 to 20 minutes, or until vegetables are very tender.

3. Puree soup in batches in a blender or food processor. Return to saucepan and return to a boil over medium-low heat. Serve hot, garnished with yogurt and chopped cilantro.

68 TOMATO AND RED BEAN SOUP
Prep: 20 minutes   Cook: 2¾ to 3 hours   Serves: 6

Beans of every kind are everyday fare all over Mexico, and many are made into flavorful soups, such as this one from Oaxaca. Oven-roasted onion and garlic contribute to its deep, satisfying flavor.

1 cup dried small red beans,
   sorted and rinsed
2 bay leaves
1 teaspoon dried oregano
1 teaspoon ground cumin
1 medium onion, halved
6 garlic cloves
1 tablespoon olive oil
1 teaspoon salt

½ teaspoon black pepper
1 (14-ounce) can Mexican-
   style stewed tomatoes
1 cup beef broth
2 fresh jalapeño peppers,
   seeded and minced
2 tablespoons chopped
   cilantro
1 lime, cut into 6 wedges

1. Preheat oven to 350°F. In a large saucepan, combine beans, bay leaves, oregano, cumin, and 3 cups of water. Bring to a boil, reduce heat to medium-low, cover, and simmer, stirring occasionally, until beans are very tender, about 2 hours. (The beans can be prepared a day ahead.)

2. Meanwhile, brush onion and garlic all over with oil. Wrap in heavy-duty aluminum foil and roast in preheated oven 30 to 40 minutes, or until very tender. Remove from oven. Chop onion and add to bean mixture. Squeeze roasted garlic into beans. Stir in salt, pepper, tomatoes, broth, and jalapeños. Cook, uncovered, 10 minutes. Remove and discard bay leaves.

3. In a food processor or blender, puree soup until smooth. Return to pan and simmer over low heat 5 to 10 minutes to blend flavors. Serve hot, garnished with chopped cilantro. Pass lime wedges to squeeze into soup.

---

69 RED DEVIL TOMATO SOUP WITH CRISP TORTILLA BITS

Prep: 15 minutes   Cook: 25 to 27 minutes   Serves: 4

Bits of crunchy corn tortilla chips are called *migas*. Here they are sprinkled on top of a zesty tomato soup, with a swirl of sour cream and a sprinkle of fresh cilantro and mint for a unique flavor treat.

2 **tablespoons unsalted butter**	1 **cup canned chicken broth**
1 **medium onion, chopped**	⅛ **teaspoon crushed hot red**
3 **garlic cloves, chopped**	**pepper**
1 **large celery rib, chopped**	½ **teaspoon salt**
1 **small red bell pepper,**	½ **cup broken-up tortilla chips**
seeded and chopped	**Sour cream, chopped**
1 **(28-ounce) can peeled plum**	**cilantro, and chopped**
tomatoes, with their	**fresh mint**
juices	

1. In a large nonreactive saucepan or flameproof casserole, melt butter over medium heat. Add onion, garlic, celery, and red bell pepper. Cover and cook, stirring often, until vegetables are tender, 5 to 7 minutes. Add tomatoes with their juices, chicken broth, hot pepper, and salt. Cover, reduce heat to medium-low, and cook 15 minutes.

2. Puree soup in a blender or food processor. There will be some texture. Return soup to pan and cook over medium heat until piping hot, about 5 minutes.

3. To serve, ladle soup into 4 bowls. Sprinkle each serving with tortilla chips, drizzle on sour cream, and top with cilantro and mint.

Chapter 3

On the Light Side

This chapter is filled with a variety of delicious salads and light first courses to kick off festive Mexican meals, add to buffets, serve with barbecues, or take along on picnics.

Salads, as we generally serve them, are not an integral part of Mexican meals, but raw vegetables and fruits garnish nearly all main-course plates and become the salad portion of a meal. There are exceptions, of course, as with Caesar Salad, Christmas Eve Salad, and Hearts of Palm Salad with Shrimp and Lime, which are true separate-course salads. Other traditional salad offerings include Jicama and Orange Salad and Sonoran Green Chile Salad. Many typical salads are quite large and are typically suited for light meals or luncheons, like Chicken Taco Salad, Shrimp Salad with Tomatoes and Cucumber, and Mexican Shredded Beef Salad.

Besides salads, there are wonderful starter courses in this chapter, such as Spicy Crab Cakes with Chipotle Mayonnaise, Poached Oysters with Salsa, and Yucatán Shrimp.

For that special brunch or breakfast, start off with Buenos Dias Fruit Plates. For barbecues and picnics, consider Mexican Potato, Carrot, and Pea Salad, Chunky Tomato and Avocado Salad, Chayote Salad with Red and Green Peppers and Lime Dressing, or Ensenada Tuna Salad.

Since most of the recipes in this chapter are to be served cold or have a marinade that improves the flavor with a little aging, many of them can be made ahead.

70   AVOCADOS WITH CRAB SALAD
Prep: 10 minutes   Cook: none   Serves: 4

Pile crab salad in avocado halves for a special luncheon dish or first course.

2 cups fresh or canned crabmeat, drained	2 tablespoons lime juice
2 scallions, finely chopped	½ teaspoon salt
½ medium red bell pepper, cut into ¼-inch dice	2 large avocados
	4 teaspoons mayonnaise
1 serrano pepper, minced	2 tablespoons chopped cilantro
1 tablespoon vegetable oil	

1. In a medium bowl, combine crab, scallions, bell pepper, serrano pepper, oil, lime juice, and salt. Toss to mix well.

2. Cut each avocado in half and remove the pits. Place each avocado half on a plate. Fill each avocado half with salad, mounding in center. Top each with 1 teaspoon mayonnaise and sprinkle with fresh cilantro. Refrigerate if not serving immediately.

71   ARTICHOKE AND PIMIENTO SALAD WITH SUNFLOWER SEED DRESSING
Prep: 15 minutes   Cook: none   Serves: 4

Artichokes are extremely popular in Mexico, both at home and in restaurants.

1 (9-ounce) package frozen artichoke hearts or 1 (14-ounce) can	1 garlic clove, chopped
	1 fresh serrano pepper, seeded and minced
1 (4-ounce) jar diced pimientos, drained	2 tablespoons dry-roasted sunflower seeds
1 (4-ounce) can sliced black olives, rinsed and drained	2 tablespoons lime juice
½ cup packed flat-leaf Italian parsley	½ cup olive oil
	1 head of butter lettuce, torn into bite-size pieces

1. Cook frozen artichoke hearts according to package directions, or rinse and drain canned artichoke hearts. Quarter artichokes and place in a medium bowl. Add pimientos and olives and toss.

2. In a food processor or blender, combine parsley, garlic, serrano peppers, sunflower seeds, and lime juice. Process to a paste. With machine on, slowly add olive oil in a stream through feed tube to form a dressing.

3. Add dressing and lettuce to artichoke mixture. Toss gently. Mound salad equally among 4 plates and serve.

72   AVOCADO AND PAPAYA SALAD
Prep: 20 minutes   Cook: none   Serves: 4

When avocados and papayas are at their peak, try this colorful first-course salad. It's an unusual seasonal treat that goes especially well before a spicy meal or seafood.

3 tablespoons olive oil
1 tablespoon white wine
  vinegar
1 teaspoon chili powder
¼ teaspoon salt

2 large ripe avocados
1 cup diced (½-inch) papaya
8 lettuce leaves, washed
1 lime, cut into slim wedges

1. In a small bowl, whisk together oil, vinegar, chili powder, and salt until smooth. Set dressing aside.

2. Cut avocados lengthwise in half and remove pit from each. Scoop out avocado in one piece, without tearing or breaking skins. Save shells. Cut avocado into ½-inch cubes.

3. In a medium bowl, combine avocado with papaya. Add dressing and toss gently to coat. Spoon salad into reserved avocado shells. Serve on lettuce-lined plates, with lime wedges.

73   CANTALOUPE AND SHRIMP WITH CITRUS VINAIGRETTE
Prep: 15 minutes   Cook: 2 minutes   Chill: 1 hour   Serves: 6 to 8

An elegant first course, or composed salad, to serve for a special meal.

1 pound medium shrimp,
  shelled and deveined
¼ cup fresh orange juice
2 tablespoons fresh lime juice
½ teaspoon Worcestershire
  sauce
3 drops of Tabasco sauce

½ teaspoon salt
¾ cup vegetable oil
1 large cantaloupe, peeled,
  halved, and cut into thin
  slices
1 bunch of cilantro, rinsed
  and dried

1. Bring a medium saucepan of lightly salted water to a boil. Add shrimp and cook until pink and loosely curled, about 2 minutes. Drain.

2. In a blender jar, place orange juice, lime juice, Worcestershire, Tabasco, salt, and oil. Blend vinaigrette well.

3. In a large bowl, place shrimp and toss with ¼ cup of reserved vinaigrette. Cover and marinate in refrigerator 1 hour.

4. To serve, arrange sliced cantaloupe on individual serving plates. Remove shrimp from marinade and divide among the plates, arranging attractively on melon slices. Garnish each plate with a bouquet of cilantro. Pass remaining vinaigrette at the table.

74   BEEF TACO SALAD

Prep: 20 minutes   Cook: 9 to 10 minutes   Serves: 4

2 tablespoons olive oil
½ pound lean ground beef
½ medium onion, minced
½ teaspoon salt
3 tablespoons chili powder
½ teaspoon dried oregano
1 medium head iceberg
    lettuce, torn into bite-size
    pieces
1 (15-ounce) can pinto beans,
    rinsed and drained

4 scallions, chopped
1 cup crushed tortilla chips
1 cup thick and chunky red
    salsa
1 cup shredded Monterey Jack
    cheese
½ cup sour cream or low-fat
    plain yogurt
1 large avocado, peeled and
    cut into ½-inch dice
¼ cup chopped cilantro

1. In a medium skillet, heat oil over medium-high heat. Add ground beef and cook, stirring and breaking it up, about 6 minutes, or until no longer pink. Add onion, salt, chili powder, and oregano. Cook, stirring, 3 to 4 minutes to blend flavors. Remove from heat.

2. In a large bowl, place lettuce, pinto beans, scallions, tortilla chips, salsa, and cooked meat. Toss to combine. Divide salad among 4 plates. Top each with a quarter of the cheese, sour cream, avocado, and cilantro.

75   MEXICAN CALAMARI SALAD

Prep: 20 minutes   Cook: 1 minute   Chill: 2 to 3 hours   Serves: 4

Calamari, commonly called squid in the United States, is low in fat and inexpensive. It makes a refreshing first course.

1 pound cleaned squid, cut
    into rings ½ inch thick;
    leave tentacles whole
1 tablespoon unseasoned rice
    vinegar
1 tablespoon fresh lime juice
¼ cup olive oil
1 tablespoon minced red
    onion

1 to 2 jalapeño peppers,
    seeded and minced
1 large tomato, seeded and cut
    into ¼-inch dice
2 tablespoons chopped
    cilantro
½ teaspoon salt
2 cups shredded lettuce
    Black olives, for garnish

1. Bring a large saucepan of lightly salted water to a boil. Add squid and cook 45 seconds to 1 minute, or until opaque. Do not overcook, or squid will be tough. Drain and rinse with cold running water. Shake excess water from squid and place in a medium bowl.

2. Add vinegar, lime juice, olive oil, red onion, jalapeño pepper, tomato, cilantro, and salt. Stir to mix well. Cover and refrigerate 2 to 3 hours. Serve chilled on a bed of lettuce. Garnish with olives.

76 CABBAGE SALAD WITH FRESH MINT
Prep: 15 minutes   Cook: none   Serves: 6

This crisp, clean refreshing salad contrasts well with really hot foods.

1 medium head of cabbage, about 1 pound
½ cup lightly packed fresh mint leaves, finely chopped
½ large green bell pepper, cut into thin strips
6 radishes, thinly sliced

½ teaspoon salt
¼ teaspoon freshly ground pepper
Cumin-Lime Vinaigrette (recipe follows) or your favorite bottled vinaigrette

1. Remove and discard tough outer cabbage leaves. Cut cabbage into quarters and cut out core. Finely shred cabbage in a food processor or on slicing blade of a hand grater.

2. In a large bowl, combine cabbage, mint, bell pepper, and radish rounds. Season with salt and pepper. Add dressing and toss to moisten. Cover and refrigerate until serving time. Serve chilled.

77 CUMIN-LIME VINAIGRETTE
Prep: 2 minutes   Cook: none   Makes: about ½ cup

3 tablespoons white wine vinegar
2 tablespoons fresh lime juice
1 tablespoon minced parsley

½ teaspoon ground cumin
½ tablespoon sugar
½ cup olive oil

In a small bowl, whisk all ingredients until well blended.

78 RED AND GREEN CABBAGE AND AVOCADO SALAD
Prep: 15 minutes   Cook: none   Serves: 6 to 8

Serve with crunchy salad with spicy sauced meat dishes for great contrast.

2 cups shredded green cabbage
1 cup shredded red cabbage
1 medium carrot, peeled and shredded
1 serrano pepper, minced
2 tablespoons chopped cilantro

Juice of 1 lime
2 tablespoons mayonnaise
¼ teaspoon salt
4 grinds of fresh black pepper
1 large ripe avocado, cut into ½-inch dice

In a large salad bowl, toss together green cabbage, red cabbage, and carrot. Add serrano pepper, cilantro, lime juice, and mayonnaise. Mix well. Season with salt and pepper. Add avocado and toss lightly.

79 MEXICAN SHREDDED BEEF SALAD

Prep: 25 minutes   Cook: 1 hour 20 to 25 minutes
Stand: 1 hour   Serves: 6

A whole meal salad to satisfy even hearty appetites. Cook the meat and potatoes ahead, then assemble just before serving. Flour tortillas, salsa, and guacamole usually accompany this salad.

1 flank steak, about 2 pounds	3 tablespoons minced onion
2 tablespoons vegetable oil	2 tablespoons red wine
1 garlic clove, minced	vinegar
1 teaspoon dried oregano	¼ cup olive oil
½ teaspoon salt	2 cups shredded romaine
¼ teaspoon pepper	lettuce
3 small red potatoes (about	½ cup crumbled queso fresco
1 pound)	or feta cheese
1 (4-ounce) can diced green	
chiles	

1. Trim fat from meat. Cut into 2-inch pieces. In a large skillet, heat oil over medium-high heat. Add meat, garlic, oregano, salt, and pepper. Cook, stirring, until meat is browned, about 5 minutes. Add 1 cup of water, cover, reduce heat to medium-low, and simmer about 1 hour, or until meat is tender. Remove pan from heat and let meat cool in stock, at least 1 hour. When cool enough to handle, remove meat from liquid and shred by pulling apart with your fingers. Place in a medium bowl. (Meat can be cooked a day ahead.)

2. Meanwhile, in a medium saucepan of boiling salted water, cook the potatoes until tender, 15 to 20 minutes. Drain and rinse under cold running water until cool enough to handle. Peel potatoes and cut into neat ½-inch dice. Place in bowl with shredded beef.

3. Add diced green chiles, onion, vinegar, oil and additional salt and pepper to taste. Toss well to mix. To serve, arrange lettuce on a serving platter. Mound salad on lettuce. Sprinkle cheese on top. Serve at room temperature.

80   CEVICHE

Prep: 15 minutes   Cook: none   Marinate: 4 hours   Serves: 4

Always insist upon impeccably fresh seafood when making a dish like this, which cooks the fish in the marinade. Ceviche is a Mexican appetizer that's light and refreshing. Serve with a basket of tortilla chips on the side.

¾ **pound very fresh firm white ocean fish, such as cod, snapper, or halibut**
½ **cup fresh lime juice**
2 **serrano peppers, minced**
1 **medium tomato, seeded and coarsely chopped**
1 **avocado, cut into ½-inch dice**

1 **tablespoon minced white onion**
2 **tablespoons chopped cilantro**
¼ **teaspoon dried oregano**
1 **tablespoon olive oil**
½ **teaspoon salt**
Lime wedges

1. Trim all skin and fat from fish and remove all bones. Cut into ½-inch dice. Place in a glass jar with lime juice. Cover and refrigerate 4 to 6 hours, turning jar over occasionally to distribute lime juice.

2. Drain fish and transfer to a medium bowl. Add serrano peppers, tomato, avocado, onion, cilantro, oregano, oil, and salt. Fold gently to mix. Cover and refrigerate about 20 minutes before serving. Serve in individual cocktail glasses, with lime wedges.

81   CAESAR SALAD

Prep: 15 minutes   Cook: none   Serves: 4

Invented by Alex-Caesar Cardini in Tijuana, Mexico, Caesar salad won great popularity in the twenties. Here's a Caesar for the nineties with a lighter dressing and without the customary egg. It's a very respectable and delicious version.

½ **cup olive oil**
2 **tablespoons red wine vinegar**
1 **tablespoon fresh lemon juice**
4 **anchovy fillets**
2 **large garlic cloves, chopped**

1 **teaspoon Dijon mustard**
¼ **cup freshly grated Parmesan cheese**
3 **grinds of fresh black pepper**
1 **large head of romaine lettuce, torn into pieces**
1 **cup croutons**

1. In blender or food processor, combine oil, vinegar, lemon juice, anchovies, garlic, and mustard. Add Parmesan cheese and black pepper and blend well. Transfer to a small bowl and set aside at room temperature, or cover and refrigerate up to 3 days. Whisk thoroughly before using.

2. In a large bowl, place lettuce and croutons. Add dressing and toss well to coat salad. Divide among 4 salad plates and serve at once.

82   CHICKEN TACO SALAD
Prep: 15 minutes   Cook: 4 to 5 minutes   Serves: 4

2 tablespoons olive oil
1 pound skinless, boneless
   chicken breasts, cut into
   1-inch pieces
½ teaspoon salt
2 tablespoons chili powder
1 medium head of iceberg
   lettuce, torn into bite-size
   pieces
1 (8-ounce) can kidney beans,
   rinsed and drained

1 (4-ounce) can sliced black
   olives, drained
3 scallions, chopped
1 cup crushed tortilla chips
1 cup thick and chunky salsa
1 cup shredded Cheddar
   cheese (about 4 ounces)
½ cup sour cream
1 large tomato, chopped
¼ cup chopped cilantro

1. In a medium skillet, heat oil over medium-high heat. Add chicken and cook, tossing, until white throughout but still juicy, 3 to 4 minutes. Add salt and chili powder. Cook, stirring, 1 minute to blend flavors. Remove from heat and set aside to cool slightly. (Chicken can be cooked ahead and refrigerated.)

2. In a large bowl, place lettuce, kidney beans, olives, scallions, tortilla chips, reserved chicken, and salsa. Toss to mix.

3. Divide salad among 4 plates. Top each with a quarter of cheese, sour cream, chopped tomato, and cilantro.

83   CHAYOTE SALAD WITH RED AND GREEN PEPPERS AND LIME DRESSING
Prep: 15 minutes   Cook: 19 to 22 minutes   Stand: 1 to 3 hours
Serves: 6

The mild flavor and lovely pale color of the chayote works well in this marinated salad. Arranged on an attractive platter, it holds up all evening on a buffet table.

2 chayotes
⅓ cup olive oil
1 medium white onion,
   halved and sliced
1 medium red bell pepper, cut
   into ½-inch-wide strips
   about 2 inches long
½ medium green bell pepper,
   cut into ½-inch-wide
   strips about 2 inches long

3 fresh serrano peppers,
   seeded and minced
½ teaspoon salt
2 tablespoons lime juice
1 tablespoon cider vinegar
1 tablespoon chopped parsley

1. Cut chayotes in half lengthwise and cook in boiling water to cover until crisp-tender when pierced with tip of a sharp knife, 18 to 20 minutes. Drain and rinse under cold running water. Peel and cut lengthwise into ¼-inch slices. Place in a medium bowl.

2. In a large skillet, heat oil over medium heat. Add onion, red and green bell peppers, and serrano peppers and cook, stirring, 1 to 2 minutes, until just barely cooked. Remove from heat. Add salt, lime juice, and vinegar. Pour at once over chayote. Stir gently to combine.

3. Cover salad and let stand 1 to 3 hours at room temperature or refrigerate overnight. Let return to room temperature and sprinkle with parsley before serving.

84 SPICY CRAB CAKES WITH CHIPOTLE MAYONNAISE

Prep: 30 minutes   Chill: 1 hour   Cook: 10 minutes   Serves: 6

Fresh crab makes incredibly good cakes, and when you give them a Mexican twist by adding smoky chipotle chiles to the other flavors, they're great. This dish is definitely contemporary Southwestern cooking and well worth the effort. Lightly dressed greens add a nice touch.

1 large cooked fresh crab, about 1½ pounds, or ½ pound fresh cooked or canned crabmeat
1 tablespoon olive oil
¼ cup finely chopped onion
¼ cup finely chopped red bell pepper
1 tablespoon chopped parsley
1 serrano pepper, minced
1 tablespoon fresh lemon juice

1 tablespoon Worcestershire sauce
¾ cup dry bread crumbs
¼ teaspoon salt
⅛ teaspoon freshly ground pepper
½ cup plus 3 tablespoons mayonnaise
1 egg, lightly beaten
½ cup fine bread crumbs
2 tablespoons mashed canned chipotle chile
¼ cup vegetable oil

1. Crack crab. Remove meat and pick over carefully. Place in a medium bowl, cover, and refrigerate.

2. In a medium skillet, heat oil over medium heat. Add onion and cook until softened, about 2 minutes. Add bell pepper and cook until barely tender, about 2 minutes longer. Transfer to a medium bowl.

3. Add crab, parsley, serrano pepper, lemon juice, Worcestershire, bread crumbs, salt, pepper, 3 tablespoons mayonnaise, and egg to bowl and mix very well. With hands, form crab mixture into 3-inch cakes. Coat with fine bread crumbs on both sides. Place on a plate, cover, and refrigerate 1 hour, or until ready to fry.

4. In a small bowl, mix remaining ½ cup mayonnaise and mashed chipotle. Cover and refrigerate chipotle mayonnaise until serving time.

5. In a medium skillet, heat oil over medium-high heat. Cook crab cakes, turning once, until crisp and brown outside and cooked through, about 3 minutes on each side. Place on individual plates and serve with chipotle mayonnaise.

85 CRAB SALAD
Prep: 10 minutes   Cook: none   Serves: 4

The best way to enjoy fresh crab in season is to prepare it very simply, as in this main-course salad. Good-quality canned crabmeat can be used as well.

4 cups shredded iceberg
   lettuce
2 cups cooked picked over
   crabmeat, about 1 pound
1 cup mayonnaise
½ cup prepared chili sauce

1 serrano pepper, minced
2 tablespoons chopped
   cilantro or Italian flat-leaf
   parsley
   Sliced avocado and lime
   wedges

1. Divide lettuce among 4 plates. Arrange crabmeat over lettuce.

2. In a medium bowl, combine mayonnaise, chili sauce, and serrano pepper. Stir to mix well. Spoon over crab. Sprinkle cilantro on top. Garnish each plate with sliced avocados and lime wedges. Serve at once.

86 FISH ESCABECHE
Prep: 20 minutes   Cook: 14 minutes
Marinate: overnight   Serves: 6

Pickled cold fish is a classic Spanish preparation that can be found all over Latin America. Remember to make it a day ahead, because it must marinate overnight. Serve escabeche as an appetizer or first course with tomatoes, avocado, lettuce, and soft, warm corn tortillas.

2 pounds firm white fish
   fillets, such as snapper or
   cod, cut into 2-inch pieces
2 tablespoons lime juice
¾ cup olive oil
⅔ cup unseasoned rice vinegar
4 garlic cloves, thinly sliced
2 serrano peppers, halved
   lengthwise

2 whole cloves
1 cinnamon stick
10 peppercorns
1 teaspoon dried oregano
1 teaspoon whole cumin seed
1 bay leaf
½ medium onion, sliced
½ teaspoon salt

1. Place fish on a plate. Drizzle lime juice over fish pieces. Let stand 15 minutes. Pat dry. In a large skillet, heat 3 tablespoons of olive oil over medium heat. Add fish and cook about 2 minutes on each side, or until white throughout. Transfer fish to a shallow dish.

2. In a medium nonreactive saucepan, combine vinegar, garlic, serrano peppers, cloves, cinnamon stick, peppercorns, oregano, cumin seed, bay leaf, onion, and salt. Simmer over medium-low heat 10 minutes, to reduce slightly and intensify flavors. Turn heat off and stir in remaining olive oil.

3. Pour warm marinade over fish. Let stand 10 minutes, then cover and refrigerate overnight. To serve, lift fish from marinade and place on a platter.

87 NOPALITOS SALAD
Prep: 8 minutes   Cook: none   Serves: 4

Nopales, the pads of the prickly-pear cactus, are cut and packed in jars or cans, ready to use. The cactus looks somewhat like green beans and has a mild, pleasant flavor.

1 (15-ounce) jar nopalitos (tender cactus pieces)
2 medium tomatoes, cut into 8 wedges each
½ medium white onion, minced
1 serrano pepper, minced
3 tablespoons vegetable oil

1 tablespoon cider vinegar
2 tablespoons chopped cilantro
4 large lettuce leaves
2 tablespoons crumbled queso fresco or feta cheese

1. Drain and rinse cactus. Shake off excess water and place in a medium bowl. Add tomatoes, onion, serrano pepper, oil, vinegar, and cilantro. Stir to mix well.

2. Line a shallow serving bowl with lettuce leaves. Mound salad on lettuce. Sprinkle crumbled cheese over top.

88 POACHED OYSTERS WITH SALSA
Prep: 20 minutes   Cook: 2½ minutes   Serves: 4

Oyster lovers really enjoy these. Inspired by market and street vendors, the oysters are cooked lightly, then chilled and served with a simple spicy salsa. Purchase the freshest oysters possible, in or out of their shells. Crisp tortilla chips or sliced French rolls, similar to Mexican *bolillos,* go very well with these oysters.

16 large fresh oysters, shucked with liquor reserved
1 medium tomato, minced
2 tablespoons minced white onion
1 serrano pepper, minced

1 tablespoon chopped fresh cilantro
2 tablespoons lime juice
½ teaspoon salt
⅛ teaspoon black pepper

1. Pour oyster liquor into a medium skillet; if purchased in jars, use about ½ cup oyster liquor from jar. Add ¼ cup water and bring to a boil over medium heat. Add oysters and cook until edges begin to curl, about 2 minutes. Turn over and cook 30 seconds. Drain and place 1 oyster on a reserved oyster shell or platter. Cover and refrigerate.

2. In a small bowl, combine tomato, onion, serrano pepper, cilantro, lime juice, salt, and pepper. Stir to mix well. Top each oyster with about 1 teaspoon of salsa. Serve cold.

89   SONORAN GREEN CHILE SALAD
Prep: 15 minutes   Cook: 10 minutes   Marinate: 1 hour   Serves: 4

A salad of marinated whole green chiles and bright red tomatoes has great eye-appeal and is vitamin-rich. Anaheim peppers range from mild to medium-hot. This popular composed salad often appears with grilled meats and seafood.

1 garlic clove, crushed
½ teaspoon dried oregano
½ teaspoon ground cumin
½ teaspoon salt
2 tablespoons cider vinegar
⅓ cup olive oil
½ teaspoon sugar
6 fresh Anaheim peppers

3 ripe tomatoes, cut into
    8 wedges each
½ medium white onion, thinly
    sliced
1 head of iceberg lettuce, torn
    into bite-size chunks
Freshly ground pepper

1. In a blender, make vinaigrette by blending garlic, oregano, cumin, salt, vinegar, olive oil, and sugar to creamy consistency. Or shake in a tight-lidded jar.

2. Preheat oven broiler. Place peppers on a baking sheet and broil as close to heat as possible, turning, until charred all over, about 10 minutes. Place peppers in a paper bag and let steam 8 to 10 minutes. Peel off blackened skin and rinse under cold running water. Slit peppers open lengthwise, retaining stems, and scoop out seeds. Rinse and pat dry. Put peppers in a medium bowl. Add tomatoes, sliced onion, and vinaigrette. Toss gently. Cover and marinate about 1 hour.

3. To serve, arrange lettuce on a large platter. Place whole peppers, tomato wedges, and sliced onion on lettuce. Sprinkle with freshly ground black pepper to taste. Pass remaining vinaigrette at table.

90   BUENOS DIAS FRUIT PLATES
Prep: 10 minutes   Cook: none   Serves: 4

Mexican morning meals nearly always feature artfully arranged fruit plates to start.

2 ripe but firm bananas, cut
    into ¼-inch rounds ¼ inch
    thick
½ medium honeydew melon,
    quartered, peeled,
    seeded, and cut into thin
    slices

1 medium cantaloupe,
    quartered, seeded,
    peeled, and cut into thin
    slices
12 ripe strawberries, whole or
    sliced
1 lime, sliced

Arrange fruits in overlapping rows on 4 salad plates. Garnish with strawberries and lime slices.

91   JICAMA AND ORANGE SALAD

Prep: 20 minutes   Cook: none   Serves: 6 to 8

Crunchy and refreshing, this is a favorite on both sides of the border.

1 **small jicama, about
   ¾ pound, peeled and cut
   into ¼ x 1½-inch strips**
1 **medium cucumber, peeled
   and thinly sliced**
1 **small red onion, halved and
   thinly sliced**
3 **navel oranges, peeled and
   cut into bite-size pieces**

1 **head of romaine lettuce,
   shredded**
¼ **cup vegetable oil**
3 **tablespoons unseasoned rice
   vinegar**
½ **teaspoon salt**

1. In a large bowl, combine jicama, cucumber, red onion, oranges, and lettuce. Toss lightly to mix.

2. In a small bowl, whisk together oil, vinegar, and salt. Pour dressing over salad and toss to coat evenly. Serve at once.

92   HEARTS OF PALM SALAD WITH SHRIMP AND LIME

Prep: 20 minutes   Cook: none   Serves: 4

Fresh hearts of palm are not readily available, but canned ones are delicious if they are thoroughly rinsed, or soaked for a few minutes in hot water to rid them of any tinny taste. A similar salad is often served in upscale Mexico City restaurants.

1 **(14-ounce) can hearts of
   palm, drained**
1 **small tomato, seeded and
   finely chopped**
1 **serrano pepper, minced**
1 **tablespoon minced parsley**
1 **garlic clove, minced**
2 **tablespoons lime juice**

2 **tablespoons olive oil**
¼ **teaspoon salt**
⅛ **teaspoon freshly ground
   pepper**
½ **pound cooked small bay
   shrimp**
3 **cups shredded romaine
   lettuce**

1. In a medium bowl, place hearts of palm in warm water to cover and soak 5 to 10 minutes; drain well. Cut spears into rounds ½ inch thick.

2. In a medium bowl, combine tomato, serrano pepper, parsley, garlic, lime juice, olive oil, salt, and pepper. Gently mix in shrimp.

3. To serve, divide lettuce among 4 salad plates. Mound shrimp salad on lettuce in center of plates. Arrange cut hearts of palm around mounded shrimp.

93 ACAPULCO SHRIMP COCKTAIL

Prep: 20 minutes   Cook: 2 to 3 minutes   Chill: 1 hour   Serves: 6

Shrimp cocktails are served just about everywhere along the coast of Mexico. It's a festive way to start a Mexican meal.

1 pound medium raw shrimp (16 to 20)
⅓ cup minced white onion
½ cup peeled, seeded, and finely diced cucumber
1 large tomato, peeled, seeded, and cut into ¼-inch dice

1 jalapeño pepper, seeded and minced
¼ cup chopped cilantro
⅓ cup ketchup
Juice of 2 limes
¼ teaspoon salt
1 large ripe avocado, cut into ½-inch dice (optional)

1. In a medium saucepan of boiling water, cook shrimp until pink and loosely curled, 2 to 3 minutes. Drain and rinse under cold running water to cool. Shell and devein shrimp.

2. Place in a medium bowl, cover, and refrigerate about 1 hour, or until cold.

3. In another medium bowl, combine onion, cucumber, tomato, jalapeño pepper, cilantro, ketchup, lime juice, and salt. Gently mix in avocado and cold shrimp. Divide among 6 cocktail glasses. Serve at once as a first course.

94 JICAMA SALAD WITH CARROT SHREDS AND CITRUS DRESSING

Prep: 15 minutes   Cook: none   Serves: 6

The crisp fresh taste of jicama with colorful carrot shreds makes a simple and healthy salad.

1 medium jicama, about 1 pound, peeled
1 small carrot, peeled and coarsely shredded
¼ cup fresh orange juice
1 tablespoon fresh lime juice

1 teaspoon unseasoned rice vinegar
1 tablespoon olive oil
1 tablespoon chopped cilantro or parsley
¼ teaspoon salt

1. Cut jicama into julienne strips, about 2 inches long and ¼ inch wide. Put in a medium bowl. Add carrot shreds and toss.

2. In a jar with a tight-fitting lid, combine orange juice, lime juice, vinegar, olive oil, cilantro, and salt. Cover and shake well. Pour dressing over salad and toss. Serve cold.

95 PINEAPPLE, JICAMA, AND BELL PEPPER SALAD

Prep: 30 minutes   Cook: none   Serves: 8

A little sweet, a little tart, and nicely crunchy, this colorful salad is terrific with poultry, pork, and grilled fish.

1 fresh pineapple, about 3 pounds
½ green bell pepper, cut into thin strips
½ red bell pepper, cut into thin strips
¾ cup finely diced jicama

2 scallions, thinly sliced
½ teaspoon salt
¼ teaspoon pepper
2 tablespoons unseasoned rice vinegar
3 tablespoons vegetable oil

1. Peel pineapple and cut away core. Cut into 1-inch bite-size pieces. Place in a large bowl. Add green and red pepper strips, jicama, and scallions. If not served immediately, cover and refrigerate up to 6 hours.

2. In a small jar, shake together salt, pepper, vinegar, and oil. Add to salad and toss to coat. Serve salad chilled or at room temperature.

96 MEXICAN THREE-MELON SALAD

Prep: 20 minutes   Cook: none   Serves: 6

A mix of summer melons makes a colorful, refreshing salad.

¼ cup vegetable oil
2 tablespoons lime juice
¼ teaspoon salt
½ cantaloupe, peeled, seeded, and cut into ½-inch chunks
½ honeydew melon, peeled, seeded, and cut into ½-inch chunks

2 cups (½-inch) chunks of seeded watermelon
¼ medium red onion, cut into thin slivers
12 leaves of butter lettuce
Freshly ground pepper

1. In a small bowl, whisk together oil, lime juice, and salt. Set dressing aside.

2. In a large bowl, combine cantaloupe, honeydew, watermelon, and red onion. Add dressing and toss gently.

3. Place 2 lettuce leaves on each of 6 salad plates. Distribute melon salad evenly. Top with a grind or 2 of fresh black pepper. Serve chilled.

97 YUCATAN SHRIMP
Prep: 20 minutes   Cook: 2 to 3 minutes   Marinate: 2 hours
Serves: 4

This starter has been a favorite in my cooking classes for years. For a really dressy dinner, cut the radishes into roses.

1 **pound large shrimp, shelled and deveined**	¼ **teaspoon salt**
2 **tablespoons red wine vinegar**	1 **large tomato, peeled, seeded, and cut into ¼-inch dice**
¼ **cup olive oil**	¼ **cup chopped cilantro**
1 **serrano pepper, minced**	2 **cups shredded lettuce**
½ **medium white onion, minced**	1 **bunch of radishes**
½ **teaspoon dried oregano**	2 **limes, quartered lengthwise**

1. In a medium saucepan of boiling water, cook shrimp until pink and loosely curled, 2 to 3 minutes. Drain and place in glass or ceramic bowl. While shrimp are still hot, stir in vinegar, oil, serrano pepper, onion, oregano, and salt. Cover and marinate in refrigerator, tossing once or twice, until cold, at least 2 hours.

2. Remove shrimp from refrigerator. Gently stir in tomato and cilantro. Divide lettuce among 4 salad plates and spoon shrimp salad over lettuce. Garnish each plate with radishes and lime wedges. Serve well chilled.

98 MEXICAN POTATO, CARROT, AND PEA SALAD
Prep: 15 minutes   Cook: 9 minutes   Serves: 4

Mexico has wonderful potatoes and uses them in many ways. This mélange of potatoes, carrots, and peas, clearly of European origin, is very typical and is often found on combination plates at lunch. This version was served to me one day in Taxco.

2 **medium red potatoes, peeled and cut into ½-inch dice**	1 **scallion, minced**
	1 **teaspoon salt**
3 **medium carrots, peeled and cut into ½-inch dice**	¼ **teaspoon freshly ground pepper**
1 **cup peas, fresh or frozen**	**Herbed Vinaigrette (recipe follows)**

1. In a medium saucepan of boiling salted water, cook potatoes until just tender, about 5 minutes. Remove with a strainer or slotted spoon and set aside. Add carrots to same saucepan and cook until just tender, about 3 minutes; remove as before. Rinse under cold running water to cool; drain well. Add peas to boiling water and cook about 30 seconds. Drain, rinse under cold running water, and drain well.

2. In a large bowl, combine potatoes, carrots, and peas. Add scallion, salt, and pepper. Pour on vinaigrette dressing and toss to mix. Serve slightly chilled or at room temperature.

HERBED VINAIGRETTE
Makes: about ⅓ cup

2 tablespoons white wine
   vinegar
½ teaspoon Dijon mustard
1 tablespoon chopped cilantro
½ teaspoon ground cumin

¼ teaspoon oregano
⅛ teaspoon freshly ground
   pepper
¼ cup extra-virgin olive oil

In a blender jar, whirl all ingredients until smooth, or shake very well in a jar.

---

99   CHRISTMAS EVE SALAD
Prep: 30 minutes   Cook: 35 minutes   Serves: 6 to 8

This imaginative composed salad of fruits and vegetables is often served as a separate course for Christmas Eve celebrations following midnight mass, when gifts are exchanged and a joyous meal is served.

3 medium beets, about
   1 pound, or 1 (16-ounce)
   can sliced beets, drained
½ medium jicama, peeled and
   cut into ¾-inch dice
2 medium oranges, peeled
   and cut into ¾-inch
   chunks
½ fresh pineapple, peeled,
   cored, and cut into ¾-inch
   chunks

1 large banana, sliced
4 large romaine lettuce leaves,
   finely shredded
2 medium red apples, cored,
   halved, and thinly sliced
½ cup dry-roasted peanuts
½ cup pomegranate seeds
¼ cup vegetable oil
2 tablespoons lime juice

1. In a large saucepan of boiling water, cook beets over medium heat, partially covered, until tender when pierced with tip of a knife, about 35 minutes. Drain and rinse under cold water to cool. Remove skins and slice beets about ¼ inch thick. Reserve on a plate.

2. In a large bowl, place jicama, oranges, pineapple, and banana. Toss very gently to combine.

3. On a large serving platter, arrange a bed of shredded lettuce. Mound jicama and fruit salad in center of platter. Place apple slices, overlapping, around salad and arrange beet slices around apples. Sprinkle peanuts and pomegranate seeds over entire composed salad.

4. In a small bowl, whisk together oil and lime juice. Drizzle over salad and serve.

100 CHUNKY TOMATO AND AVOCADO SALAD

Prep: 15 minutes   Cook: none   Serves: 4 to 6

Put this terrific salad on your fiesta buffet for a colorful addition. It takes very little time to prepare.

2 ripe medium tomatoes, cut
    into 8 wedges each
1 medium cucumber, peeled,
    halved lengthwise, and
    sliced
½ red onion, quartered
    lengthwise and thinly
    sliced
1 jalapeño pepper, minced

Juice of 2 limes
2 tablespoons vegetable oil
½ teaspoon salt
⅛ teaspoon pepper
2 large avocados, peeled and
    cut into ½-inch dice
2 tablespoons chopped
    cilantro

In a large bowl, toss together tomatoes, cucumber, red onion, jalapeño pepper, lime juice, oil, salt, and pepper. Gently stir in avocado and cilantro and serve.

101 SALAD TOSTADA ISADORA

Prep: 15 minutes   Cook: none   Serves: 4

Tostadas are crisp fried corn tortillas topped with just about anything. This refreshing and light topping comes from Isadora Restaurant in Mexico City. Serve as a salad or first course.

1 cup shredded carrots
1 cup shredded jicama
¾ cup very thin strips of red
    bell pepper, about 1 inch
    long
1 cup shredded Monterey Jack
    cheese (about 4 ounces)
1 serrano pepper, minced

3 tablespoons chopped
    cilantro
¼ cup olive oil
3 tablespoons unseasoned rice
    vinegar
½ teaspoon salt
4 packaged tostadas or crisply
    fried corn tortillas

1. In a large bowl, combine carrots, jicama, bell pepper, cheese, serrano pepper, cilantro, olive oil, vinegar and salt. Toss to mix well.

2. When ready to serve, place tostadas on individual serving plates. Spoon salad onto tostadas, mounding it up in centers, and leaving ½-inch edge of tostada showing. Serve at once, so tostadas retain their crispness.

102 PUERTO VALLARTA MIXED VEGETABLE SALAD

Prep: 20 minutes   Cook: 8 to 11 minutes   Serves: 4 to 6

2 medium red potatoes, peeled and cut into ¼-inch dice
2 medium carrots, peeled and cut into ¼-inch dice
1 cup green beans, cut into 1-inch lengths
1 cup cauliflower florets
½ teaspoon salt
¼ cup bottled Italian salad dressing
2 medium tomatoes, sliced
1 cucumber, sliced

1. In a medium pan of boiling water, cook each vegetable separately over medium heat until just tender: 3 to 4 minutes for potatoes and carrots, 4 to 6 minutes for green beans, and 45 seconds to 1 minute for cauliflower. Use a slotted spoon to remove vegetables, from boiling water, as they are cooked. Place in a strainer and cool under running water. Place in a large bowl.

2. Add salt and dressing to salad and toss to coat. Mound salad in center of a round platter. Arrange overlapping slices of tomato and cucumber around edge. Serve cold.

103 SHRIMP SALAD WITH TOMATOES AND CUCUMBER

Prep: 10 minutes   Cook: none   Serves: 4

4 cups shredded iceberg lettuce
2 tablespoons fresh lime juice
2 tablespoons olive oil
⅛ teaspoon salt
2 cups cooked tiny shrimp (about ½ pound), rinsed and drained
1 fresh jalapeño pepper, seeded and minced
1 tablespoon chopped cilantro or parsley
2 medium tomatoes, sliced
½ medium cucumber, peeled and sliced

Divide shredded lettuce among 4 plates. In a medium bowl, whisk together lime juice, olive oil, and salt. Stir in shrimp, jalapeño pepper, and cilantro. Arrange evenly over lettuce. Garnish each plate with tomato and cucumber slices. Serve at once.

104 SPICY ZUCCHINI SALAD WITH CARROT AND PICKLED JALAPENO PEPPERS

Prep: 10 minutes   Cook: 6 to 8 minutes   Chill: 4 to 6 hours
Serves: 4

Many of us welcome more ways to prepare zucchini. Mexican cooks use them often in a variety of dishes. In this salad the vegetables are barely cooked, then marinated to enhance the flavors. Serve this salad as a separate course or with grilled poultry or roasted meats. *Queso fresco*, a crumbly fresh cheese, is scattered over the top. It is available in Latino markets and some specialty stores. Feta cheese can be substituted.

¼ cup olive oil
3 medium zucchini (about 1 pound), sliced ¼ inch thick
1 medium carrot, sliced ¼ inch thick
½ medium red onion, thinly sliced
½ teaspoon ground cumin
¼ teaspoon paprika
½ teaspoon salt

1 teaspoon sugar
3 tablespoons unseasoned rice vinegar
1 tablespoon chopped pickled jalapeño peppers
1 teaspoon jalapeño juice from jar
Freshly ground pepper
¼ cup crumbled queso fresco or feta cheese

1. In a large nonstick skillet, heat 2 tablespoons of oil over medium-high heat. Add zucchini and cook, tossing, until barely tender, 2 to 3 minutes. Remove with a slotted spoon and transfer to a medium bowl. Add carrot to same skillet and cook, tossing, until barely tender, about 3 minutes. Place in bowl with zucchini.

2. Add onion to same skillet and cook over medium-high heat, tossing, until barely tender, about 1 minute. Add cumin, paprika, salt, sugar, vinegar, jalapeños, and jalapeño juice. Cook, stirring, until sugar dissolves, 30 to 60 seconds. Immediately scrape contents of skillet into bowl with zucchini and carrot. Add remaining 2 tablespoons olive oil and a grinding of black pepper to taste. Toss and let cool to room temperature, then cover and marinate in refrigerator 4 to 6 hours.

3. To serve, arrange in a shallow bowl and scatter queso fresco over salad.

105 ENSENADA TUNA SALAD

Prep: 15 minutes   Cook: 4 to 6 minutes   Serves: 6

Ensenada lies on the Pacific Coast of Baja, south of Tijuana. Many big game fish are caught in these waters, and tuna is popular—both fresh and canned. Here's a tasty tuna salad that's quite versatile. Serve as a light entree, or use as a filling for avocados or tomatoes. It's good wrapped in a soft warm flour tortilla, too.

2 medium carrots, peeled and cut into ¼-inch dice
1 medium red potato, cut into ¼-inch dice
½ teaspoon dried oregano
¼ teaspoon salt

2 (6⅛-ounce) cans solid white tuna, drained and flaked
⅓ cup mayonnaise
3 pickled jalapeño peppers, seeded and minced
3 grinds of fresh black pepper

1. In a medium saucepan of boiling water, cook carrots and potatoes until just tender, 4 to 6 minutes. Drain and rinse under cold running water to cool. Drain well.

2. In a medium bowl, combine carrots and potatoes. Season with oregano and salt.

3. Add tuna, mayonnaise, jalapeños, and black pepper. Mix well. Transfer to a shallow serving bowl. Cover and refrigerate up to 3 days until ready to serve.

Chapter 4

Salsas, Sauces, and Condiments Olé

Many of the unique and characteristic flavors of Mexican foods come from the vast array of spicy fresh salsas and cooked sauces, the wet and dry seasoning mixtures, and the typical condiments that are so important to complete a dish.

This may be the hottest chapter in the book, for these recipes are where the majority of the chiles lurk, to add their fiery flavor and tongue-tingling excitement to Mexican cooking. Recipes explain where to find them and how to use them.

Table salsas and customary condiments are added at will to suit individual tastes, from mild to wild. Sauces and seasoning mixtures flavor foods while cooking, to give zip, zing, color, and texture. The recipes from this chapter can be mixed and matched with different foods to create great variety for your dining pleasure. Be adventurous and experiment.

Some recipes, such as Guacamole, Salsa Fresca Mexicana, Pickled Onions, and Fresh Tomatillo Salsa, are classics that you'll make often and serve with just about everything. There are also raw fruit and vegetable salsas, like Mango Lime Salsa, Spicy Fresh Corn Salsa, Black Bean Salsa, and Red Onion–Zucchini Salsa, that are so popular now and that go very well with grilled and roasted meats, poultry, and fish. Don't forget the bottled sauces and other commercial products that add fire by the drop, dash, or spoonful. New products appear constantly, so check Mexican sections of markets and specialty gourmet shops to help you with your cooking.

Explore this chapter for special touches to make your foods taste and look really authentic. Part of the fun with Mexican cooking and eating is plenty of color, texture, and variety, and the recipes in this chapter can add all of these qualities to your cooking.

106 CRISP ANCHO CHILE STRIPS
Prep: 4 minutes   Cook: 10 to 15 seconds   Serves: 4

Special additions add authenticity and distinctive taste to Mexican food. The dried brick-red ancho chile is often crisp fried and used to garnish soups or top tostadas and other dishes. They can even be eaten as an appetizer with chunks of cheese. The strips can also be crumbled into small pieces and sprinkled over soups or salads.

4 **large ancho chiles, rinsed**   2 **tablespoons vegetable oil**
   and dried

1. Cut chiles open by slitting lengthwise. Remove stems and seeds. Open out flat. With a sharp knife or kitchen scissors, cut into thin strips about ¼ inch wide.

2. In a large skillet, heat oil over medium heat. Add chile strips and fry 10 to 15 seconds, or until slightly blistered and color changes. Do not burn, or they will be bitter. With a slotted spatula, immediately remove from oil and drain on paper towels. They will become crisp when cool. Store in a plastic bag. Use within 3 days.

107 RED CHILE SAUCE
Prep: 20 minutes   Steep: 1 hour   Cook: 19 minutes
Makes: about 2 cups

This classic sauce can be used whenever red chile sauce is called for. It's commonly used to sauce enchiladas.

4 **ancho chiles**   2 **tablespoons chopped**
2 **medium tomatoes, peeled,**   **cilantro**
   seeded, and chopped   1 **tablespoon vegetable oil**
½ **medium onion, chopped**   ½ **teaspoon salt**
2 **garlic cloves, chopped**   1 **tablespoon red wine vinegar**
1 **teaspoon dried oregano**

1. Cut open chiles. Remove seeds and stems. Rinse and place in a medium saucepan with enough water to barely cover. Bring to a boil over medium heat and cook 2 minutes. Remove pan from heat, cover, and let chiles steep about 1 hour. Drain, reserving soaking water.

2. In a blender or food processor, place chiles, tomatoes, onion, garlic, oregano, cilantro, and ½ cup reserved chile water. Blend to a puree. Add additional soaking water to make a sauce with consistency of heavy cream.

3. In a medium saucepan, heat oil over medium heat. Add chile puree and cook, stirring, 2 minutes. Reduce heat to low and stir in salt and vinegar. Cover and simmer, stirring frequently, until there is no taste of raw garlic or onion, about 15 minutes. If not used within several hours, cover and refrigerate up to 1 week, or freeze up to 3 months.

108   CHILE DE ARBOL SAUCE

Prep: 5 minutes   Toast: 3½ to 4½ minutes   Makes: about 1 cup

Here is a traditional table sauce, made by toasting and grinding hot dried chiles, tomatillos, and garlic to a rustic mixture by hand in a *molcajete* (a Mexican mortar) or nowadays, quite often in an electric blender. Be forewarned —this is a hot one! Chiles de arbol are one of the spiciest varieties used in cooking. Look for them in Mexican markets and specialty food shops, or see the mail-order source on page 9.

½ pound fresh tomatillos
2 garlic cloves, unpeeled
6 chiles de arbol

¼ teaspoon salt
1 tablespoon chopped cilantro

1. Heat a heavy dry skillet or a Mexican *comal*, or griddle, over medium heat. Add tomatillos with their husks on and toast, turning often, until slightly charred and softened, about 3 minutes. At the same time, toast garlic with skin on, until slightly charred, 3 to 4 minutes. Remove husks from tomatillos and outer papery skin from garlic. Put into a blender or food processor.

2. Add chiles to same skillet, reduce heat to low, and toast, turning, about 30 seconds per side, until they are aromatic and a few lighter spots appear. Remove stems, shake out a few seeds, and crumble into blender jar.

3. Add salt and ¼ cup water; puree. Add cilantro and puree again. Finished sauce will have a characteristic rough texture. Transfer to a small bowl. Serve as a condiment at room temperature and add to foods cautiously.

109   BLACK BEAN SALSA

Prep: 20 minutes   Cook: none   Serves: 6

Black beans are rated very high on my bean list. They are delicious served in many different ways. For cold dishes, canned beans work really well, and their use makes speedy work when creating this colorful salsa.

2 (15-ounce) cans black beans
½ teaspoon ground cumin
¼ teaspoon ground oregano
2 ripe medium tomatoes,
    peeled, seeded, and
    chopped
½ medium white onion, finely
    diced

3 serrano peppers, minced
2 tablespoons unseasoned rice
    vinegar
2 tablespoons lime juice
½ teaspoon salt
¼ cup olive oil
2 tablespoons chopped
    cilantro

In a large colander, drain and rinse beans under cold running water. Shake off excess water and place beans in a large bowl. Add remaining ingredients and stir to combine. Serve at once or cover and set aside at room temperature up to 2 hours or refrigerate overnight.

110   CABBAGE AND CARROT SALSA
Prep: 12 minutes   Cook: none   Chill: 30 minutes   Makes: 2½ cups

You could think of this as a Mexican coleslaw. Pickled jalapeño peppers give cabbage and carrot salsa an unexpected zip that goes especially well with grilled meats and potato dishes. I like it with Carnitas (page 147) and soft tortillas.

½ **small cabbage, finely shredded (about 2 cups)**
1 **medium carrot, finely shredded**
1 **tablespoon chopped parsley**
1 **tablespoon finely chopped pickled jalapeño peppers**

1 **tablespoon unseasoned rice vinegar**
1 **teaspoon sugar**
½ **teaspoon salt**
1 **tablespoon olive oil**

In a medium bowl, toss cabbage, carrot, parsley, jalapeño peppers, vinegar, sugar, salt, and olive oil. Cover and marinate in refrigerator at least 30 minutes or up to a day before serving. Serve as a condiment with grilled meats, poultry, and potato dishes.

111   CHIPOTLE CHILE SALSA
Prep: 5 minutes   Cook: 12 to 14 minutes   Makes: about 1½ cups

Chipotle chiles are dried smoked jalapeños, and they have been discovered north of the border. Southwestern chefs and home cooks, too, have created a demand, making it easier to find a variety of prepared chipotle sauces or the canned whole peppers packed in a saucy mixture called *adobo*. It is quick to make your own chipotle salsa, and it keeps just fine for up to 6 months in the refrigerator. Its unique hot and smoky flavor adds something special to many dishes.

1 **tablespoon vegetable oil**
1 **medium onion, minced**
1½ **teaspoons dried oregano**
½ **teaspoon ground cumin**
½ **teaspoon dried marjoram**
¾ **cup ketchup**

1 **tablespoon unseasoned rice vinegar**
1½ **tablespoons brown sugar**
½ **(7-ounce) can chipotle chiles in adobo sauce**

1. In a nonreactive medium saucepan, heat oil over medium heat. Add onion and cook, stirring, until onion is softened, about 3 minutes. Stir in oregano, cumin, and marjoram and cook 1 minute. Add ketchup, vinegar, brown sugar, chiles in sauce, and 1 tablespoon water. Reduce heat to low, cover, and cook, stirring occasionally, until thick and fragrant, 8 to 10 minutes.

2. Transfer to a blender or food processor and puree until smooth. Strain through a wire-mesh strainer into a small bowl and let cool to room temperature. Transfer to a jar, cover, and refrigerate.

112 SPICY FRESH CORN SALSA

Prep: 15 minutes   Cook: 2 to 3 minutes   Makes: about 3 cups

Choose wonderful fresh ears of corn to make this salsa. It's a seasonal favorite. Spoon it next to grilled steaks or chicken, and if there's a fisherman in your family, try it with fresh trout.

4 ears of fresh corn
½ medium white onion, finely
    diced
2 tablespoons finely diced red
    bell pepper
1 to 2 serrano peppers, minced
1 medium tomato, seeded and
    chopped

¼ cup fresh lime juice
½ teaspoon ground cumin
½ teaspoon salt
2 tablespoons chopped
    cilantro

1. Shuck corn and cook ears in a large saucepan of boiling water until barely tender, 2 to 3 minutes. Drain and rinse under cold running water until cool. Cut kernels off cobs and place in a medium bowl.

2. Add onion, bell pepper, serrano pepper(s), tomato, lime juice, cumin, salt, and cilantro. Stir to combine. Serve at room temperature.

113 CORN AND TOMATO SALSA

Prep: 10 minutes   Cook: 1 minute   Makes: about 2½ cups

2 cups corn kernels, fresh or
    frozen
1 (4-ounce) can diced green
    chiles
2 tablespoons finely chopped
    white onion

1 medium tomato, chopped
    Juice of 1 lime
½ teaspoon salt
1 tablespoon chopped fresh
    mint

1. In a medium saucepan of boiling water, cook corn 1 minute. Drain in a sieve and rinse under cold running water to cool. Shake to remove excess water. Put corn in a medium bowl.

2. Add diced green chiles, onion, tomato, lime juice, salt, and fresh mint. Stir to combine. Serve at room temperature or slightly chilled. For best flavor and texture, use within 4 hours.

114   CREMA

Prep: 3 minutes   Cook: none   Stand: overnight
Chill: 4 to 6 hours   Makes: 1 cup

To make the wonderful tangy, slightly sour Mexican cream, called *crema*, that's drizzled over many Mexican dishes or stirred into sauces, start 2 days before needed. This lovely metamorphosis adds an authentic touch when used instead of ordinary sour cream.

1 cup heavy cream	2 tablespoons plain yogurt or buttermilk

In a pint glass jar, stir together cream and yogurt (or buttermilk) until very well mixed. Cover with lid, but do not tighten. Set aside at room temperature and let stand overnight, or until thickened and set. Stir gently, tighten lid, and refrigerate 4 to 6 hours to finish thickening. Crema keeps up to 10 days covered in refrigerator.

115   EASY RED ENCHILADA SAUCE

Prep: 5 minutes   Cook: 16½ minutes   Makes: about 2½ cups

Pure chili powder in place of whole dried chiles speeds up the process of preparing red enchilada sauce, and the results are very good. New Mexican chili powder is available in specialty food shops and in some supermarkets; or see mail-order sources on page 9.

3 tablespoons vegetable oil	1 (10-ounce) can tomato puree
1 tablespoon flour	1 teaspoon dried oregano
¼ cup pure New Mexico chili powder	½ teaspoon ground cumin
1 (14½-ounce) can beef broth or reduced-sodium chicken broth	Salt (optional)

1. In medium nonreactive saucepan, heat oil over medium-low heat. Add flour and cook, stirring, 1 minute. Add chili powder and cook, stirring, until aromatic, about 30 seconds.

2. Add broth, tomato puree, oregano, and cumin. Bring to a boil, stirring. Reduce heat to low and cook, stirring often, until sauce is smooth and thickened, about 15 minutes. Season with salt, if needed. Cover and refrigerate up to 5 days before using, or freeze up to 3 months.

116   GREEN ENCHILADA SAUCE

Prep: 20 minutes   Cook: 20 to 30 minutes   Makes: about 3 cups

This is the classic way to prepare green enchilada sauce using fresh ingredients.

4 poblano or Anaheim peppers	1 teaspoon ground cumin
2½ pounds tomatillos, husked and quartered	1 teaspoon dried oregano
	½ cup chicken broth
½ cup fresh cilantro sprigs	½ teaspoon sugar
2 serrano peppers, minced	½ teaspoon salt
¼ medium onion, chopped	⅛ teaspoon pepper
1 garlic clove, chopped	1 tablespoon vegetable oil

1. Preheat oven broiler. Place peppers on a baking sheet and broil as close to heat as possible, turning, until charred all over, about 10 minutes. Or roast peppers directly over a gas flame, turning, until charred, about 5 minutes. Place peppers in a paper bag and let steam 10 minutes. Peel off blackened skin and rinse under cold running water. Cut peppers open; discard stems and seeds. Chop peppers and put in a food processor. Add tomatillos, cilantro, serrano peppers, onion, garlic, cumin, oregano, chicken broth, sugar, salt, and pepper. Process about 10 seconds, until nearly smooth. There will be some texture.

2. In a heavy medium saucepan, heat oil over medium heat. Add pureed sauce and bring to a boil. Reduce heat to low, cover, and cook 15 to 20 minutes, stirring frequently, until there is no taste of raw onion or garlic. This sauce keeps, covered and refrigerated, up to 5 days, or frozen up to 3 months.

117   CHIPOTLE MAYONNAISE

Prep: 2 minutes   Cook: none   Makes: 1 cup

This spicy mayonnaise is used to spread on tortas, quesadillas, tacos, and burritos; it can also be added to salads, such as chicken or corn salad. The smoky taste of the chipotle chile is quite distinctive and is becoming extremely popular. Prepared *salsa de chipotle* or canned chipotle peppers in adobo are available in Latin American markets and in the Mexican food section of some supermarkets.

1 cup mayonnaise	2 tablespoons chipotle salsa

In a small bowl, combine mayonnaise and chipotle salsa. Mix well. Store refrigerated, in a covered jar, for up to 6 months.

118   PEGGY'S PANTRY ENCHILADA SAUCE
Prep: 8 minutes   Cook: 12 to 13 minutes   Makes: about 3½ cups

Peggy Pfardresher's sauce, for enchiladas and tamales, relies on convenience ingredients from the larder when you need something reliable and easy. Note the "secret ingredient"—peanut butter. Plus, it freezes well.

⅓ cup vegetable oil
⅓ cup flour
3 tablespoons chili powder
1 tablespoon ground cumin
1 teaspoon dried oregano
1 (14½-ounce) can reduced-sodium chicken broth

1 teaspoon peanut butter
2 garlic cloves, minced
⅓ cup canned tomato sauce
⅛ teaspoon sugar

1. In a nonreactive medium saucepan, combine oil, flour, chili powder, cumin, and oregano. Stir to make a thick paste. Cook over very low heat, stirring, until paste sizzles and is fragrant, 2 to 3 minutes. Take care not to burn roux. Remove from heat and whisk in chicken broth. Add peanut butter, garlic, tomato sauce, sugar, and ½ cup water. Whisk to combine.

2. Return pan to medium heat and cook, stirring, until sauce boils and thickens. Reduce heat to low and simmer, uncovered, stirring frequently, 10 minutes.

119   SALSA FRESCA MEXICANA
Prep: 15 minutes   Cook: none   Stand: 15 minutes
Makes: about 2 cups

This basic fresh tomato salsa goes with almost everything, and it has gained such popularity in the United States that it's often referred to as just "salsa." If good ripe tomatoes are not available, try the recipe for Pantry Salsa (page 91), which uses canned tomatoes.

3 large, ripe tomatoes (about 1¼ pounds), finely chopped
½ medium white onion, finely chopped

3 tablespoons chopped fresh cilantro
2 to 3 serrano peppers, minced
3 tablespoons fresh lime juice
½ teaspoon salt

In a medium bowl, stir all ingredients together. Cover and let stand about 15 minutes to blend flavors. For fresh taste and texture, serve within a few hours of preparing.

120   CALIFORNIA MEXICAN GARDEN SALSA

Prep: 15 minutes   Cook: none   Chill: 1 hour   Makes: about 3 cups

An innovative and refreshing salsa made of garden vegetables. The fresher the better, so mix it up and use it right away. Enjoy this saucy condiment on hamburgers and steaks at a summer cookout, as well as with tacos and burritos.

3 large ripe tomatoes, seeded
    and coarsely chopped
1 celery rib, finely chopped
3 scallions, finely chopped
1 small cucumber, peeled,
    seeded, and coarsely
    chopped
1 small carrot, peeled and
    finely shredded
2 jalapeño peppers, seeded
    and finely chopped

2 tablespoons minced fresh
    thyme, preferably lemon
    thyme
2 tablespoons finely chopped
    Italian parsley
2 tablespoons balsamic or red
    wine vinegar
1 teaspoon sugar
1 teaspoon salt

In a large nonreactive bowl, mix all ingredients together. Cover and refrigerate until chilled, about 1 hour.

121   GUACAMOLE

Prep: 10 minutes   Cook: none   Serves: 4

Avocados are native to Mexico, and there are many varieties. In the United States, the preferred avocado for guacamole is the dark, pebbly-skinned Hass variety, which has a buttery texture and rich flavor. The Fuerte variety is a close second choice. Guacamole is simple to make and a perfect appetizer with crisp tortilla chips for dipping.

2 large ripe avocados
½ medium white onion, finely
    chopped
1 to 2 serrano peppers, minced

1 tablespoon chopped cilantro
   Juice of 1 lime, about
    2 tablespoons
½ teaspoon salt

1. Cut avocados in half. Remove seeds. Hold one unpeeled half in the palm of your hand and mash avocado meat with a fork right in its shell. Repeat with remaining avocado halves.

2. Scoop out mashed avocado into a medium bowl. Add onion, serrano pepper(s), cilantro, lime juice, and salt. Mix well. Pile into a pretty bowl and place a piece of plastic wrap right on surface to retain color. Serve as soon as possible or refrigerate up to 2 hours for best color and flavor.

Variation

Guacamole with Tomato:
In step 2, add 1 small tomato, chopped.

122   OAXACA RED MOLE

Prep: 45 minutes   Cook: 45 to 46 minutes   Stand: 1 hour
Makes: about 2 cups

There are many rich and wonderful authentic moles. These complex sauces take time to prepare, but are worth the effort. If you can't find guajillo chiles, use all anchos. For best flavor, make mole at least a day ahead; freeze any left over. This sauce is traditionally served with turkey, chicken, or pork.

6 guajillo chiles	1 tablespoon dried oregano
2 ancho chiles	1 teaspoon cumin seeds
1 large ripe tomato	2 cups chicken broth
3 tablespoons vegetable oil	½ teaspoon ground cinnamon
½ medium onion, chopped	½ teaspoon ground allspice
3 garlic cloves, minced	½ teaspoon salt
3 slices of ripe plantain, cut	⅛ teaspoon pepper
¼ inch thick	½ ounce Mexican chocolate, or
2 slices of French bread	unsweetened baking
2 tablespoons sesame seeds	chocolate

1. Wipe chiles clean with a damp cloth, cut open, and remove stems and seeds. In a large dry skillet, toast chiles over medium heat, pressing down with a spoon, until chiles are fragrant, about 20 seconds total. Put in a medium pan of boiling water to cover and cook 2 minutes. Cover and soak off heat 1 hour.

2. Meanwhile, over a direct gas flame or under a broiler as close to heat as possible, broil tomato, turning, until charred all over, about 2 minutes. Put in a small bowl with skin on. In a medium skillet, heat oil over medium heat. Add onion and garlic and cook, stirring, until they begin to brown, about 3 minutes. Transfer to bowl with tomato. In same skillet, fry plantain slices until golden brown on both sides, about 2 minutes. Put in bowl with other ingredients. In same pan, fry bread until lightly browned on both sides. Reserve with other ingredients.

3. In a small dry skillet, toast sesame seeds, tossing, until lightly browned, about 2 minutes. Transfer to a small bowl and reserve. In same pan, toast oregano and cumin together until fragrant, about 1 minute. Add to bowl with sesame seeds. Remove chiles from soaking water; reserve ½ cup of water.

4. In a blender or food processor, combine chiles with 1 cup of chicken broth and ¼ cup of reserved soaking water. Process to a thick puree. Add roasted tomato, onion, garlic, plantain, bread, sesame, oregano, cumin, cinnamon, allspice, salt, pepper, and remaining 1 cup broth. Puree as smooth as possible, in 2 batches, if necessary. There will be some texture.

5. Transfer puree to a large saucepan and cook over medium-low heat, stirring frequently, 10 minutes. Correct consistency of sauce, if too thick, by adding more chile soaking water. Sauce should coat back of a wooden spoon. Add chocolate and cook, stirring, until melted, 2 to 3 minutes. Reduce heat to low and cook, stirring frequently to prevent sticking, 20 minutes. If made ahead, refrigerate up to 1 week, or freeze up to 6 months in a tightly covered container.

123   MUY PRONTO COOKED GREEN SAUCE

Prep: 7 minutes   Cook: 5 minutes   Makes: about 2 cups

Here's an easy, quick sauce to rely on when you're in a rush.

1 (12-ounce) can tomatillos, drained and rinsed	¼ cup loosely packed cilantro leaves
⅓ cup prepared thick and chunky green salsa	½ teaspoon ground cumin
1 cup canned reduced-sodium chicken broth	½ teaspoon dried oregano
	½ teaspoon sugar

In a blender or food processor, blend all ingredients to a smooth puree. Transfer to a nonreactive medium saucepan. Bring to a boil, reduce heat to medium, and cook, stirring often, 5 minutes. Let cool, cover, and refrigerate up to 5 days. Bring to a boil and use hot whenever cooked green sauce is called for.

124   MANGO LIME SALSA

Prep: 15 minutes   Cook: none   Stand: 30 minutes
Makes: about 2½ cups

Juicy ripe mangoes mixed with sweet and hot peppers make a lively salsa with bright color and taste appeal. Try it with poultry, pork, or fish.

2 large ripe mangoes, peeled and finely diced	2 serrano peppers, minced
½ medium onion, finely chopped	¼ cup fresh lime juice
	2 tablespoons finely chopped fresh mint leaves
½ red bell pepper, finely diced	¼ teaspoon salt

In a medium bowl, mix all ingredients. Cover and let stand 30 minutes to 1 hour before serving. Serve at room temperature. If made ahead, cover and refrigerate no more than 4 hours for best flavor and texture.

125   BLACK BEAN MOLE

Prep: 20 minutes   Cook: 9 minutes   Makes: about 3 cups

This is a different mole based on black beans, and it goes with almost everything. Use as an enchilada sauce or over grilled or roasted meats and poultry. It's also great with tamales.

2 ancho chiles, or
    2 tablespoons ground
    ancho or pasilla chili
	1 medium tomato, peeled
	1 tablespoon Worcestershire
	    sauce

1½ teaspoons cumin seeds	1 cup chicken broth
1½ teaspoons dried oregano	1 teaspoon dark brown sugar
1 tablespoon sesame seeds	2 teaspoons lime juice
1 cup cooked or canned black beans, drained	½ teaspoon salt 2 tablespoons butter

1. Stem and seed ancho peppers; tear into pieces. Place in a small saucepan with water to barely cover. Bring to a boil and cook 2 minutes. Remove pan from heat and soak chiles 15 minutes. Drain and set aside.

2. In a small skillet, toast cumin, oregano, and sesame seeds over medium heat, stirring, until aromatic, about 2 minutes. Transfer to a blender or food processor. Add reserved anchos, black beans, tomato, Worcestershire, chicken broth, brown sugar, lime juice, and salt. Puree until smooth.

3. In a medium saucepan, melt butter over medium heat. Add pureed sauce and cook, stirring frequently, until sauce is consistency of thick gravy, about 5 minutes.

126   QUICK MOLE

Prep: 5 minutes   Cook: 9 to 11 minutes   Serves: 4 to 6

A prepared mole paste is used to make this sauce. It is available in jars and cans in Mexican markets and in the Mexican section of many supermarkets. For better flavor and added convenience, cook the sauce ahead, then store in the refrigerator for up to 3 days, or freeze up to 6 months. The cooked mole is then ready to reheat and serve with cooked chicken or turkey. This recipe makes enough sauce for about 4 pounds of chicken or turkey pieces, which can be roasted, grilled, or fried, then covered with the precooked sauce and served. Sprinkle your finished dish with sesame seeds for an authentic touch.

1 (8-ounce) jar prepared mole
    poblano paste
	1 (14½-ounce) can reduced-
	    sodium chicken broth

In a large heavy saucepan, heat oil that has risen to the top of jar of mole paste over medium heat. Add thick paste from jar and cook, stirring, until paste warms and softens, about 3 minutes. Gradually stir in broth and ½ cup water. Bring to a boil, reduce heat to low, and simmer until sauce thickens, 6 to 8 minutes.

127   YUCATAN RED ONIONS IN ORANGE JUICE

Prep: 8 minutes   Cook: 1½ to 2 minutes   Stand: 1 hour
Makes: about 1½ cups

Make these terrific onions ahead. You'll find many ways to use them as a tangy condiment.

2 tablespoons vegetable oil
1 large red onion (about
    8 ounces), quartered and
    thinly sliced
½ teaspoon dried oregano
¼ teaspoon salt

⅛ teaspoon freshly ground
    pepper
2 tablespoons orange juice
1 tablespoon cider vinegar or
    red wine vinegar

1. In a medium skillet, heat oil over medium-high heat. Add onion, oregano, salt, and pepper. Cook, stirring, until onion is barely tender, 1½ to 2 minutes. Transfer to a small bowl.

2. Stir in orange juice and vinegar. Marinate about 1 hour. Serve at room temperature. If made ahead, cover and refrigerate up to 1 week.

128   RED ONION–ZUCCHINI SALSA

Prep: 15 minutes   Cook: 2 minutes   Stand: 10 minutes
Makes: about 2 cups

Contemporary salsas are inventive and exciting. Their fresh taste and vivid colors appeal to everyone. It's no wonder new ones keep appearing all the time. Zucchini salsa is a natural with all your Southwestern barbecues.

3 tablespoons olive oil
1 medium red onion, finely
    diced
½ teaspoon dried oregano
½ teaspoon salt
⅛ teaspoon freshly ground
    pepper
2 tablespoons unseasoned rice
    vinegar

2 small zucchini (about
    ¼ pound), cut into ¼-inch
    dice
1 small tomato, peeled,
    seeded, and finely
    chopped
2 jalapeño peppers, seeded
    and minced
1 tablespoon chopped cilantro

1. In a large nonreactive skillet, heat 1 tablespoon of olive oil over medium-high heat. Add onion and cook for 1 minute, stirring. Add oregano, salt, pepper, and vinegar. Cook until vinegar boils, about 1 minute. Stir in remaining 2 tablespoons oil and diced zucchini.

2. Immediately remove from heat and transfer to a medium bowl. Let stand 10 minutes. Stir in tomato, jalapeño peppers, and cilantro. For best color and texture, serve at room temperature within 4 hours of preparing.

129   TANGY RED ONION SAUCE

Prep: 8 minutes   Cook: 9 to 11 minutes   Makes: about 1 cup

A quick-to-make cooked onion sauce with an intriguing color from red jalapeño jelly, which is available in most supermarkets. This sauce goes very well with grilled chicken, roasted pork, and seafood. It's a great dipping sauce for appetizer meatballs.

2 tablespoons vegetable oil
1 large red onion, minced
1 teaspoon salt
⅛ teaspoon pepper
2 tablespoons unseasoned rice
  vinegar

½ cup fresh orange juice
3 tablespoons red jalapeño
  pepper jelly

1. In a nonreactive medium saucepan, heat oil over medium-high heat. Add onion and cook, stirring, until it begins to brown, 4 to 5 minutes. Add salt and pepper. Reduce heat to low and cook 2 minutes.

2. Stir in vinegar, orange juice, and jelly. Cook, stirring, until jelly is completely melted and sauce is slightly thickened and glossy, 3 to 4 minutes. Serve hot. (This sauce can be made a day ahead and reheated.)

130   PICKLED ONIONS

Prep: 10 minutes   Cook: 1 minute   Stand: 3 hours
Makes: about 1½ cups

Red pickled onions are a Yucatán specialty, but white onions are prepared in a similar way in other regions to accompany grilled meats, top enchiladas, or have on the table with other pickled vegetables.

1 large red or white onion,
  halved and thinly sliced
1 teaspoon dried oregano

1 bay leaf
½ teaspoon salt
⅓ to ½ cup cider vinegar

1. Place onion in a medium saucepan with enough cold water to cover. Bring to a boil over medium heat. When water begins to boil, cook 1 minute. Immediately remove from heat and drain.

2. Place onion in a medium bowl. Add oregano, bay leaf, salt, and vinegar. Add enough water to barely cover and let marinate at room temperature 3 to 4 hours, or cover and refrigerate overnight.

3. To use, drain onion well. Serve as a garnish or as a condiment in a bowl on the table.

131   PANTRY SALSA
Prep: 10 minutes   Cook: none   Makes: about 3 cups

When winter rolls around, a tasty salsa is still possible by using good canned tomatoes. This one has the advantage of keeping about 5 days refrigerated. Salt is not called for because canned ingredients contain salt. If you think it needs a touch, season with salt to taste.

1 (28-ounce) can peeled whole tomatoes
1 (4-ounce) can diced green chiles
½ green bell pepper, finely diced
2 tablespoons thick and chunky prepared salsa

½ medium onion, finely chopped
1 tablespoon unseasoned rice vinegar
1 teaspoon sugar
2 tablespoons chopped cilantro

Drain tomatoes very well and coarsely chop them. (Save juice for another purpose.) Place tomatoes in a medium bowl and add diced chiles, bell pepper, salsa, onion, vinegar, sugar, and cilantro. Stir to mix.

132   FRESH PINEAPPLE SALSA
Prep: 20 minutes   Cook: none   Makes: about 4½ cups

Fresh ripe pineapple combined with hot chile peppers and bright bell pepper is a natural with grilled fish and other seafood dishes. Plan to make it shortly before serving for best flavor.

1 medium ripe pineapple
½ large red bell pepper, finely chopped
3 to 4 serrano peppers, minced
4 scallions, minced
2 tablespoons unseasoned rice vinegar

1 teaspoon sugar
⅛ teaspoon salt
3 tablespoons chopped cilantro

1. Cut top and bottom off pineapple. Cut lengthwise into quarters and cut away tough center core. Cut off skin and remove eyes. Chop pineapple and place in a large bowl.

2. Add red bell pepper, serrano peppers, scallions, vinegar, sugar, salt, and cilantro. Mix well. Serve at room temperature, or cover and refrigerate up to 4 hours.

133 FRESH TOMATILLO SALSA

Prep: 8 minutes   Cook: 3 to 5 minutes   Makes: about 1½ cups

Green sauce, or *salsa verde*, of one kind or another, appears on the table for nearly every meal in Mexican homes and restaurants, too. It is very versatile, easy to make, and extremely popular.

½ pound fresh tomatillos, husked and rinsed	2 serrano peppers, minced
½ medium white onion, finely chopped	3 tablespoons chopped cilantro
1 garlic clove, minced	½ teaspoon sugar
	¼ teaspoon salt

1. In a medium saucepan of boiling water, cook tomatillos over high heat until barely tender, 3 to 5 minutes. Drain and place in a food processor or blender. Process to a coarse puree.

2. In a medium bowl, combine pureed tomatillos with onion, garlic, serrano peppers, cilantro, sugar, and salt. Stir to mix well. Serve right away or set aside at room temperature for up to 3 hours.

NOTE: *This sauce tends to separate if it sits too long. Just give it a good stir to bring it back together.*

134 ELLIE'S MEXICAN SALAD DRESSING

Prep: 5 minutes   Cook: none   Makes: about 1½ cups

Ellie Farnsworth, of Fair Oaks, California, gave me this recipe for a creamy salad dressing with a Mexican accent. It's best on mixed greens.

½ cup sour cream or plain low-fat yogurt	2 scallions, minced
½ cup salsa picante	1 garlic clove, minced
¼ cup mayonnaise	2 tablespoons chopped cilantro
½ medium tomato, finely chopped	¼ teaspoon salt
	⅛ teaspoon pepper

In a medium bowl, combine all ingredients and mix well. Cover and refrigerate up to 1 day before using.

135 GRILLED SCALLIONS
Prep: 10 minutes   Cook: 5 to 8 minutes   Serves: 4 to 6

These are fabulous tucked into a taco, with fajitas, or with any grilled meats.

4 bunches of scallions	½ teaspoon salt
2 tablespoons vegetable oil	¼ teaspoon freshly ground
2 tablespoons lime juice	pepper

1. Rinse scallions and remove wilted leaves. Cut about 2 inches from green ends to make them all even. Barely trim roots. Place in a large shallow dish. Add oil, lime juice, salt, and pepper. Toss to coat with marinade.

2. Prepare a hot fire in a barbecue grill. Lay scallions on an oiled grill rack and cook, basting with marinade and turning several times, 5 to 8 minutes, or until barely charred on both sides. Serve hot.

136 TOMATILLO-AVOCADO SALSA
Prep: 10 minutes   Cook: 2 minutes   Chill: 1 hour
Makes: about 2 cups

An all-green salsa combining tart tomatillos and creamy avocados goes especially well with grilled fish and seafood. The extra acidity of the tomatillos allows you to make this salsa several hours ahead, or even the day before. Stored in a bowl, covered tightly with plastic wrap pressed directly onto the surface, it stays green and appetizing for up to 2 days.

½ pound fresh tomatillos, husked and rinsed	2 ripe medium avocados, halved and pitted
1 tablespoon chopped onion	Juice of 1 fresh lime, about
1 serrano pepper, minced	2 tablespoons
½ cup loosely packed fresh cilantro, chopped	½ teaspoon salt

1. In a medium saucepan of boiling water, cook tomatillos about 2 minutes. Drain and rinse under cold running water to cool. Place in a food processor or blender. Add onion, serrano pepper, and cilantro. Puree to a coarse texture.

2. In a medium bowl, mash avocados, leaving some texture. Add tomatillo mixture, lime juice, and salt. Mix well. Cover and refrigerate until chilled, at least 1 hour. Serve cold.

137   TOMATO-TOMATILLO SALSA
Prep: 10 minutes   Cook: none   Makes: about 2 cups

Ripe red tomatoes combined with tart green tomatillos make yet another tasty salsa to serve as a dip with crisp tortilla chips.

3 medium tomatoes, finely chopped
3 medium tomatillos, husked and finely chopped
1 tablespoon minced onion
2 tablespoons chopped cilantro

1 fresh jalapeño pepper, seeded and minced
¼ teaspoon ground cumin
1 tablespoon fresh lime juice
¼ teaspoon salt
   Tortilla chips

In a medium bowl, mix together all ingredients except tortilla chips. Serve right away with crisp chips for dipping, or cover and refrigerate up to 8 hours for best flavor and texture.

138   FRESH TOMATO SAUCE
Prep: 5 minutes   Cook: 7 minutes   Makes: about 2 cups

Wonderful vine-ripened red tomatoes with lots of flavor grow in Mexico. This sauce is often served over Huevos Rancheros or with meat, poultry, or fish.

4 ripe medium tomatoes, peeled and chopped
2 serrano peppers, minced
¼ medium onion, chopped

½ teaspoon salt
⅛ teaspoon pepper
2 tablespoons vegetable oil

1. In a blender or food processor, place tomatoes, serrano peppers, onion, salt, and pepper. Blend to a coarse puree. There should be some texture.

2. In a nonreactive medium saucepan, heat oil over medium heat. Pour in blended sauce. Cook, stirring, 2 minutes. Reduce heat to low, cover, and simmer 5 minutes.

139   ROASTED TOMATO SAUCE

Prep: 5 minutes   Cook: 33 to 50 minutes   Makes: 3 cups

Broiling and roasting the tomatoes before simmering them into a sauce adds a more intense flavor.

6 **medium, ripe tomatoes, cored**	1 **medium white onion, chopped**
3 **serrano peppers, minced**	½ **teaspoon salt**
3 **tablespoons vegetable oil**	⅛ **teaspoon pepper**

1. Preheat oven to 475°F. Place tomatoes on a small baking sheet. Roast tomatoes 20 to 30 minutes, or until they are soft and skins are wrinkled.

2. In a blender or food processor, combine roasted tomatoes with serrano peppers. Blend to a coarse puree.

3. In a medium saucepan, heat oil over medium heat. Add onion and cook, stirring frequently, until edges begin to brown, 3 to 5 minutes. Add pureed tomatoes, salt, and pepper. Cover and cook over medium-low heat, stirring occasionally, 10 to 15 minutes for flavors to blend.

140   MEXICAN TARTAR SAUCE

Prep: 5 minutes   Cook: none   Makes: 1 cup

Add this to your cache of table sauces. It's something a bit different to serve with fish.

1 **cup mayonnaise**	1 **serrano pepper, seeded and minced**
2 **tablespoons chopped capers**	
1 **tablespoon minced white onion**	1 **tablespoon chopped cilantro**
	Juice of 1 lime

In a small bowl, combine all ingredients. Stir to mix well. Serve within 2 to 3 hours for best flavor.

Chapter 5

Savory Fish and Shellfish

Mexicans take their seafood dishes seriously, and no wonder, since Mexico's coastlines run the length of the country, both east and west. The Mexican appreciation for fresh seafood was established long before the discovery of the New World, for it is recorded that the great Aztec emperor, Montezuma, sent swift runners to both coasts from the valley of Mexico, now the site of Mexico City, to satisfy his demands for fresh fish. Modern day shoppers still look for the best, and there is usually great choice and excellent quality. Fine seafood reaches the larger markets all over the country.

Among the most plentiful shellfish and other fresh fish from Mexican waters are shrimp, crab, clams, lobsters, squid, octopus, red snapper, swordfish, sea bass, shark, tuna, and any number of smaller fish. This bounty from the sea is prepared in many ways, to enhance the natural goodness of the seafood. Techniques include rubbing with spicy seasoning pastes, then grilling or steaming in banana leaves or other wrappings; stewing with onions, tomatoes, chiles, and spices; frying in lard, butter, or oil, then serving with fresh lime juice, chiles, pickled vegetables, or chopped toasted nuts. Cooked fish is often chopped or flaked and used to fill tortillas, sand-wiches, or tamales. Raw seafood cocktail, *ceviche*, cooks the fish in lime juice with chiles, onions, herbs, and tomatoes. Many of the dishes reflect the influence of Spain and other for-eign nations, whose products reached Mexico and became important in the cuisine, such as sauces using oranges, almonds, olives, and capers, which are often used to flavor seafood. And, of course, fresh salsas nearly always accom-pany the dishes, to be added by the desire and discretion of the diner.

Since fish is highly recommended for healthy bal-anced diets, give it zest and excitement by preparing it the Mexican way. The real key to successful fish cookery is fresh! So be a picky shopper, and search for the best fish market in your area. The outcome of the dish depends on quality.

Most fish and seafood preparations are amazingly simple, as the recipes in this chapter will show, such as Sau-téed Sea Bass with Garlic and Lime, Grilled Shrimp Brochettes with Chili Butter, or fabulous Crispy Fried Scallops. For a whole meal in a bowl, Shrimp Stew with Corn, Peppers, and Rice is unique, delicious, and satisfying. Soup lovers will really go for Red Snapper and Shrimp Stew. The Mexican way with fish opens a whole new way to treat the ocean's bounty, so scout out some good sources and try some of these delicious dishes.

141 SAUTEED SEA BASS WITH GARLIC AND LIME

Prep: 15 minutes   Cook: 6½ minutes   Serves: 6

A variety of fresh fish, simply prepared, is typical along Mexico's extensive coastline. *Robalo* is a favorite type of sea bass. Its delicate flavor is enhanced by this quick and easy recipe. Other firm white fish fillets can be used in place of the sea bass. Black Bean Salsa (page 79) is a good accompaniment.

2 **pounds sea bass fillets**	2 **tablespoons vegetable oil**
1 **teaspoon salt**	6 **scallions, thinly sliced**
½ **teaspoon pepper**	3 **garlic cloves, minced**
3 **tablespoons flour**	3 **tablespoons fresh lime juice**
3 **tablespoons unsalted butter**	

1. Cut fish into 6 serving pieces. Season with salt and pepper. Dust with flour to coat. Shake off excess.

2. In a large skillet, melt 1 tablespoon of butter in oil over medium heat. When butter begins to sizzle, add fish and cook, turning once, until lightly browned outside and opaque throughout, about 3 minutes on each side. Remove fish to a warm plate. Wipe out skillet with paper towels.

3. Melt remaining 2 tablespoons butter in skillet over medium heat. Add scallions and garlic. Cook, stirring, until garlic is softened and fragrant, 30 to 40 seconds. Add lime juice. Bring to a boil and immediately pour over fish. Serve at once.

142 SEA BASS WITH MANGO SALSA

Prep: 5 minutes   Cook: 5 to 7 minutes   Serves: 4 to 6

2 **pounds sea bass fillets, about ½ inch thick**	1 **ripe mango, peeled and cut into ¼-inch dice**
½ **teaspoon salt**	¼ **cup fresh lime juice**
⅛ **teaspoon pepper**	**Pinch of crushed hot red**
2 **tablespoons flour**	**pepper**
2 **tablespoons vegetable oil**	1 **tablespoon chopped cilantro**
2 **tablespoons butter**	**or parsley**

1. Cut fish fillets into 4 serving pieces. Season with salt and pepper. Dust with flour to coat. Shake off excess.

2. In a large skillet, heat oil over medium-high heat. Add fish and cook, turning once, until golden brown outside and just opaque inside, 2 to 3 minutes on each side. Transfer fish to a serving platter.

3. In same skillet, melt butter. Add mango, lime juice, and hot pepper. Cook, tossing, until heated through, about 1 minute. Spoon salsa over fish fillets. Garnish with cilantro and serve.

143   CRISPY FRIED SCALLOPS
Prep: 10 minutes   Cook: 3 to 4 minutes   Serves: 4

A little crusty and brown on the surface, sweet and moist inside, large sea scallops coated with cornmeal and pan-fried to perfection are sure to be popular even with finicky seafood eaters. Serve with lemon wedges, rice, and Salsa Fresca Mexicana (page 84).

1 pound sea scallops	½ teaspoon paprika
½ cup finely ground yellow cornmeal	¼ teaspoon pepper
½ teaspoon salt	¼ cup corn oil
	Lemon wedges

1. Blot scallops with paper towels and place on a plate. In a small bowl, mix cornmeal, salt, paprika, and pepper. Dredge scallops in seasoned cornmeal to coat; shake off excess. Place scallops on wax paper as they are coated.

2. In a large nonstick skillet, heat oil over medium heat. Add scallops and cook, turning, until golden brown all over, 3 to 4 minutes. Do not overcook or scallops will toughen. Drain briefly on paper towels. Serve hot, with lemon wedges.

144   CLAMS MEXICANA
Prep: 25 minutes   Cook: 11 to 13 minutes   Serves: 4

Clams served with *bolillos*, Mexican rolls, or any good country bread to sop up the juices make for an informal feast.

3 pounds (about 30) small hard-shell clams	2 serrano peppers, cut into thin rings
2 tablespoons olive oil	½ cup dry white wine
¼ cup chopped white onion	1 cup canned reduced-sodium chicken broth
3 garlic cloves, minced	
1 teaspoon dried oregano	1 tablespoon chopped cilantro
½ medium red bell pepper, cut into ¼-inch dice	3 tablespoons lime juice
	½ teaspoon salt
2 medium tomatoes, peeled, seeded, and finely chopped	¼ teaspoon freshly ground pepper

1. Scrub clams, rinse well, and drain. In a large deep skillet or flameproof casserole, heat olive oil over medium heat. Add onion, garlic, oregano, and bell pepper. Cook, stirring occasionally, until onion is softened, 3 to 4 minutes.

2. Add tomatoes and cook, stirring, until juices evaporate and tomatoes thicken, 3 to 4 minutes. Add serranos, wine, chicken broth, and 1 cup water. Bring to a boil.

3. Add clams, cover, and cook until all clams have opened, about 5 minutes. (Remove any clams that do not open.) Stir in cilantro, lime juice, salt, and pepper. Serve hot in shallow bowls with the broth.

145   COLD FISH FILLETS WITH GUACAMOLE
Prep: 8 minutes   Cook: 3 minutes   Chill: 2 hours   Serves: 4

Very fresh, firm fish fillets are necessary for this easy poached preparation. Because it's made in advance, it's a wonderful dish for a hot summer evening or for a buffet table.

4 firm white fish fillets, such
    as sea bass or snapper
    (about 1 pound)
	2 garlic cloves, chopped
	2 parsley sprigs
	1 teaspoon salt

½ small onion, sliced
¼ cup unseasoned rice vinegar
1 teaspoon dried oregano
	4 grinds of fresh black pepper
	    Guacamole and salsa, as
	    accompaniments

1. In a medium nonreactive skillet, place fish fillets in a single layer. Add onion, vinegar, oregano, garlic, parsley, salt, and pepper. Add enough hot water to barely cover. Place pan over medium heat. When water begins to steam, reduce heat to low, cover skillet, and simmer 3 minutes. With a slotted spatula, lift fish from liquid and place on a plate. Cover and refrigerate about 2 hours, or until very cold.

2. To serve, blot fish with paper towels and place 1 fish fillet on each of 4 serving plates. Spoon guacamole and salsa in separate bands over center of each fillet.

146   FISH FILLETS WITH ORANGE, GARLIC, AND PARSLEY SAUCE
Prep: 20 minutes   Cook: 12 to 15 minutes   Serves: 4

A light and lively preparation for almost any catch-of-the-day. Serve with rice or Potato Patties (page 206).

4 large garlic cloves, minced
3 tablespoons olive oil
½ teaspoon salt
4 skinless, boneless fish
    fillets, about 1½ pounds
2 tablespoons orange juice
	1 tablespoon unseasoned rice
	    vinegar
	¼ cup finely chopped parsley
	12 to 16 cherry tomatoes,
	    halved

1. Preheat oven to 375°F. In a small bowl, mix half of minced garlic with 1 tablespoon of olive oil. Add salt and stir to mix. Rub all over fish fillets and place in a single layer in a baking dish. Bake, uncovered, 12 to 15 minutes, or until opaque throughout.

2. While fish bakes, prepare sauce. In a small skillet, heat remaining 2 tablespoons olive oil over medium heat. Add remaining garlic and cook, stirring, until softened and fragrant, about 1 minute. Add orange juice and vinegar. Bring to a boil, about 30 seconds. Remove pan from heat and stir in parsley.

3. To serve, place cooked fish on individual plates. Stir fish juices from baking dish into parsley sauce. Spoon an equal amount over each serving. Garnish with cherry tomatoes.

147   FISH FILLETS WITH TOASTED GARLIC AND PAPAYA SAUCE

Prep: 30 minutes   Cook: 8½ to 11½ minutes   Serves: 6

During a culinary holiday in Puerto Vallarta, my friends Gloria Bowers and Bernice Hagen teamed up to create this unusual, tasty recipe. It is typical of much modern Mexican cooking.

¼ cup olive oil
10 to 12 large garlic cloves, cut into tiny dice
1 papaya, peeled, seeded, and chopped (about 1 cup)
2 serrano peppers, seeded and minced
¼ cup fresh lime juice

¾ teaspoon salt
¼ teaspoon pepper
1 cup loosely packed cilantro leaves, chopped
6 (6- to 7-ounce) fish fillets, such as snapper, cod, or sea bass
½ cup flour

1. In a small heavy skillet, heat 2 tablespoons of olive oil over medium-low heat. Add garlic and cook, stirring, until golden, 2 to 3 minutes. Do not burn, or garlic will be bitter. With a slotted spoon, transfer garlic to a paper towel to drain. Save oil.

2. In a small saucepan, heat reserved garlic oil over medium heat. Add papaya, serrano peppers, lime juice, ¼ teaspoon of salt, and ⅛ teaspoon of pepper. Bring to a boil, stirring, and cook 30 seconds. Remove from heat and stir in chopped cilantro. Set papaya sauce aside.

3. Dust fish fillets lightly with flour to coat. Shake off any excess. In a large nonstick skillet, heat remaining 2 tablespoons olive oil over medium heat. Add fish and remaining ½ teaspoon salt and ⅛ teaspoon pepper. Cook, turning once, until fish is golden brown on both sides and opaque throughout, 6 to 8 minutes total. With a wide spatula, carefully transfer fish to a warm platter. Top with reserved papaya sauce and scatter garlic bits over all.

148 FOIL-BAKED FISH FILLETS WITH TOMATO AND GREEN CHILES

Prep: 15 minutes   Cook: 12 minutes   Serves: 4

San Angel Inn restaurant in Mexico City serves incredibly fresh fish in this fashion. Simple steamed rice and buttered chayote or zucchini are the perfect accompaniments.

3 tablespoons olive oil
1 medium white onion, quartered and thinly sliced
1 garlic clove, minced
2 serrano peppers, minced
Juice of 2 limes

4 (6-ounce) firm white fish fillets, such as sea bass or snapper
½ teaspoon salt
1 large ripe tomato, cut into ¼-inch dice
4 parsley sprigs

1. Preheat oven to 450°F. In a large skillet, heat 2 tablespoons of olive oil over medium-high heat. Add onion and garlic and cook, stirring, until onion is softened, about 3 minutes. Stir in serrano peppers and lime juice. Remove from heat.

2. Brush fish with remaining 1 tablespoon olive oil. Place 1 fish fillet on each of 6 pieces of aluminum foil 9 x 12 inches. Season with salt. Spoon cooked onion mixture over fish fillets, dividing evenly. Distribute diced tomato over each portion, and put a parsley sprig on top. Fold foil to enclose and seal fish.

3. Put foil packets on a large baking sheet and place in middle of preheated oven. Bake 9 minutes. To serve, unfold and turn back foil. Place open packets on individual serving plates, so no juices will be lost.

149 SHRIMP IN ALMOND SAUCE

Prep: 20 minutes   Cook: 16 to 21 minutes   Serves: 4

1 pound large shrimp (16 to 20), shelled and deveined
½ teaspoon salt
½ cup chopped cilantro
½ cup sliced almonds, toasted and chopped

4 tablespoons butter
3 garlic cloves, minced
1 to 2 serrano peppers, minced
3 tablespoons fresh lime juice

1. Preheat oven to 350°F. In a medium baking dish, place shrimp in a single layer. Season with salt. Scatter chopped cilantro and almonds evenly over shrimp.

2. In a small skillet, melt butter over medium heat. Add garlic and cook, stirring, until softened and fragrant, about 1 minute. Add serrano peppers and lime juice. Pour over shrimp.

3. Cover dish with foil and bake in preheated oven 15 to 20 minutes, or until shrimp are pink and curled and sauce is bubbling.

150 SHRIMP STEW WITH CORN, PEPPERS, AND RICE

Prep: 30 minutes   Cook: 40 to 45 minutes   Serves: 4

This is a terrific whole meal in a bowl. For extra heat, offer a small bowl of Chipotle Chile Salsa (page 80) to be added at the table with great discretion. A little dab will usually do.

1 cup long-grain white rice	¾ cup dry white wine
1 teaspoon salt	1 pound large shrimp (16 to
2 tablespoons olive oil	20), shelled and deveined
1 medium onion, chopped	1 cup cooked corn kernels,
3 garlic cloves, minced	fresh or frozen
1 (14½-ounce) can ready-cut	½ green bell pepper, cut into
tomatoes with juices	¼-inch dice
1 teaspoon dried oregano	1 jalapeño pepper, minced
½ teaspoon dried marjoram	Chopped cilantro and lime
2 (14½-ounce) cans reduced-	wedges
sodium chicken broth	

1. In a medium saucepan, bring 1¾ cups water to a boil. Stir in rice and ½ teaspoon of the salt. Reduce heat to low, cover, and simmer 18 to 20 minutes, or until all liquid is absorbed. Remove from heat and let stand, covered, about 10 minutes.

2. Meanwhile, in a large nonreactive saucepan or flameproof casserole, heat oil over medium heat. Add onion and garlic and cook until they begin to brown, 4 to 5 minutes. Add tomatoes, oregano, marjoram, broth, and wine. Bring to a boil, reduce heat to low, cover, and simmer 15 minutes to blend flavors.

3. Add shrimp, remaining ½ teaspoon salt, corn, bell pepper, and jalapeño pepper. Raise heat to medium and cook 3 to 5 minutes, or until shrimp are pink and loosely curled.

4. Divide stew evenly among 4 shallow soup plates. For each bowl of soup, pack about ¾ cup hot cooked rice in a custard cup and invert into center of soup. Garnish with cilantro. Serve with lime wedges.

151 SKILLET SHRIMP IN GARLIC SAUCE
Prep: 20 minutes   Cook: 5 to 7 minutes   Serves: 4

Wherever seafood is served, you're bound to find some form of *camerones al mojo de ajo*, or shrimp in garlic sauce. This easy version is all done in one pan. Serve with crusty bread or rice to soak up the juices.

2 tablespoons unsalted butter	½ teaspoon salt
2 tablespoons olive oil	½ teaspoon paprika
6 garlic cloves, minced	3 tablespoons lime juice
1 pound large shrimp (16 to 20), shelled and deveined, with tails left on	

1. In a large skillet, melt butter in olive oil over medium heat. Add garlic and cook, stirring, until golden brown, about 2 minutes. Do not burn, or it will be bitter.

2. Add shrimp, salt, and paprika. Cook shrimp, turning several times, until pink outside, curled, and opaque throughout, 3 to 5 minutes. Remove from heat.

3. Add lime juice and toss to combine. Transfer shrimp to a warm serving platter, drizzle on pan juices, and serve.

152 GARLIC SHRIMP WITH RED PEPPER, TOMATO, AND CHIPOTLE SAUCE
Prep: 25 minutes   Cook: 21 to 28 minutes   Serves: 4

A delicious sauce of red bell peppers sparked with smoky-hot chipotle chiles served with shrimp fairly sings with flavor. Add plain rice to soak up extra sauce.

¼ cup olive oil	1 tablespoon fresh lemon juice
2 large red bell peppers, seeded and chopped	1 teaspoon salt
1 large ripe tomato, peeled, seeded, and chopped	1 pound large shrimp (16 to 20), shelled and deveined
1 tablespoon imported sweet paprika	4 garlic cloves, minced
1 tablespoon mashed canned chipotle chile	½ cup canned chicken broth
	8 sprigs of fresh cilantro or parsley

1. In a medium nonreactive saucepan, heat 2 tablespoons of olive oil over high heat. Add red peppers and tomato. Cook, tossing, 1 minute. Add 2 tablespoons water, cover, and reduce heat to medium-low. Cook, stirring occasionally, until peppers are very tender, 15 to 20 minutes. Add paprika, mashed chipotle, lemon juice, and ½ teaspoon of salt. Transfer mixture to a food processor or blender and puree until smooth. Return chipotle sauce to pan and set aside.

2. In a large skillet, heat remaining 2 tablespoons oil over medium-high heat. Add shrimp in a single layer and cook, turning with tongs, 30 seconds on each side. Add garlic and remaining ½ teaspoon salt. Cook, stirring, until garlic is softened and fragrant, about 1 minute. Add chicken broth. Cook 2 minutes, or until shrimp curl and are pink.

3. With tongs or a slotted spoon, remove shrimp to a plate. Pour pan juices into red pepper sauce. Bring sauce to a boil over medium heat. Cook, stirring, until sauce is slightly thickened and coats back of a wooden spoon, stirring, 1 to 3 minutes.

4. To serve, divide sauce among 4 individual serving plates. Distribute shrimp over sauce. Garnish with cilantro sprigs.

153   GRILLED SHRIMP BROCHETTES WITH CHILI BUTTER

Prep: 25 minutes   Marinate: 45 minutes   Cook: 4 to 6 minutes
Serves: 4

Accompany these spicy shrimp brochettes with Green Rice Puebla Style (page 166) and Mango Lime Salsa (page 87) for a terrific combination plate.

1 pound large shrimp, shelled
   and deveined
4 tablespoons butter, softened
2 tablespoons mayonnaise
2 tablespoons lemon juice
2 garlic cloves, crushed
   through a press

1 tablespoon chili powder
½ teaspoon ground cumin
¾ cup ketchup
1 tablespoon chopped cilantro
   or parsley

1. Prepare a hot fire in a barbecue grill. Thread shrimp onto 4 metal skewers or wooden skewers that have been soaked in cold water at least 30 minutes. Place skewered shrimp on a tray. In a small bowl, combine 2 tablespoons of softened butter with mayonnaise, lemon juice, and garlic. Stir until well blended. Brush this basting mixture over top side of skewered shrimp. Cover and refrigerate shrimp 45 minutes.

2. In a small saucepan, melt remaining 2 tablespoons butter over low heat. Stir in chili powder, cumin, ketchup, and cilantro. Remove chili butter from heat.

3. Place shrimp on an oiled grill rack and set 4 to 6 inches above coals, buttered side down. Brush mayonnaise basting mixture on top side of shrimp. Grill, turning once, until shrimp are pink and begin to curl, 4 to 6 minutes. Serve hot with chili butter as a dipping sauce.

154   CRISP FISH TACOS
Prep: 10 minutes   Cook: 2 minutes   Serves: 3

A crisp fish taco will surprise and delight fish fans. Be sure fish is very fresh. These make a great snack, starter, or light lunch dish.

1 **(8-ounce) boneless white fish fillet, such as red snapper or scrod**	2 **tablespoons olive oil**
1 **teaspoon flour**	¼ **cup mayonnaise**
1 **teaspoon cornmeal**	2 **tablespoons thick and chunky salsa**
½ **teaspoon chili powder**	½ **cup finely shredded cabbage**
¼ **teaspoon salt**	6 **purchased taco shells**
	Lime wedges

1. Check fish for bones. Cut fillet crossways into 4 equal pieces. In a small bowl, combine flour, cornmeal, chili powder, and salt. Mix well. Dust fish pieces with flour mixture.

2. In a medium nonstick skillet, heat oil over medium heat. Add fish and fry 1 minute on each side, or until lightly browned outside and white to center. Drain on paper towels. Flake fish coarsely with a fork.

3. In a small bowl, mix mayonnaise and salsa. Divide shredded cabbage among 6 taco shells. Top equally with flaked fish and mayonnaise mixture. Serve at once, with lime wedges.

155   CHILLED SALMON STEAKS WITH CILANTRO-MINT SAUCE
Prep: 15 minutes   Cook: 7 to 8 minutes   Chill: 2 hours   Serves: 4

This is a popular dish in warm weather. The bright pink salmon and green sauce are very attractive. Serve smaller portions as a first course, if you like.

2 **scallions, coarsely chopped**	1 **tablespoon fresh mint leaves**
1 **medium carrot, sliced**	2 **tablespoons hulled raw pumpkin seeds (pepitas)**
1½ **teaspoons salt**	2 **serrano peppers, chopped**
4 **(6-ounce) salmon steaks, about ¾ inch thick**	2 **tablespoons unseasoned rice vinegar**
½ **cup stemmed parsley, loosely packed**	2 **tablespoons lime juice**
1 **cup cilantro leaves, loosely packed**	¼ **cup vegetable oil**

1. In a medium skillet over medium heat, bring 2 cups water to a boil. Add scallions, carrot, and 1 teaspoon of salt. Reduce heat to low and place salmon in water. Simmer, uncovered, 4 minutes. With a slotted spatula, carefully turn salmon over and cook 3 to 4 minutes, or until opaque throughout. Remove fish with slotted spatula and place on a platter. Blot excess water with a paper towel. Cover and refrigerate until cold, about 2 hours.

2. In a food processor, place parsley, cilantro, mint, pumpkin seeds, serrano peppers, vinegar, lime juice, and remaining ½ teaspoon salt. Process until cilantro and mint are finely chopped. Add oil and process until thick and smooth, about 10 seconds. Scrape down sides and blend 5 seconds. Transfer to a medium bowl. Cover and refrigerate until shortly before serving.

3. Place chilled salmon steaks on individual serving plates. Spoon 2 to 3 tablespoons sauce over center of each serving. Pass remaining sauce. Serve cold.

156 SALMON FILLET WITH FRESH TOMATILLO SAUCE
Prep: 12 minutes   Cook: 7 minutes   Serves: 4

Fresh salmon treated in a California-style interpretation of Mexican cooking is sure to please. Tiny buttered new potatoes and black bean salad make a stunning plate with the salmon.

¾ **pound fresh tomatillos**
½ **medium red onion, finely chopped**
1 **jalapeño pepper, seeded and minced**
1 **tablespoon chopped cilantro**
1 **tablespoon unseasoned rice vinegar**

2 **tablespoons olive oil**
1 **teaspoon salt**
¼ **teaspoon sugar**
4 **salmon fillets, about 4 ounces each**
3 **tablespoons vegetable oil**
1 **(4-ounce) jar pimiento strips, drained**

1. Rinse tomatillos and remove papery outer husks. In a medium saucepan of boiling water, cook tomatillos until barely cooked, about 3 minutes. Drain and rinse under cold running water. Put in a food processor or blender and blend to a coarse puree. Transfer to a medium bowl. Add red onion, jalapeño pepper, cilantro, vinegar, olive oil, ½ teaspoon salt, and sugar. Stir until well mixed. Set tomatillo sauce aside.

2. Remove skin from salmon. Season fish with remaining ½ teaspoon salt. In a large skillet, heat vegetable oil over medium-high heat. Add salmon fillets and cook, turning once, until just opaque throughout, about 2 minutes on each side. Do not overcook.

3. Transfer salmon to a warmed serving platter. Spoon about 2 tablespoons of tomatillo sauce in a ribbon across each piece of salmon. Garnish with strips of pimiento. Pass remaining sauce on the side.

157   TROUT WITH PARSLEY AND LIME
Prep: 10 minutes   Cook: 8 to 10 minutes   Serves: 4

Trout, called *trucha* in Spanish, are available in some mountainous regions of Mexico. For nonfishermen, fresh boneless trout is shipped almost everywhere in the United States.

4 whole boned trout, about 10 ounces each	1 teaspoon salt
3 tablespoons olive oil	3 tablespoons butter, melted
3 garlic cloves, crushed through a press	3 tablespoons finely chopped fresh parsley
½ teaspoon chili powder	Juice of 1 lime

1. Preheat broiler. Place trout skin side up on a foil-lined broiler pan. In a small bowl, mix together olive oil, garlic, chili powder, and salt. Brush over trout inside and out.

2. Broil trout about 4 inches from heat 5 minutes, or until skin is brown. With a wide spatula, turn trout over and broil 3 to 5 minutes longer, or until trout are opaque throughout.

3. Meanwhile, in a small bowl, combine melted butter, parsley, and lime juice. Spoon over cooked trout and serve at once.

158   RED SNAPPER AND SHRIMP STEW
Prep: 20 minutes   Cook: 39 to 43 minutes   Serves: 4

Seafood stews and soups are common along both coasts of Mexico. This one is a meal in a bowl, though you could serve it as a first course, in which case it would be enough for six.

1 medium chayote, cut in half lengthwise	½ cup dry white wine
3 tablespoons olive oil	1 large bay leaf
1 medium onion, chopped	2 tablespoons chopped parsley
3 garlic cloves, minced	½ teaspoon salt
1 cup stewed Mexican-style tomatoes, with juices	½ pound boneless, skinless red snapper fillet, cut into ½-inch pieces
2 medium carrots, peeled and cut into ¼-inch dice	½ pound medium shrimp, shelled and deveined
1 large celery rib, thinly sliced	Chopped cilantro and fresh lime wedges, as garnish
1 (14½-ounce) can reduced-sodium chicken broth	

1. In a medium saucepan of boiling salted water, cook chayote in water to cover about 20 minutes, until just tender when pierced with tip of a small knife. Rinse under cold running water to cool. Peel and cut into ½-inch dice.

2. In a large nonreactive saucepan or flameproof casserole, heat olive oil over medium heat. Add onion and garlic and cook, stirring, until onion is soft and translucent, about 3 minutes. Add tomatoes and boil until most of juices evaporate, about 3 minutes. Add chayote, carrots, celery, chicken broth, wine, bay leaf, parsley, and salt. Cook, partially covered, stirring occasionally, 10 to 12 minutes, or until vegetables are tender.

3. Add red snapper and shrimp. Cook until fish is firm and opaque throughout and shrimp are pink and curled, 3 to 5 minutes. Serve hot, sprinkled with cilantro. Pass lime wedges to squeeze juice into stew.

159 RED SNAPPER VERACRUZANA
Prep: 15 minutes   Cook: 20 to 25 minutes   Serves: 4

Huachinango Veracruzana, red snapper prepared in the Veracruz style, appears on restaurant menus all over Mexico. It is an extremely tasty and colorful dish. If red snapper is not available, use another firm white fish fillet.

4 skinless boneless red snapper fillets (about 1½ pounds)
Juice of 1 lime
½ teaspoon salt
2 tablespoons olive oil
½ medium white onion, chopped
3 garlic cloves, minced
3 medium ripe tomatoes (about 1 pound), peeled and chopped, or 1 (14-ounce) can Italian peeled tomatoes, drained and chopped

3 pickled jalapeño peppers, seeded and cut into very thin strips
8 pitted green olives, sliced
½ teaspoon dried oregano
¼ teaspoon ground cinnamon
2 tablespoons capers
Juice of 1 medium orange
Juice of ½ lemon
2 tablespoons chopped Italian flat-leaf parsley

1. Place fish fillets in a single layer in a medium nonreactive greased oven-proof casserole. Sprinkle with lime juice and salt.

2. Preheat oven to 350°F. In a large nonreactive skillet, heat oil over medium heat. Add onion and garlic and cook, stirring, until they begin to brown, 3 to 5 minutes. Add tomatoes, pickled jalapeño peppers, olives, oregano, cinnamon, capers, orange juice, and lemon juice. Bring to a boil. Reduce heat to low and simmer, uncovered, 5 minutes.

3. Spoon sauce over fish, cover casserole loosely with aluminum foil, and bake 12 to 15 minutes, or until fish is opaque throughout. Sprinkle with parsley and serve.

160 GRILLED SWORDFISH WITH GREEN CHILE PESTO

Prep: 20 minutes   Cook: 8 to 10 minutes   Serves: 4

Southwest cooks dream up pesto sauces using Mexican ingredients. I think the results are terrific, especially on seafood.

¼ cup grated Parmesan cheese
2 garlic cloves, chopped
2 fresh jalapeño peppers, seeded and chopped
⅓ cup blanched almonds
½ cup cilantro leaves, lightly packed
¼ cup parsley sprigs

¼ cup plus 2 tablespoons olive oil
2 tablespoons lime juice
½ teaspoon salt
4 swordfish steaks, 6 to 8 ounces each, cut ¾ inch thick

1. Prepare a hot fire in charcoal or gas grill.

2. In a blender or food processor, combine Parmesan cheese, garlic, jalapeño peppers, almonds, cilantro, parsley, ¼ cup of olive oil, lime juice, and ¼ teaspoon salt. Process to a smooth paste. Transfer pesto to a small bowl, cover, and set aside at room temperature.

3. Brush fish with remaining 2 tablespoons olive oil and season with remaining ¼ teaspoon salt. Place fish on an oiled grill rack about 6 inches from heat and grill, turning once, until just opaque in center, about 8 to 10 minutes. Top each swordfish steak with green chile pesto and serve.

161 SWORDFISH WITH SERRANO SAUCE

Prep: 15 minutes   Cook: 26 to 28 minutes   Serves: 4

Other firm fish steaks, such as tuna or halibut, are equally delicious with this silky smooth sauce ignited with the spicy flavor of serrano peppers.

3 fresh serrano peppers, stemmed and sliced into rounds
2 shallots, chopped
3 garlic cloves, chopped
¼ cup unseasoned rice vinegar
1 cup canned reduced-sodium chicken broth
1 cup heavy cream

1 teaspoon salt
¼ teaspoon pepper
4 swordfish steaks, 6 to 8 ounces each, cut ¾ inch thick
2 tablespoons flour
3 tablespoons vegetable oil
Lime wedges

1. In a medium nonreactive saucepan, place serrano peppers, shallots, garlic, and vinegar. Bring to a boil over medium-high heat and boil until reduced by half, about 3 minutes. Add chicken broth and cream. Boil, stirring frequently, until sauce is reduced to about 1½ cups and is thick enough to coat back of a wooden spoon, about 15 minutes. Strain sauce through a fine-mesh strainer into a medium bowl. Return sauce to pan. Season with ½ teaspoon of salt and pepper.

2. Dust fish with flour to coat. Shake off excess. Season with remaining ½ teaspoon salt. In a large skillet, heat oil over medium heat. Add fish and cook, turning once, until lightly browned outside and just opaque throughout but still moist, 4 to 5 minutes per side.

3. Meanwhile, reheat sauce over low heat. Transfer swordfish to plates and pour sauce over fish. Garnish with lime wedges.

---

162 TUNA STEAKS WITH TOMATOES, JALAPEÑO PEPPERS, AND ZUCCHINI

Prep: 20 minutes   Soak: 30 minutes   Cook: 16 minutes   Serves: 4

Raging hot jalapeño peppers are given a cold salt water bath to lessen their heat, but retain crispness and flavor in this saucy fresh tuna dish.

4 large fresh jalapeño peppers
3 tablespoons olive oil
1 small onion, minced
1 garlic clove, minced
2 medium tomatoes, peeled, seeded, and chopped
1 teaspoon salt
1 small zucchini, cut into ¼-inch dice
4 tuna steaks, about 6 ounces each, cut ¾ inch thick

1. Cut jalapeño peppers in half lengthwise and remove seeds and veins. Cut peppers lengthwise into long, thin strips ⅛ inch wide. Place in a small bowl with salted cold water to cover. Soak at least 30 minutes or up to 2 hours. Drain and rinse pepper strips. Drain well and blot dry on paper towels.

2. Meanwhile, in a medium nonreactive saucepan, heat 1 tablespoon of olive oil over medium heat. Add onion and garlic and cook, stirring, until they begin to brown, about 3 minutes. Add tomatoes and ½ teaspoon of salt. Cook, uncovered, stirring frequently, until juices reduce and sauce is thick, about 5 minutes. Add zucchini and cook until crisp-tender, about 2 minutes. Remove from heat and set aside, covered to keep warm.

3. Season tuna steaks with remaining ½ teaspoon salt. In a large skillet, heat remaining 2 tablespoons olive oil over medium-high heat. Add tuna and cook, turning once, until browned on both sides and just opaque in center, about 6 minutes total.

4. To serve, place 1 tuna steak on each of 4 plates. Spoon tomato sauce equally over each tuna steak. Scatter jalapeño pepper strips evenly over tuna steaks. Serve at once.

163   SQUID WITH PEPPERS AND ONIONS

Prep: 15 minutes   Cook: 3 minutes 15 seconds   Serves: 4

The trick to preparing tender squid is not to overcook it. Yellow Rice with Peas (page 171) makes a fine partner with this dish.

1 **pound cleaned squid, cut into rings ½ inch thick; leave tentacles whole**
2 **tablespoons olive oil**
1 **medium red bell pepper, cut into 2 x ¼-inch strips**
1 **medium onion, quartered and sliced**

2 **pickled jalapeño peppers, seeded and cut into very thin strips**
1 **tablespoon lime juice**
½ **teaspoon salt**
⅛ **teaspoon pepper**

1. Rinse squid well. Drain and pat dry on paper towels. In a large skillet, heat oil over medium-high heat. Add squid and cook, tossing, about 45 seconds, until just opaque and firm. Immediately remove with a slotted spoon to a bowl.

2. To same skillet, add red pepper, onion, and jalapeño peppers. Cook over medium-high heat, stirring, until crisp-tender, about 2 minutes. Add lime juice, reserved squid, salt, and pepper. Cook, stirring, just until heated through, about 30 seconds. Serve at once.

Chapter 6

South of the Border Birds

Chicken is the preferred bird in today's Mexican cookery. Although wild turkeys, ducks, and other game birds were widely used in pre-Hispanic cooking, domestic chickens were introduced by the Spaniards. Since they are easy to raise and provide a sure supply of eggs, they were quickly accepted. Now chickens rule the roost.

Turkey, a bird indigenous to the New World, is also much favored, particularly at holiday time, and for special fiestas. Ducks and small game birds, such as quail, appear on some restaurant menus, but are not commonly cooked at home.

Poultry and wonderfully spiced Mexican sauces belong together, and there are some special combinations in this chapter, such as the classic Arroz con Pollo, Chicken Breasts in Creamy Pumpkin Seed Sauce, Chicken Breasts in Adobo Sauce, and Drunken Chicken. These are zesty dishes to build a menu around. Some, like Chiapas Fiesta Chicken Stew and Maverick Turkey Chili, become complete meals in themselves by adding tortillas and a salad. For a taste of new-style light cooking, try Lime Chicken with Cilantro or Turkey Cutlets with Red Onion Marmalade. An alternative holiday meal, in place of the usual plain roasted turkey, might feature Yucatan Turkey Stuffed with Pork, Olives, and Almonds, which is served with an intriguing white sauce with tomatoes. Cookouts and barbecues call for Chicken Fajitas or Grilled Chicken Breasts with Poblano Chiles, Onions, and Cheese.

The lone duck recipe in this chapter is very special and not difficult, so I encourage you to try it. Of course, roasted duck or sautéed or grilled duck breasts can be paired with other sauces in this chapter, or with the sauces found in chapter 4, as can any simple chicken or turkey breast.

164   ARROZ CON POLLO
Prep: 25 minutes   Cook: 1 hour   Serves: 6

Rice with chicken is well known throughout Mexico and Latin America. Served directly from a rustic clay casserole, arroz con pollo is an ideal party dish.

6 skinless, boneless chicken breast halves	1 teaspoon dried oregano
1 teaspoon salt	1¼ cups long-grain white rice
¼ teaspoon pepper	1 (14½-ounce) can reduced-sodium chicken broth
2 tablespoons olive oil	1 cup corn kernels
2 garlic cloves, minced	1 cup thick and chunky salsa
½ medium onion, chopped	1 tablespoon chopped fresh cilantro or parsley
1 teaspoon ground cumin	

1. Preheat oven to 350°F. Season chicken breasts with ½ teaspoon of salt and pepper. In a large skillet, heat olive oil over medium heat. Add chicken and cook, turning once, until lightly browned, 2 to 3 minutes on each side. (Meat interior may still be slightly pink in center.) Transfer to a plate.

2. Add garlic, onion, cumin, and oregano to skillet. Cook, stirring, until onion is softened, about 3 minutes. Add rice and remaining ½ teaspoon salt. Cook, stirring, until rice is opaque, about 2 minutes. Stir in broth, corn, and salsa. Bring to a boil. Transfer mixture to a 3-quart casserole.

3. Cover and bake 30 minutes, or until liquid is almost absorbed. Remove cover and tuck reserved cooked chicken breasts into casserole along with any juices that have accumulated on plate. Cover and bake 20 minutes longer, or until chicken is white throughout, liquid is all absorbed, and rice is tender. Garnish with cilantro. Serve from casserole.

165   CHICKEN FAJITAS
Prep: 15 minutes   Marinate: 1 to 2 hours
Cook: 8 to 11 minutes   Serves: 6

A platter of grilled chicken, hot off the fire, surrounded by do-it-yourself garnishes and soft warm tortillas, is extremely popular fare for outdoor entertaining.

3 tablespoons lime juice	6 skinless, boneless chicken breast halves
3 garlic cloves, minced	12 flour tortillas
½ teaspoon dried oregano	Guacamole, salsa, shredded lettuce, pickled jalapeño peppers, and sour cream, as accompaniment
¼ teaspoon crushed hot red pepper	
1 teaspoon salt	
2 tablespoons olive oil	

1. In a large bowl, combine lime juice, garlic, oregano, hot pepper, salt, and oil. Add chicken and toss to coat. Cover and marinate at room temperature 1 to 2 hours.

2. Prepare a hot fire in a barbecue grill. Put chicken on an oiled grill rack and grill, turning and basting with marinade several times, until chicken is white throughout, 8 to 10 minutes. Remove to a cutting board.

3. Place tortillas directly on grill. Heat 10 to 20 seconds, turning with tongs. Wrap in a cloth napkin and place in a basket to keep warm.

4. Cut chicken into large strips and place on a platter. Serve with guacamole, salsa, lettuce, pickled jalapeño peppers, and sour cream for each person to roll their own.

---

166   CHICKEN BREASTS IN ADOBO SAUCE
Prep: 20 minutes   Cook: 48 minutes   Serves: 6

In Mexican cooking, adobo is a thick and spicy red chile sauce. It goes especially well with boneless breast of chicken. Serve with Mexican Rice (page 166) and sliced avocados.

4 ancho chiles, about
    2 ounces, stems and seeds
    removed
	1 tablespoon red wine vinegar

	1 teaspoon salt
2 medium tomatoes, peeled seeded, and chopped	½ teaspoon sugar
	½ cup canned chicken broth
1 tablespoon chopped onion	6 skinless, boneless chicken breast halves
½ teaspoon dried marjoram	
¼ teaspoon dried oregano	3 tablespoons flour
¼ teaspoon ground cinnamon	3 tablespoons olive oil

1. Rinse chiles and place in a small pan of hot water to barely cover. Bring to a boil over medium-high heat and cook 1 minute. Remove from heat, cover, and soak about 20 minutes; drain.

2. In a blender or food processor, combine tomatoes, onion, marjoram, oregano, cinnamon, vinegar, ½ teaspoon of salt, sugar, and chicken broth. Puree until smooth. Add reserved chiles and puree again until smooth. Set sauce aside.

3. Preheat oven to 350°F. Dust chicken breasts with flour. Shake off excess. In a medium skillet, heat oil over medium heat. Place chicken breasts in skillet and season with remaining ½ teaspoon salt. Cook 3 minutes. Turn and cook 2 minutes. Transfer chicken to an ovenproof casserole large enough to hold them in a single layer.

4. Set heat and add sauce (caution: it will splatter). Cook 2 minutes, stirring. Cover and simmer 10 minutes, stirring frequently.

5. Pour sauce over chicken, cover loosely with foil, and bake 30 minutes.

167 CHICKEN CHILAQUILES WITH GREEN CHILE STRIPS

Prep: 30 minutes   Cook: 51 to 59 minutes   Serves: 6

Chilaquiles make an easy tortilla casserole that's rich and delicious. With salad, it's a complete meal.

Vegetable oil, for frying	1 **bay leaf**
10 **corn tortillas, halved and cut**	1 **medium onion, chopped**
into ½-inch strips	1 **(14½-ounce) can ready-cut**
2 **large poblano peppers**	**salsa tomatoes**
3 **chicken breast halves (about**	½ **cup heavy cream**
1½ pounds)	1 **cup shredded Monterey Jack**
1 **(14½-ounce) can reduced-**	**cheese, packed (about**
sodium chicken broth	**5 ounces)**
¼ **cup dry white wine**	

1. In a medium skillet, heat ½ inch vegetable oil over medium heat. Add tortilla pieces in batches and fry until light golden brown, 1 to 2 minutes. Drain on paper towels.

2. Roast poblano peppers over a gas flame or under a broiler as close to heat as possible, turning, until blistered and charred all over, 5 to 10 minutes. Place in bag to steam for about 5 minutes. Rub skins off; remove seeds and veins. Rinse and pat dry. Cut peppers into strips ¼ inch wide and 2 inches long.

3. In a medium nonreactive saucepan, place chicken breasts with chicken broth, wine, and bay leaf. Bring to a boil over medium-high heat, reduce heat to low, cover, and cook 12 to 14 minutes, or until chicken is white in center but still moist. Let cool in broth. When cool enough to handle, pull meat off bones and shred. Discard skin and bones. Reserve 1 cup of broth for sauce.

4. In another medium nonreactive saucepan, heat 2 tablespoons vegetable oil over medium heat. Add onion and cook, stirring, until it begins to brown, about 3 minutes. Add tomatoes and cook, uncovered, stirring frequently, until liquid almost evaporates, about 5 minutes. Add reserved 1 cup broth, poblano pepper strips, and cream. Cook 5 minutes.

5. Preheat oven to 350°F. Place half of tortilla pieces in bottom of a greased 2½- to 3-quart ovenproof casserole. Spoon on half of chicken and half of tomato sauce. Repeat layers. Top with shredded cheese. Bake, uncovered, in preheated oven 20 minutes, or until cheese is melted and casserole is heated through.

168 CHICKEN BREASTS WITH PINE NUTS, POBLANO PEPPERS, AND SUN-DRIED TOMATOES

Prep: 30 minutes   Cook: 17 to 24 minutes
Marinate: 20 minutes   Serves: 6

Although sun-dried tomatoes are not a traditional Mexican ingredient, I like their color and intensity in combination with flavors that are.

½ cup pine nuts
6 skinless, boneless chicken
   breast halves
2 garlic cloves, crushed
   through a press
1 teaspoon fresh lemon juice
1 teaspoon salt
3 tablespoons olive oil

3 poblano peppers
½ medium onion, minced
1 teaspoon dried oregano
2 tablespoons chopped
   parsley
12 sun-dried tomato halves, cut
   into thin strips
¼ cup dry white wine

1. In a medium dry skillet, toast pine nuts over medium heat, shaking pan, until nuts are golden brown and fragrant, about 2 minutes. Watch carefully to prevent burning.

2. Place chicken breasts, 1 at a time, between sheets of plastic wrap and flatten to uniform thickness, about ½ inch, with flat side of a wooden meat mallet or a rolling pin. Place chicken breasts on a plate. In a small bowl, combine garlic, lemon juice, ½ teaspoon of salt, and 1 tablespoon of olive oil. Rub mixture all over chicken. Cover with plastic wrap and let marinate at room temperature 20 minutes.

3. Preheat oven broiler. Place poblano peppers on a baking sheet and broil as close to heat as possible, turning until charred all over, about 10 minutes. Or roast peppers directly over gas flame, turning, about 5 minutes, until charred. Place peppers in a paper bag and let steam 10 minutes. Peel off blackened skin and rinse under cold running water. Cut peppers open; discard stems and seeds. Cut peeled peppers into strips, ¼ inch x 2 inches.

4. In a medium saucepan, heat 1 tablespoon of olive oil over medium-high heat. Add onion and cook, stirring occasionally, until it begins to brown, about 3 minutes. Add oregano, parsley, sun-dried tomato strips, pine nuts, wine, poblano pepper strips, and remaining ½ teaspoon salt. Cook, stirring, 2 to 3 minutes to soften dried tomato strips and blend flavors. Remove from heat, cover, and set aside.

5. In a large skillet, heat remaining 1 tablespoon olive oil over medium heat. Add chicken breasts and cook until lightly browned on bottom, about 3 minutes. Turn chicken over and cook until white throughout but still juicy, about 2 minutes. Transfer chicken to a warm platter. Add reserved vegetable mixture to the skillet. Stir to combine with pan juices and cook about 2 minutes, or until completely heated through. Spoon over chicken and serve.

169   BREAST OF CHICKEN WITH ALMONDS
Prep: 20 minutes   Cook: 11 to 13 minutes   Serves: 4

Chicken prepared this way is called *pollo almendrado*. It's quick and light.

¾ cup whole almonds, with
    skins on
4 skinless, boneless chicken
    breast halves, about
    5 ounces each
3 tablespoons flour
½ teaspoon salt

3 tablespoons olive oil
2 garlic cloves, minced
1 serrano pepper, minced
6 scallions, thinly sliced
¾ cup chopped cilantro
3 tablespoons lime juice
2 tablespoons unsalted butter

1. In a dry medium skillet, toast almonds over medium heat until they begin to brown and are fragrant, 3 to 5 minutes. Set nuts aside to cool slightly and then finely chop.

2. Flatten chicken breasts with flat side of a wooden mallet or rolling pin to even thickness. Dust chicken pieces with flour and season with salt. In a large skillet, heat oil over medium heat. Add chicken and cook until lightly browned on both sides and white throughout but still juicy, about 6 minutes total. Place on a platter and cover to keep warm.

3. In same skillet, cook garlic, serrano pepper, and scallions over medium heat, stirring, until fragrant, about 1 minute. Add cilantro, chopped toasted almonds, and lime juice. Toss together until just beginning to boil, about 1 minute. Stir in butter until melted. Spoon almond sauce over chicken and serve.

170   LIME CHICKEN WITH CILANTRO
Prep: 15 minutes   Cook: 8 minutes   Serves: 4

3 tablespoons vegetable oil
1 medium onion, halved and
    thinly sliced
2 garlic cloves, minced
4 skinless, boneless chicken
    breast halves, cut into
    2-inch pieces

½ teaspoon salt
¼ teaspoon pepper
¼ cup lime juice
½ cup chopped cilantro
4 jalapeño peppers, seeded
    and thinly sliced

1. In a large skillet, heat oil over medium-high heat. Add onion and cook until soft, about 3 minutes. Add garlic and cook, stirring, 1 minute.

2. Add chicken, salt, and pepper to skillet. Cook, stirring occasionally, until lightly browned, about 4 minutes. Stir in lime juice and cilantro. Transfer chicken to a serving dish.

3. Pour pan juices over chicken. Scatter jalapeño slices on top.

171 CHICKEN SONORAN WITH RED CHILI SAUCE AND TOASTED SESAME SEEDS
Prep: 15 minutes   Cook: 30 to 33 minutes   Serves: 4

A flavorful dish from northern Mexico that's quick and easy to prepare. Serve with steamed white rice and sliced avocados.

¼ cup vegetable oil
⅓ cup pure California red chili powder
¾ cup drained and chopped canned tomatoes
½ teaspoon dried oregano
½ teaspoon ground cumin
2 garlic cloves, minced
½ cup canned chicken broth

1 teaspoon salt
4 skinless, boneless chicken breast halves
2 tablespoons flour
¼ teaspoon pepper
1 medium onion, halved and thinly sliced
⅓ cup sesame seeds

1. In medium saucepan, heat 2 tablespoons of oil over medium heat. Add chili powder, tomatoes, oregano, cumin, garlic, chicken broth, and ½ teaspoon of salt. Bring to a boil, reduce heat to low, cover, and simmer 10 minutes. Strain sauce through a wire strainer into a medium bowl. Set chili sauce aside.

2. Dust chicken with flour. Season with remaining ½ teaspoon salt and pepper. In a medium skillet, heat remaining 2 tablespoons oil over medium-high heat. Add chicken breasts and cook, turning once, until lightly browned, 2 to 3 minutes on each side. With tongs, remove to a plate and reserve.

3. Add onion to same skillet and cook, stirring, until limp and aromatic, about 4 minutes. Return chicken to pan and pour reserved chili sauce over chicken. Cover and cook over low heat 10 minutes.

4. Meanwhile, in a medium dry skillet, toast sesame seeds over medium heat, stirring often, until golden brown and fragrant, 2 to 3 minutes.

5. To serve, arrange chicken on a platter. Spoon sauce with onion on top. Sprinkle generously with sesame seeds.

172 CHICKEN BREASTS WITH OREGANO, HONEY, AND LIME

Prep: 10 minutes   Marinate: 30 minutes   Cook: 12 to 15 minutes
Serves: 4

This simple and delicious low-fat chicken preparation, with the typical flavor of oregano and a touch of hot pepper, is a winner. Tangy Red Onion Sauce (page 90) goes very well with the chicken.

4 boneless chicken breast halves	½ teaspoon salt
2 garlic cloves, crushed through a press	1 tablespoon honey Juice of 1 lime
1½ teaspoons dried oregano	1 tablespoon olive oil
⅛ teaspoon crushed hot red pepper	

1. Remove excess fat from chicken. Rinse, blot dry, and place in a medium nonreactive baking dish. In a small bowl, mix together garlic, oregano, hot pepper, salt, honey, and lime juice. Coat chicken pieces with mixture, rubbing some under skin. Cover and let stand at room temperature, turning once, about 30 minutes.

2. Meanwhile, preheat oven to 425°F. Place chicken on a baking sheet, skin side up, about 1 inch apart. Brush with olive oil. Roast in preheated oven 12 to 15 minutes, until skin is lightly browned and meat is white throughout but still juicy. Serve hot, at room temperature, or chilled.

173 CHICKEN BREASTS IN SESAME SEED SAUCE

Prep: 25 minutes   Cook: 22 to 25 minutes   Serves: 6

Traditional Mexican sauces are often flavored and thickened with ground nuts or seeds. Toasted sesame seeds combined with dried red chiles, tomatoes, and other seasonings is a well-known and tasty example.

3 ancho chile peppers, seeded and rinsed	¾ teaspoon salt
¼ cup sesame seeds	3 tablespoons vegetable oil
⅛ teaspoon aniseed	6 skinless, boneless chicken breast halves
1 garlic clove, chopped	¾ to 1 cup canned chicken broth
3 medium tomatoes, peeled, and quartered	2 scallions, thinly sliced
½ teaspoon ground cinnamon	

1. In a medium saucepan of boiling water, cook ancho chiles over medium heat 2 minutes. Remove from heat, cover, and soak about 20 minutes to soften; drain.

2. Meanwhile, heat a small dry skillet over medium heat. Add sesame seeds and aniseed and toast, stirring, until fragrant and sesame seeds are golden, 3 to 4 minutes. Pour onto a plate and let cool completely; then grind to a powder in a spice grinder. In a blender or food processor, place ancho chiles, ground sesame seeds, aniseed, garlic, tomatoes, cinnamon, and ¼ teaspoon of salt. Blend to a thick puree.

3. In a large skillet, heat vegetable oil over medium-high heat. Add chicken breasts and cook, turning once, until lightly browned on both sides, 2 to 3 minutes per side. Season with remaining ½ teaspoon salt. Remove chicken to a plate.

4. Drain off all but 1 teaspoon fat from skillet. Add chile puree and ¾ cup of chicken broth. Cook over medium heat, stirring, until sauce is simmering, about 3 minutes. Add additional chicken broth, if needed, for sauce to achieve consistency of heavy cream.

5. Return chicken to skillet, reduce heat to low, partially cover, and simmer 10 minutes. Transfer chicken to a serving platter, pour sauce on top, and garnish with sliced scallions.

---

174   CHIAPAS FIESTA CHICKEN STEW
Prep: 25 minutes   Cook: 49 to 54 minutes   Serves: 6

Here is a special dressed-up chicken stew with wonderful flavors from the region of Chiapas in southern Mexico.

3 tablespoons vegetable oil	1 teaspoon dried oregano
12 skinless chicken thighs, on the bone	½ cup dry white wine
	1 cup chicken broth
1 medium white onion, halved and sliced	3 medium zucchini, cut into ½-inch rounds
4 garlic cloves, chopped	½ medium head of cabbage, coarsely chopped
3 medium carrots, peeled and cut into ½-inch rounds	12 pitted dried prunes
1½ teaspoons salt	¼ teaspoon freshly ground pepper
½ teaspoon ground cinnamon	Pickled jalapeño peppers
½ teaspoon ground allspice	and cilantro, for garnish
½ teaspoon dried thyme	

1. Preheat oven to 350°F. In a flameproof casserole, heat oil over medium heat. Add chicken thighs and cook, turning, until lightly browned on both sides, about 6 minutes total. Add onion, garlic, and carrots. Sprinkle on salt, cinnamon, allspice, thyme, and oregano. Cook, stirring, 1 minute.

2. Add wine and chicken broth. Bring to a boil, stirring up browned bits from bottom of pan, and cook 2 minutes. Cover casserole and transfer to oven. Bake 20 minutes.

3. Add zucchini, cabbage, and prunes. Cover and bake 20 to 25 minutes, or until vegetables are tender. Stir in freshly ground black pepper. Serve stew garnished with sliced pickled jalapeño peppers and cilantro.

175 BREAST OF CHICKEN WITH SWEET RED PEPPER SAUCE

Prep: 25 minutes   Cook: 43 to 46 minutes   Serves: 4

A fancy contemporary dish that's easy to prepare. To complete a picture-perfect plate, serve Yellow Rice with Peas (page 171) as accompaniment.

2 large red bell peppers
1 tablespoon chili powder
½ cup heavy cream
1 teaspoon salt
4 skinless, boneless chicken
  breast halves

2 tablespoons flour
2 tablespoons olive oil
¼ cup chicken broth
2 tablespoons brandy
1 cup shredded Swiss cheese
  (about 4 ounces)

1. Preheat oven broiler. Cut bell peppers in half lengthwise. Scoop out seeds and cut out stems. Place peppers, skin side up, on a baking sheet and broil as close to heat as possible until skin is charred all over, about 10 minutes. Place peppers in a paper bag and let steam 10 minutes. Peel off blackened skin and rinse under cold running water. Chop coarsely and place in a blender or food processor. Add chili powder, cream, and ½ teaspoon of salt. Puree until smooth.

2. Preheat oven to 350°F. Place chicken breasts between sheets of plastic wrap and pound to flatten to even thickness with flat side of a wooden mallet or with a rolling pin. Dust lightly with flour and season with remaining ½ teaspoon salt.

3. In a large skillet, heat olive oil over medium heat. Add chicken pieces and cook, turning once, 2 to 3 minutes on each side, or until lightly browned. Place in a single layer in a shallow heatproof casserole.

4. Add chicken broth and brandy to same skillet. Boil 1 minute over medium heat, scraping up browned bits from bottom of pan. Add red pepper puree and bring to a boil, stirring. Reduce heat to low and cook, stirring, until sauce thickens, 3 to 4 minutes. Pour over chicken.

5. Bake in preheated oven about 20 minutes, or until sauce bubbles around edges. Top with shredded cheese and bake 5 minutes longer, or until cheese is melted.

176   CHICKEN BREASTS IN CREAMY PUMPKIN SEED SAUCE

Prep: 20 minutes   Cook: 27 to 32 minutes   Serves: 6

Boneless breast of chicken blanketed with an elegant version of pumpkin seed sauce is perfect with steamed rice and fresh corn salsa. Unroasted hulled pumpkin seeds are sold in Hispanic markets and in health food stores. They are sometimes called *pepitas.*

6 skinless, boneless chicken
    breast halves
2 cups boiling water
1 teaspoon salt
½ teaspoon dried oregano
1 bay leaf
¾ cup hulled, unroasted,
    unsalted pumpkin seeds
½ cup loosely packed cilantro
    leaves

2 garlic cloves, chopped
2 serrano peppers, chopped
4 tomatillos, husked, rinsed,
    and quartered
2 tablespoons chopped onion
2 tablespoons butter
⅓ cup heavy cream
¼ teaspoon ground white
    pepper

1. In large deep frying pan, place chicken pieces in a single layer. Add boiling water, ½ teaspoon of salt, oregano, and bay leaf. Bring to a boil over medium heat, reduce heat to low, cover, and cook 10 minutes. Remove pan from heat and let chicken remain in cooking liquid.

2. In a medium dry skillet, toast pumpkin seeds over medium heat, stirring often, until they begin to pop, about 2 minutes. Transfer to a paper towel to cool. In a blender or food processor, grind toasted pumpkin seeds as fine as possible. Add cilantro, garlic, serrano peppers, tomatillos, onion, and ½ cup broth from cooking chicken. Puree until smooth.

3. In a large saucepan, melt butter over medium heat. Add pumpkin seed sauce, cream, remaining ½ teaspoon salt, and white pepper. Bring to a boil, reduce heat to low, and cook, uncovered, 12 to 15 minutes, stirring frequently, until thickened.

4. With a slotted spoon, lift chicken breasts from cooking liquid and put in pan with sauce. Simmer until heated through, 3 to 5 minutes. Transfer to a serving platter. Garnish with additional cilantro leaves and serve at once.

177 GRILLED CHICKEN BREASTS WITH POBLANO CHILES, ONIONS, AND CHEESE

Prep: 20 minutes   Cook: 17 to 26 minutes   Serves: 4

Grilled chicken breasts are topped with a skillet-cooked mixture of onions, chiles, and cheese. Timing the outcome is important, but the cooking is simple and the results are delicious. Serve with black beans and rice.

2 poblano peppers	¼ teaspoon salt
2 tablespoons unsalted butter	⅛ teaspoon pepper
1 medium white onion, quartered and sliced	1 tablespoon vegetable oil
4 skinless, boneless chicken breast halves	1½ cups shredded Monterey Jack cheese (about 6 ounces)
1 garlic clove, crushed through a press	

1. Prepare a hot fire in a barbecue grill. Meanwhile, preheat oven broiler. Place peppers on a baking sheet and broil as close to heat as possible, turning, until charred all over, about 10 minutes. Or roast peppers directly over gas flame, turning, about 5 minutes, until charred. Place peppers in a paper bag and let steam 10 minutes. Peel off blackened skin and rinse under cold running water. Cut peppers open, discarding stems and seeds. Cut peppers into thin strips ¼ inch wide and 2 inches long.

2. In a medium skillet, melt butter over medium heat. Add onion and cook, stirring, until beginning to brown, about 3 minutes. Stir in pepper strips. Remove from heat and set aside.

3. Place chicken breasts on a platter. Rub with garlic, salt, pepper, and oil. Cover lightly with plastic wrap until fire is ready. When coals are hot, put chicken skinned side down on an oiled grill rack and cook 3 to 5 minutes, until lightly browned. Turn and cook 3 to 4 minutes, or until just firm to the touch. Place chicken in a single layer on a warm platter and cover with foil to keep warm.

4. Reheat onions and peppers over medium-high heat, stirring until mixture sizzles, about 2 minutes. With a wide spatula, spread vegetables flat in skillet. Reduce heat to low and quickly sprinkle cheese over entire surface. Do not stir. Cover and cook until cheese begins to melt, 1 to 2 minutes. With a spatula, lift out a quarter of the mixture to top each chicken breast. Serve at once.

178   ROTISSERIE CHICKEN WITH ESCABECHE

Prep: 30 minutes   Marinate: 2 hours   Cook: 19 to 23 minutes
Serves: 4

Here the authentic vinaigrette flavors of classic *escabeche* are captured in a heady mix of herbs, spices, chiles, onions, and orange juice. They are simmered with a purchased rotisserie-cooked chicken from the deli section of a supermarket (sometimes called barbecued chicken) to put this classic dish in the easy category.

1 large white onion, halved and thinly sliced	½ teaspoon ground cinnamon
¼ cup white wine vinegar	3 garlic cloves, crushed through a press
1½ teaspoons dried oregano	½ cup orange juice
¾ teaspoon salt	2 tablespoons red wine vinegar
2 poblano or Anaheim peppers	½ cup canned reduced-sodium chicken broth
¼ teaspoon whole black peppercorns	1 rotisserie-cooked chicken, about 2 pounds, quartered
1 teaspoon cumin seeds	
½ teaspoon ground allspice	

1. In a medium saucepan of boiling water, cook onion 1 minute. Drain and place in a medium bowl. While onion is still warm, add white vinegar, ½ teaspoon of oregano, ½ teaspoon of salt, and ½ cup water. Let marinate 2 to 4 hours.

2. Preheat oven broiler. Place poblano peppers on a baking sheet and broil as close to heat as possible, turning, until charred all over, about 10 minutes. Place peppers in a paper bag and let steam 10 minutes. Peel off blackened skin and rinse under cold running water. Cut peppers open and discard stems and seeds. Cut into thin strips 2 inches long and ¼ inch wide.

3. In a small dry skillet, toast remaining 1 teaspoon oregano, peppercorns, and cumin seeds over medium heat, stirring, until fragrant, 1 to 2 minutes. Grind fine in a spice grinder or with a mortar and pestle. Put toasted spices in a small bowl. Add allspice, cinnamon, garlic, remaining ¼ teaspoon salt, orange juice, red wine vinegar, and chicken broth. Stir to mix well.

4. Place cooked chicken pieces in a large nonreactive skillet or flameproof casserole. Spoon vinegar-spice mixture evenly over each quarter. Bring to a boil over medium heat. Cook, turning chicken 2 to 3 times and basting, until sauce is reduced by half and chicken is hot throughout, 6 to 8 minutes. Place chicken on a platter.

5. Drain marinated onion and add to skillet juices along with roasted pepper strips. Cook, tossing, until hot, 1 to 2 minutes. Spoon onion-pepper mixture over chicken and serve.

179   POACHED AND SHREDDED CHICKEN

Prep: 15 minutes   Cook: 40 minutes   Makes: about 3 cups

This is the chicken to use for any Mexican recipe that calls for cooked shredded chicken: tacos, enchiladas, chilaquiles, or salad. It's also wonderful for chicken salad. It's economical and easy to gently poach a whole chicken, then hand-shred the meat for many useful purposes. The resulting stock is handy for soups and such.

1 (3- to 3½-pound) whole chicken	2 parsley sprigs
1 medium onion, quartered	2 bay leaves
1 large carrot, scrubbed and cut into 2-inch chunks	1 teaspoon dried oregano
1 celery rib, cut into 2-inch chunks	1 teaspoon salt
	½ teaspoon whole black peppercorns

1. Place all ingredients in a large pot and add enough cold water to barely cover. Bring to a boil over high heat; then reduce heat to low, partially cover, and simmer until chicken is tender and there is no trace of pink near thigh bone, about 40 minutes. Remove chicken to a platter and let cool. Strain stock through a fine-mesh sieve into a large bowl. Discard solids. Refrigerate stock, covered, up to 3 days. When cold, remove fat from top. Freeze for longer storage.

2. When chicken is cool enough to handle, pull meat from bones and tear into large shreds. For best flavor, use chicken meat the day it is cooked, or store in a heavy-duty plastic bag up to 2 days. Freeze, if necessary, but flavor and texture will not be as good.

180   DRUNKEN CHICKEN

Prep: 20 minutes   Cook: 49 to 54 minutes   Serves: 4

Liquor-laced sauces are amusingly labeled *borracha* ("drunken") in Mexican cooking, and they make delicious eating. Nearly all the alcohol cooks away, leaving only a bit of flavor. Serve this dish with steamed rice and Savory Zucchini Pudding (page 211).

3 to 4 ancho chiles	2 tablespoons fresh lime juice
¼ cup olive oil	¼ cup tequila
½ medium onion, chopped	8 chicken thighs (about 2 pounds), skinned
½ teaspoon dried oregano	
¼ teaspoon cinnamon	½ teaspoon salt
¼ teaspoon allspice	⅛ teaspoon pepper
½ cup orange juice	

1. Rinse ancho chiles and pat dry with paper towels. Cut chiles lengthwise in half and remove stems and seeds. In a large skillet, preferably nonstick, heat 2 tablespoons of olive oil over medium heat. Add ancho pieces and cook about 20 seconds, or until fragrant. Do not brown, or they will be bitter. With a slotted spoon, remove chiles to a blender or food processor.

2. In same skillet, cook onion, oregano, cinnamon, and allspice, stirring, until onion begins to soften, about 3 minutes. Transfer to blender with chiles. Add orange juice, lime juice, and tequila. Puree until sauce is smooth.

3. Preheat oven to 350°F. In same skillet, heat remaining 2 tablespoons olive oil over medium heat. Add chicken thighs and cook until lightly browned, about 3 minutes on each side. Season with salt and pepper. Pour chile sauce over chicken and bring to a boil, stirring frequently. Transfer contents to an ovenproof casserole.

4. Cover and bake 40 to 45 minutes, or until chicken is very tender. If sauce separates during baking, stir well to recombine.

---

181 SKILLET CHICKEN, SONORA STYLE

Prep: 25 minutes   Cook: 16 to 19½ minutes   Serves: 4

Mexican main dishes are often presented with cooked and raw vegetables and other condiments. All contribute to the flavors and textures of the dish.

4 small new potatoes, peeled and cut into ½-inch dice	½ teaspoon dried oregano
4 small zucchini, cut into ½-inch dice	2 teaspoons chili powder
3 tablespoons olive oil	2 tablespoons white wine vinegar
4 chicken breast halves with bone (about 2 pounds)	3 romaine lettuce leaves, shredded
½ teaspoon salt	2 medium tomatoes, sliced
⅛ teaspoon pepper	Pickled jalapeño peppers

1. In a medium saucepan of boiling salted water, cook diced potatoes until barely tender, about 2 minutes. With a slotted spoon, transfer potatoes to a colander. Rinse under cold running water to cool, drain, and reserve in a medium bowl. In same saucepan, boil diced zucchini until barely tender, 20 to 30 seconds; do not overcook. Drain and cool under running water. Put in bowl with potatoes.

2. In a large skillet, heat olive oil over medium-high heat. Add chicken, skin side down, and cook until golden brown, about 4 minutes. Turn and season with salt, pepper, oregano, and 1 teaspoon of chili powder. Reduce heat to medium-low and cook until white throughout but still juicy, 6 to 8 minutes. With tongs, transfer to a large platter and keep warm in 200°F. oven.

3. In pan juices in same skillet, cook reserved potatoes and zucchini over medium-high heat, tossing frequently, until they are tender and begin to brown, 4 to 5 minutes. Sprinkle with vinegar and remaining 1 teaspoon chili powder. Stir to combine.

4. Arrange vegetables around chicken on a platter. Garnish with shredded romaine and sliced tomatoes. Accompany with pickled jalapeños.

182   CHICKEN IN TOMATILLO AND PUMPKIN SEED SAUCE

Prep: 20 minutes   Cook: 53 to 57 minutes   Serves: 6

Pipian verde, as this sauce is called, is an ancient recipe that has changed little since it was first recorded by the Spaniards. Toasted pumpkin seeds, available in health food stores, give the sauce its wonderful nutty taste. Serve this dish with rice or soft, warm tortillas.

¾ cup hulled, unroasted pumpkin seeds (pepitas)
½ cup loosely packed cilantro leaves
3 serrano peppers, chopped
½ pound tomatillos, husked, rinsed, and quartered, or 1 (10-ounce) can, drained
3 tablespoons chopped onion
1 teaspoon dried oregano
1 teaspoon salt
½ to ¾ cup canned chicken broth
3 tablespoons vegetable oil
6 chicken breast halves (about 8 ounces each)
6 chicken thighs (about 5 ounces each)
¼ teaspoon pepper

1. In a dry medium skillet, toast pumpkin seeds over medium heat, stirring, until they pop around the pan, begin to brown, and are very aromatic, 2 to 3 minutes. Transfer to a small bowl and let cool; then grind to a fine powder in a spice grinder or blender.

2. In a blender or food processor, combine pumpkin seeds, cilantro, serrano peppers, tomatillos, onion, oregano, and ½ teaspoon of salt. Add ½ cup chicken broth and puree until smooth. Sauce should be consistency of heavy cream. If too thick, add remaining ¼ cup chicken broth.

3. In a heavy medium saucepan, heat 1 tablespoon of oil over medium heat. Add pumpkin seed sauce and cook, stirring often, until it boils, 1 to 2 minutes. Reduce heat to low and simmer, stirring frequently, until thickened, 10 to 12 minutes. Remove from heat.

4. Preheat oven to 350°F. In a large skillet, heat remaining 2 tablespoons oil over medium heat. Add chicken and cook, turning once, until lightly browned on both sides, about 10 minutes total. Season with pepper and remaining ½ teaspoon salt. Transfer to a shallow 9 x 13-inch baking dish. Pour reserved sauce over chicken and loosely cover with aluminum foil. Bake 30 minutes, or until chicken is tender and sauce is bubbling.

183 BONELESS CHICKEN TINGA WITH CHORIZO

Prep: 20 minutes   Cook: 50 to 52 minutes   Serves: 4

Tinga is a typical regional stew, from the town of Puebla, about 90 miles east of Mexico City. This version uses boneless chicken thigh meat for easier preparation. It's wonderful wrapped in soft warm tortillas, with slices of buttery ripe avocado. Canned chipotle chile peppers or bottled chipotle salsa is available in the Mexican section of most supermarkets.

2 pounds skinless, boneless chicken thigh meat, cut into 2-inch pieces	½ teaspoon dried oregano
¾ cup canned chicken broth	3 medium tomatoes, peeled, seeded, and chopped
½ pound chorizo sausage, casing removed	2 canned chipotle chiles, minced, or 1 teaspoon bottle chipotle salsa
1 medium onion, chopped	1 tablespoon chopped cilantro
2 garlic cloves, minced	Salt

1. In a large saucepan, bring chicken pieces and broth to a boil over medium heat. Reduce heat to low, cover, and simmer until chicken is tender, about 30 minutes.

2. Meanwhile, in a medium skillet, cook chorizo over medium heat, stirring to break up lumps, until cooked through, 4 to 5 minutes. If chorizo is fatty, drain off all but 1 tablespoon of fat from pan. Add onion, garlic, and oregano. Cook until onion is limp, about 3 minutes. Add tomatoes, chipotles, and cilantro. Boil until juices almost evaporate, 3 to 4 minutes. Transfer contents to pan with chicken. Cook over medium-low heat, stirring occasionally, 10 minutes. Season with salt to taste.

184 SPICY TURKEY PATTIES

Prep: 15 minutes   Cook: 7 to 8 minutes   Serves: 4

1 pound ground turkey	1 jalapeño pepper, seeded and minced
⅓ cup fresh bread crumbs	½ teaspoon dried oregano
2 tablespoons dry white wine	½ teaspoon salt
½ medium onion, minced	⅛ teaspoon freshly ground pepper
2 garlic cloves, minced	2 tablespoons olive oil
2 tablespoons minced red bell pepper	

1. In a medium bowl, combine all ingredients except olive oil. Mix very well. Form into 8 patties 2½ inches across and ¾ inch thick.

2. In a large skillet, preferably nonstick, heat oil over medium heat. Add patties and cook without crowding, in 2 batches if necessary, until golden brown on bottom, about 4 minutes. Turn and cook until brown on second side, 3 to 4 minutes.

185 TURKEY PIE MEXICANA WITH CORNMEAL CRUST

Prep: 30 minutes   Cook: 39 to 46 minutes   Serves: 6

This easy turkey pie is a complete meal and special enough for company. Make it with leftover roast turkey or cooked turkey breast.

3 tablespoons olive oil	½ cup chicken broth
½ medium onion, minced	½ cup heavy cream
2 garlic cloves, minced	½ teaspoon salt
1 (4-ounce) can diced green chiles	⅛ teaspoon pepper
	1 cup corn kernels
½ cup chopped red bell pepper	2 cups bite-size cubes of cooked turkey (about ¾ pound)
4 to 5 small fresh tomatillos, husked, rinsed, and cut into ½-inch pieces	
1 teaspoon ground cumin	Cornmeal Dough (recipe follows)
2 tablespoons flour	

1. In a large skillet, heat oil over medium heat. Add onion and cook, stirring, until it begins to brown, about 3 minutes. Add garlic, chiles, bell pepper, and tomatillos. Cook, stirring, about 3 minutes. Stir in cumin and flour. Stir in chicken broth and cream all at once. Cook, stirring, until mixture boils and thickens, 3 to 5 minutes. Season with salt and pepper. Add corn and turkey. Remove from heat and let cool to room temperature.

2. Preheat oven to 450°F. Remove dough from refrigerator and divide into 2 parts. On a lightly floured board, roll out half of dough to a round about ⅛ inch thick. Use to line a 10-inch pie plate. Put cooled turkey mixture into pie shell. Roll out remaining dough and place on top of pie. Crimp edges. Cut steam vents in center of top.

3. Bake in preheated oven 15 minutes. Reduce oven temperature to 350°F. and bake 15 to 20 minutes longer, until crust is golden brown. Cut pie into wedges and serve hot.

CORNMEAL DOUGH
Makes: double crust for 10-inch pie

2 cups flour	1 stick (4 ounces) cold unsalted butter, cut into pieces
¼ cup yellow cornmeal	
½ teaspoon paprika	
½ teaspoon salt	2 tablespoons cold vegetable shortening

1. In a food processor, place flour, cornmeal, paprika, and salt. Pulse 4 to 6 times to blend. Add cold butter pieces and shortening. Process until crumbly, 10 to 15 seconds.

2. Remove processor lid and drizzle ¼ cup cold water over flour mixture. Process until mixture begins to clump together; do not overprocess. Remove dough and form into a ball. Then flatten into a disk, wrap in plastic wrap, and refrigerate. Use as directed in recipe.

186 TURKEY CUTLETS WITH RED ONION MARMALADE

Prep: 20 minutes   Cook: 20 to 23 minutes   Serves: 6

An innovative way to enjoy the convenience of fresh sliced turkey breast. The red onion topping takes on a great color and extra spice with the addition of red jalapeño jelly, which can be purchased in many supermarkets and in specialty food shops.

3 tablespoons vegetable oil	6 turkey cutlets (1½ to
2 medium red onions, minced	1¾ pounds)
½ teaspoon sugar	3 garlic cloves, crushed
1 teaspoon salt	through a press
¼ teaspoon pepper	½ cup flour
2 tablespoons unseasoned rice	½ cup canned chicken broth
vinegar	4 tablespoons butter
2 tablespoons fresh orange	3 tablespoons bottled red
juice	jalapeño jelly

1. In a nonreactive medium saucepan, heat 1 tablespoon of vegetable oil over medium-high heat. Add red onions and cook, stirring, until they soften, about 3 minutes. Add sugar, ½ teaspoon of salt, and pepper. Cook, stirring, 1 minute. Add vinegar and orange juice. Bring to a boil and cook, stirring, 1 minute longer. Remove from heat.

2. Rub turkey cutlets with garlic and season with remaining ½ teaspoon salt. Dust lightly with flour. In a large nonreactive skillet, heat remaining 2 tablespoons oil over medium heat. Add turkey and cook until edges begin to look opaque, 3 to 4 minutes. Turn pieces over and cook until tender and white throughout, about 2 minutes. Transfer to a warm platter and cover with foil to keep warm.

3. Add reserved onion mixture to same skillet and cook over medium-high heat, stirring, until it boils, about 2 minutes. Stir in chicken broth and boil until reduced by half, 4 to 5 minutes. Reduce heat to low and stir in butter, 1 tablespoon at a time, until melted and blended into sauce, about 2 minutes. Add jalapeño jelly and cook, stirring, until it melts, 2 to 3 minutes longer. Spoon sauce over turkey slices and serve.

187   TURKEY SAUSAGE 'N CHIPS CASSEROLE

Prep: 8 minutes   Cook: 25 minutes   Serves: 4

Youngsters and teens love this super convenient casserole. Lean smoked turkey sausage, which is low in fat, is available in all supermarkets.

½   pound smoked fully cooked turkey sausage, sliced ¼ inch thick
½   cup mayonnaise
½   cup plain yogurt
1   cup thick and chunky salsa
1   (15-ounce) can pinto beans, drained and rinsed

1   (2¼-ounce) can sliced olives
4   scallions, chopped
2½   cups coarsely broken corn tortilla chips (about 5 ounces)
2   cups shredded Cheddar cheese (about 8 ounces)

1. Preheat oven to 350°F. In a medium bowl, combine sliced sausage, mayonnaise, yogurt, salsa, beans, olives, and scallions. Stir to mix well.

2. In a 2-quart casserole, layer half of meat mixture, half of tortilla chips, and half of cheese. Repeat layers with remaining ingredients.

3. Bake in preheated oven 25 minutes, or until casserole is bubbly and cheese is melted. Serve hot.

188   TURKEY CUTLETS WITH MELON SALSA

Prep: 12 minutes   Cook: 4 minutes   Serves: 4

½   small cantaloupe, peeled, seeded, and cut into ¼-inch dice
½   red bell pepper, seeded and cut into ¼-inch dice
1   tablespoon minced white onion
1   tablespoon minced fresh mint
2   teaspoons unseasoned rice vinegar

Juice of 1 lime
1   jalapeño pepper, seeded and minced
¾   teaspoon salt
4   slices uncooked turkey breast, about ½ inch thick (1 to 1¼ pounds)
3   tablespoons vegetable oil

1. In a medium bowl, combine cantaloupe, red pepper, onion, mint, vinegar, lime juice, jalapeño pepper, and ¼ teaspoon of salt. Mix salsa well, cover, and refrigerate.

2. Season turkey slices with remaining ½ teaspoon salt. In a large skillet, heat oil over medium-high heat until it shimmers. Add turkey and cook, turning once, until white throughout but still moist, about 2 minutes per side. Overlap slices on a warm platter. Serve with melon salsa.

189 MAVERICK TURKEY CHILI
Prep: 15 minutes   Cook: 41 to 50 minutes   Serves: 6 to 8

Healthy and hot, this different breed of chili has plenty of kick and flavor. Make it several hours or a day ahead for best flavor.

3 tablespoons vegetable oil	1 (14½-ounce) can reduced-sodium chicken broth
2 medium onions, chopped	
4 garlic cloves, chopped	1 (14½-ounce) can ready-cut tomatoes
2 pounds ground turkey	
2½ tablespoons chili powder	1 (12-ounce) bottle beer
1 tablespoon dried oregano	2 tablespoons masa harina or cornmeal
1 tablespoon ground cumin	
1 teaspoon salt	2 (15-ounce) cans small white beans, drained but not rinsed
1 teaspoon bottled chipotle salsa	
1 teaspoon Worcestershire sauce	Chopped cilantro
1 medium green bell pepper, chopped	

1. In large heavy saucepan or flameproof casserole, heat oil over medium heat. Add onions and garlic and cook, stirring occasionally, until onions begin to brown, 4 to 6 minutes. Add turkey and cook, stirring to break up lumps, until meat is no longer pink, 6 to 8 minutes. Add chili powder, oregano, cumin, and salt. Cook 1 minute, stirring to distribute seasonings.

2. Add chipotle salsa, Worcestershire, bell pepper, chicken broth, tomatoes, beer, and masa harina. Mix well. Reduce heat to low, cover, and cook, stirring occasionally, 20 to 25 minutes, or until juices thicken.

3. Stir in beans and simmer 10 minutes. Serve chili hot, garnished with chopped cilantro. If made ahead, cover and refrigerate up to 2 days.

190 YUCATAN TURKEY STUFFED WITH PORK, OLIVES, AND ALMONDS

Prep: 30 minutes   Cook: 1 hour 49 minutes to 1 hour 55 minutes
Serves: 8

A Mayan way to prepare our native bird, called in Mexico *pavo en relleno blanco*. Here, just the meaty breast is used, topped with a traditional creamy tomato sauce. This dish is special enough for a holiday dinner, and the sauce is great over other meats, too.

1 turkey breast, about
   5 pounds
3 garlic cloves, crushed
   through a press
1½ teaspoons salt
½ teaspoon pepper
1 tablespoon white wine
   vinegar
¾ pound fresh ground pork
1 teaspoon dried oregano
½ cup chopped pimiento-
   stuffed green olives

½ cup currants or raisins
⅓ cup chopped blanched
   almonds
2 tablespoons capers, rinsed
8 slices of day-old French
   bread, cut or torn into
   ½-inch pieces (about
   4 cups)
1 cup chicken or turkey broth
1 tablespoon vegetable oil
   White Sauce with Tomatoes
   (recipe follows)

1. Preheat oven to 350°F. Trim excess fat from turkey. In a small bowl, combine crushed garlic, 1 teaspoon of salt, pepper, and vinegar. Rub seasonings all over turkey breast and under skin. Set turkey aside at room temperature.

2. In a medium nonstick skillet, cook ground pork and oregano, stirring to break up lumps, until meat is no longer pink, 4 to 5 minutes. Transfer to a large bowl. Add olives, currants, almonds, capers, bread, and remaining ½ teaspoon salt. Toss to mix. Add broth and mix until stuffing is moist.

3. Mound stuffing in a loaf shape in center of a buttered medium roasting pan. Brush turkey skin with vegetable oil. Place turkey on top of stuffing. Fold strips of aluminum foil around outer edges of stuffing to avoid overbrowning. Cover pan tightly with aluminum foil.

4. Roast in oven 1 hour. Remove foil cover, reduce oven temperature to 325°F., and roast 45 to 50 minutes longer, or until turkey is golden brown and cooked through; a meat thermometer should register 170°F. Transfer turkey breast to a cutting board. Place stuffing on a large platter. Slice turkey and arrange over stuffing. Spoon about ½ cup tomato sauce over turkey. Pass remaining sauce on the side.

191   WHITE SAUCE WITH TOMATOES

Prep: 15 minutes   Cook: 16 to 18 minutes   Makes: about 3 cups

This wonderful "saucy" white gravy traditionally tops Yucatán Turkey, but don't stop there. Use it with turkey cutlets, game hens, and Mexican meatloaf.

3 tablespoons unsalted butter	12 pimiento-stuffed green
½ medium white onion, finely	olives, sliced into thirds
chopped	½ teaspoon salt
3 tablespoons flour	⅛ teaspoon pepper
½ medium green bell pepper,	2 medium tomatoes, peeled,
cut into ¼-inch dice	seeded, and cut into
1 serrano pepper, minced	½-inch pieces
1 (14½-ounce) can reduced-	
sodium chicken broth	

1. In a medium saucepan, melt butter over medium heat. Add onion and cook 3 to 4 minutes, or until onion begins to soften. Sprinkle on flour and cook, stirring, 1 minute.

2. Remove from heat and add bell pepper, serrano pepper, chicken broth, olives, salt, and pepper. Stir to combine and return pan to heat. Cook, uncovered, stirring frequently, about 10 minutes, or until sauce is thickened.

3. Stir in tomatoes. Cook until sauce simmers, 2 to 3 minutes. Cover and keep warm, or if made ahead, refrigerate up to 2 days.

192   TURKEY LOAF MEXICANA

Prep: 15 minutes   Cook: 50 minutes   Rest: 10 minutes   Serves: 8

Low-fat turkey fits today's life-style, and the naturally light meat has been used for centuries in Mexico. This loaf, or *albondigon*, is tasty served with a fresh salsa, such as Mango Lime (page 87) or Spicy Fresh Corn (page 81).

2 pounds fresh ground turkey	½ medium red bell pepper,
½ cup dry bread crumbs	finely diced
1 egg	2 garlic cloves, minced
¼ cup milk or dry white wine	¾ teaspoon dried oregano
1 medium onion, minced	¾ teaspoon salt
2 tablespoons minced parsley	¼ teaspoon pepper
2 to 3 fresh jalapeño peppers,	
seeded and minced	

Preheat oven to 350°F. In a large bowl, mix all ingredients very thoroughly. Using hands, shape into 2 equal loaves and place in 2 greased loaf pans 7¼ x 3¾ inches or set freeform on a large baking sheet. Bake in preheated oven until juices run clear, about 50 minutes. Let rest 10 minutes before slicing.

193 ROAST GAME HENS WITH PICKLED RED ONIONS

Prep: 20 minutes   Marinate: 1 hour   Cook: 30 to 35 minutes
Serves: 4

Small chickens or game birds are often seasoned in this way and served with a topping of pickled fried onions. It's a delicious and slightly unusual rendition. Serve with oven-roasted potatoes and corn or zucchini.

2 Cornish game hens (about 1¼ pounds each), cut in half, rinsed, and patted dry
2 garlic cloves, crushed through a press
1 teaspoon salt
1 teaspoon white wine vinegar

2 tablespoons orange juice
1 tablespoon lime juice
½ teaspoon dried oregano
1 tablespoon vegetable oil
Pickled Red Onions (recipe follows)

1. Place game hens skin side up on a work surface. In a small bowl, mix garlic with salt and vinegar to make a paste. Rub mixture all over game hens. Lay skin side down in a single layer in a nonreactive dish. Mix orange and lime juices and drizzle over hens. Sprinkle with crumbled oregano, well rubbed in palm of hand. Cover and marinate in refrigerator 1 to 2 hours.

2. Preheat oven to 400°F. Remove hens from marinade and rub all over with vegetable oil. Lay skin side up on a foil-lined baking sheet. Roast in middle of oven 30 to 35 minutes, or until skin is lightly browned and juices run clear when thigh is pricked at thickest point. Transfer to a serving platter. Pour pan juices over game hens and top with pickled onions.

194 PICKLED RED ONIONS

Prep: 5 minutes   Cook: 4 to 5 minutes   Makes: about 1½ cups

2 tablespoons vegetable oil
2 medium red onions, halved and thinly sliced
1 tablespoon red wine vinegar

½ teaspoon dried oregano
½ teaspoon sugar
¼ teaspoon salt
⅛ teaspoon pepper

In large nonreactive skillet, heat oil over medium-high heat. Add red onions and cook, stirring occasionally, until softened, about 2 minutes. Add vinegar, oregano, sugar, salt, and pepper. Cook, stirring, until limp and tender, 2 to 3 minutes. Serve hot.

195 BARBECUED GAME HENS

Prep: 25 minutes   Cook: 22 to 26 minutes   Serves: 4

Game hens are convenient to prepare and serve. Barbecuing them over hot coals adds a smoky edge that is terrific with tortillas, salsa, guacamole, and all the trimmings. Provide plenty of napkins for this is finger-licking fare.

4 game hens, about
   1½ pounds each
1 teaspoon salt
¼ teaspoon pepper
2 garlic cloves, crushed
   through a press
1 tablespoon olive oil
½ cup ketchup
1 tablespoon red wine vinegar

1 teaspoon Worcestershire
   sauce
1 tablespoon brown sugar
½ teaspoon ground cumin
¼ teaspoon crushed hot red
   pepper
2 tablespoons apricot
   preserves

1. Prepare a hot fire in a barbecue grill. Rinse game hens under cold running water inside and out. Pat dry. Cut hens in half with a cleaver or poultry shears. Trim off excess fat. Place bone side down on baking sheet. Season with salt, pepper, and garlic. Rub all over with olive oil. Set aside at room temperature.

2. In a medium nonreactive saucepan, combine ketchup, vinegar, Worcestershire, brown sugar, cumin, hot pepper, and apricot preserves. Bring to a boil over medium heat. Reduce heat to low and simmer, stirring frequently, about 5 minutes to blend flavors.

3. Place game hens, skin side down, on an oiled grill rack set 4 to 6 inches from coals. Grill hens until skin is lightly browned, 6 to 8 minutes. Turn hens over and grill until second side is browned, 6 to 8 minutes. With a brush, baste hens on both sides with reserved marinade, turning and grilling, until well coated with barbecue marinade, well browned but not charred, and juices run clear when meat is pierced near leg joint, about 5 minutes longer. Serve hot, at room temperature, or cold.

196   DUCK IN PUMPKIN SEED SAUCE

Prep: 25 minutes   Cook: 1 hour 8 to 40 minutes   Serves: 6

In traditional Mexican cooking, *pipian* is an important sauce, flavored and thickened with toasted seeds and nuts. This pumpkin seed sauce is served with duck, which is cooked in two ways. The legs and thighs are oven-braised, until very tender, and the breasts are sautéed briefly, then thinly sliced in the new style. (If you are not handy with a boning knife, ask your butcher to cut up the ducks for you.) It's a special dish, worth the time and effort. Accompany with Mexican Rice (page 166) and black beans.

2 (5-pound) ducks	⅓ cup dry white wine
½ teaspoon salt	1 recipe Pumpkin Seed Sauce
¼ teaspoon pepper	(recipe follows)
2 tablespoons vegetable oil	
1 medium onion, peeled and	
quartered	

1. Preheat oven to 350°F. Rinse ducks and pat dry. With a boning knife, cut leg and thigh away from body of duck in 1 piece. Repeat for all leg-thigh pieces. Set aside. Cut each breast half away from carcass, leaving skin on meat. (Use remaining carcasses for duck stock, if desired, or discard.) Remove excess fat from all duck pieces. Season duck with salt and pepper.

2. In a large skillet, heat oil over medium heat, add leg-thigh pieces, and cook, turning frequently, until lightly browned on both sides, 6 to 8 minutes. Transfer to an ovenproof casserole. In same skillet, cook onion, stirring, until softened, 2 to 3 minutes. Put in casserole with duck. Add wine and ⅓ cup water to skillet. Pour juices over duck. Cover and transfer to oven. Bake 1 to 1½ hours, or until duck is very tender. (The legs and thighs can be cooked up to a day ahead. Refrigerate, covered; reheat before proceeding.)

3. About 20 minutes before ready to serve, heat a large, heavy skillet over medium heat. Arrange duck breasts skin side down in dry pan. Cook without turning until skin is nicely browned, about 10 minutes. Fat will render as meat cooks, and skin will become crisp. Take care not to blacken skin. Turn and cook second side until medium-rare, 4 to 5 minutes. Transfer to a plate and let rest about 5 minutes.

4. Meanwhile, reheat pumpkin seed sauce over medium heat. Spoon some of sauce onto 6 plates. Slice each duck breast crosswise on a diagonal and fan out on top of sauce. Arrange cooked legs beside sliced breast meat, or put on a platter and pass separately along with remaining sauce.

197   PUMPKIN SEED SAUCE
Prep: 10 minutes   Cook: 20 to 21 minutes   Makes: about 2½ cups

¾ cup hulled, unroasted
  pumpkin seeds (pepitas)
½ cup lightly packed cilantro
½ pound tomatillos, husked,
  rinsed, and quartered
2 serrano peppers, chopped

3 tablespoons chopped onion
½ teaspoon dried oregano
½ teaspoon salt
½ to 1 cup canned chicken
  broth or duck stock
1 tablespoon vegetable oil

1. In a dry heavy medium skillet, toast pumpkin seeds over medium heat, stirring constantly, until they pop around in pan and begin to brown, 3 to 4 minutes. Transfer to a bowl to cool. When cool, grind to a fine powder in a spice grinder or blender.

2. In a blender or food processor, combine pumpkin seeds, cilantro, tomatillos, serrano peppers, onion, oregano, salt, and ½ cup broth. Puree until smooth. If sauce is too thick, add enough broth to make mixture consistency of very heavy cream.

3. In a heavy medium saucepan, heat vegetable oil over medium heat. Add sauce and cook, stirring, 2 minutes. Turn heat to low. Simmer, uncovered, stirring frequently, 15 minutes. Cover and reserve until ready to use.

Chapter 7

Meats Go Mexican

The recipes in this chapter reflect the spectrum of beef, pork, and lamb dishes that are typically prepared all over Mexico: Chile Verde, Pork in Adobo Sauce, Shepherd's Lamb Stew, and Ranchero Steak with Potatoes, for example. A few new-style dishes with authentic taste, such as Grilled Flank Steak with Chili-Corn Sauce and Pork Tenderloin with Ancho Citrus Sauce, are offered as well. All of these are main-course entrees around which a complete Mexican menu can be built. Or they can be used as a centerpiece accompanied by simple side dishes with which you are already familiar.

Domestic livestock was introduced to Mexico by the Spanish. Cattle, pigs, sheep, and goats were quickly accepted, and these domesticated meats broadened the culinary picture considerably, making much greater variety possible. Cattle-raising went north, and even today, northern Mexico is known for its superior, more tender beef. Generally, Mexican beef is tough and stringy, but well suited to long, slow cooking with spicy sauces, thinly sliced steaks for asadas and fajitas, and shredded for many tortilla-wrapped specialties. Mexican pork is excellent, and is probably the most commonly used meat among cooks all over the country. Lamb and goat, particularly barbecued kid, are favorites for fiestas.

Today's trend toward eating less red meat makes these dishes especially important, for Mexican meat dishes stretch a small amount of meat to serve more people. Corn, beans, and tortillas add extra protein, with fresh salsas and vegetables completing the plate. The recipes in this book do not use lard, and the amount of oil and butter used in preparation is kept to a minimum, where possible, to achieve flavorful results. The recipes for the meat dishes have been carefully chosen for their wide appeal, delicious authentic flavors, and availability of ingredients to make them.

198 BEEF TENDERLOIN WITH CHILI RUB

Prep: 30 minutes   Chill: 3 hours   Stand: 1 hour
Cook: 45 to 50 minutes   Serves: 8 to 10

For a special party, you can't miss with this succulent, Mexican-style roasted tenderloin of beef, accompanied by rice, beans, salsa, and a salad. The recipe is quick and easy to prepare and cook, but the meat does need to marinate in the refrigerator for several hours and then return to room temperature, so plan your time accordingly.

1 (5-pound) beef tenderloin, trimmed of all excess fat and silver membrane	½ teaspoon salt
	1 tablespoon fresh lime juice
	3 tablespoons olive oil
3 large garlic cloves, crushed through a press	Chili Rub (recipe follows)

1. Place tenderloin on a large piece of plastic wrap. In a small bowl, make a paste of garlic, salt, lime juice, and olive oil. Rub all over meat. Wrap beef tightly in plastic wrap and refrigerate 3 to 4 hours. About 1 hour before roasting, remove meat from refrigerator, unwrap, and coat all over with chili rub. Place meat on a rack in a baking pan and let stand at room temperature 1 hour.

2. Preheat oven to 425°F. Roast beef, uncovered, 45 to 50 minutes for medium-rare, 150°F. on a meat thermometer; do not overcook. Remove from oven and let rest about 10 minutes before slicing.

199 CHILI RUB

Prep: 5 minutes   Toast: 2 minutes   Makes: about ½ cup

3 tablespoons cumin seeds	¼ cup New Mexico chili powder
1 teaspoon coriander seeds	
½ teaspoon aniseed	2 tablespoons dark brown sugar
1½ tablespoons dried oregano	
	1 teaspoon salt

1. In a dry medium skillet, toast cumin, coriander, aniseed, and oregano over medium heat, stirring, until very aromatic, about 2 minutes. Seeds may brown lightly, but do not let burn, or mixture may taste bitter. Immediately transfer to a plate and let cool. Grind until very fine in a spice grinder or blender, or with a mortar and pestle.

2. In a small bowl, combine ground seasonings with chili powder, brown sugar, and salt. Mix well. Store in a plastic bag or covered jar in freezer. Will keep 6 months to 1 year before flavor deteriorates.

3. To use, massage chili rub into both sides of meat, poultry, or fish 2 or 3 hours before cooking. Cover and refrigerate. Let seasoned items return to room temperature before cooking.

200 GRILLED FLANK STEAK WITH CHILI-CORN SAUCE

Prep: 25 minutes   Cook: 28 to 37 minutes   Serves: 4

This easy-to-prepare red chili sauce should be made a day ahead, if possible, for a deeper, more mellow flavor. The fresh corn, red pepper, and zucchini garnish adds color and texture, and it tastes great.

3 tablespoons vegetable oil
3 medium shallots, minced
1½ tablespoons chili powder
2 teaspoons masa harina or cornmeal
1 teaspoon ground cumin
1½ tablespoons tomato paste
1 teaspoon Worcestershire sauce
¼ cup dry red wine
1 cup canned beef broth

1 flank steak, about 2 pounds
½ teaspoon salt
2 garlic cloves, crushed through a press
½ medium red bell pepper, cut into ¼-inch dice
1 cup corn kernels, fresh or frozen
1 small zucchini, cut into ¼-inch dice
Chopped fresh cilantro

1. In a heavy medium saucepan, heat 1 tablespoon of vegetable oil over medium-low heat. Add shallots, stirring, until they are golden brown, about 3 minutes. Do not burn, or they will be bitter. Add chili powder, masa harina, cumin, tomato paste, Worcestershire, wine, and broth. Stir to combine. Reduce heat to medium and bring to a boil. Reduce heat to low and cook, partially covered, stirring frequently, until thickened, 15 to 18 minutes. Strain sauce through a wire strainer set over a small saucepan. Set sauce aside. (Sauce can be made up to a day ahead to this point. Cover and refrigerate.)

2. Light a hot fire in a barbecue grill. Trim fat from steak. Rub with salt, garlic, and 1 tablespoon of oil.

3. Place steak on an oiled grill rack set 4 to 6 inches from coals. Grill until steak is browned on bottom, 4 to 6 minutes. Turn and grill second side until nicely browned outside and still pink and juicy inside, 4 to 6 minutes, or longer to taste. Transfer steak to a cutting board and let stand 5 minutes.

4. Meanwhile, in a medium skillet, heat remaining 1 tablespoon oil over medium heat. Add red bell pepper, corn, and zucchini. Cook, tossing, until heated through and sizzling, 2 to 4 minutes. Reheat sauce.

5. Cut steak into thin slices crosswise on a diagonal. Divide steak evenly among 4 plates. Spoon chili sauce over steak and scatter hot vegetables on top. Sprinkle with chopped cilantro and serve.

201 ROPA VIEJA

Prep: 25 minutes   Cook: 1 hour 26 minutes to 1 hour 35 minutes
Serves: 6

Homey and simple, this shredded beef with chiles—known as Ropa Vieja ("old clothes")—can be served as a hash with scrambled eggs, or as a filling for burritos or tacos.

1 pound beef stew meat, cut into 1-inch pieces	½ medium green bell pepper, cut into ¼-inch dice
2 medium red potatoes, peeled, about ¾ pound	1 teaspoon dried oregano
3 tablespoons vegetable oil	½ cup bottled red salsa
1 medium onion, minced	½ teaspoon salt
3 garlic cloves, minced	¼ teaspoon pepper
	3 tablespoons chopped cilantro

1. Place beef in a medium saucepan. Add enough lightly salted water to barely cover. Bring beef to a boil over medium-high heat. Reduce heat to low, cover, and simmer until meat is fork-tender, about 1 hour. Let meat cool in broth. When cool enough to handle, shred meat.

2. Meanwhile, in a medium saucepan, place potatoes in cold water to cover. Bring to a boil over medium-high heat. Reduce heat to medium and cook until potatoes are tender, 20 to 25 minutes. Drain and rinse under running cold water to cool. Drain again and cut into ½-inch cubes.

3. In a large skillet, heat oil over medium heat. Add onion, garlic, and bell pepper and cook, stirring often, until onion begins to brown, 3 to 5 minutes. Add oregano, potatoes, and shredded meat. Cook, stirring frequently, until sizzling, 3 to 5 minutes. Stir in salsa, salt, pepper, and cilantro and serve.

202 STEAK WITH ONION AND CHEESE TOPPING

Prep: 15 minutes   Cook: 12 to 15 minutes   Serves: 4

A tender juicy steak reaches new heights when topped with sizzled onions, melted cheese, and a garnish of hot pickled jalapeño peppers.

4 boneless beef rib-eye steaks, cut 1 inch thick (about 6 ounces each)	1 large onion, halved and thinly sliced
1 garlic clove, minced	2 tablespoons vegetable oil
½ teaspoon salt	1 cup shredded Monterey Jack cheese (about 4 ounces)
⅛ teaspoon pepper	Sliced pickled jalapeño peppers
2 tablespoons unsalted butter	

1. Trim all fat from steaks. Rub with garlic, ¼ teaspoon of salt, and pepper.

2. In a large skillet, melt butter over medium heat. Add onion and remaining ¼ teaspoon salt and cook, stirring, until onion begins to brown, 3 to 5 minutes. Remove from heat.

3. In another large skillet, heat vegetable oil over medium-high heat until hot but not smoking. Add steaks and cook 1 minute on each side. Turn steaks again and cook 2 minutes longer on each side for medium-rare. Place on a warm platter. Cover with foil to keep warm.

4. Reheat onion mixture over medium-high heat, stirring, until onion begins to sizzle, about 2 minutes. With a spatula, spread onion out flat and scatter shredded cheese evenly over surface. Reduce heat to medium-low and cook until cheese melts into hot onion mixture, 1 to 2 minutes. Top each steak with about 2 tablespoons of topping and a few jalapeño slices.

203 BEEF FAJITAS
Prep: 20 minutes   Marinate: 3 hours   Cook: 12 to 15 minutes
Serves: 6

Fajitas originally implied skirt steak, but the excitement of discovery led to broader interpretation, and the dish is now commonly made with other meats, chicken, and even fish.

1½ to 2 pounds beef skirt or flank steak	½ teaspoon ground cumin
2 garlic cloves, minced	½ teaspoon salt
2 tablespoons fresh lime juice	¼ teaspoon crushed hot red pepper
1 tablespoon Worcestershire sauce	12 (7-inch) flour tortillas
2 tablespoons vegetable oil	Guacamole, salsa, shredded lettuce, and sour cream as
1 teaspoon dried oregano	accompaniment

1. Trim all fat and membrane from steak. In a large bowl, combine garlic, lime juice, Worcestershire, oil, oregano, cumin, salt, and hot pepper. Add meat and turn to coat. Cover and marinate about 3 hours at room temperature, turning occasionally, or overnight, refrigerated.

2. Prepare a hot fire in a barbecue grill. Place steak on an oiled grill rack 4 to 6 inches from coals and cook, turning once, until browned outside and pink and juicy inside, 12 to 15 minutes for medium-rare. Remove from grill and let stand while heating tortillas.

3. Place tortillas directly on grill. Heat 10 to 20 seconds, turning with tongs, until hot and pliable. Wrap in cloth napkin and place in a basket.

4. Cut meat against grain on a diagonal into thin slices. Place on a large platter. Serve with tortillas, guacamole, salsa, lettuce, and sour cream for each person to fill, roll, and eat.

204   MEXICAN MEATLOAF
Prep: 8 minutes   Cook: 1 hour   Serves: 4

Meatloaf is known as *albondigon,* and it's home cooking in Mexico, just as it is here.

1½ **pounds lean ground beef**
½ **cup bread crumbs**
1 **egg, beaten**
2 **shallots, minced**
½ **teaspoon dried oregano**
½ **teaspoon ground cumin**

¼ **teaspoon dried thyme leaves**
⅓ **cup red salsa**
2 **teaspoons unseasoned rice vinegar**
½ **teaspoon salt**
⅛ **teaspoon pepper**

1. Preheat oven to 350°F. In a large bowl, combine all ingredients. Mix thoroughly. On a baking sheet form meat mixture into a loaf about 9 x 5 inches.

2. Bake 1 hour, or until nicely browned and cooked in center and juices run clear. Remove from oven; drain off excess grease. Slice and serve.

205   RANCHERO STEAK WITH POTATOES
Prep: 25 minutes   Cook: 52 minutes   Serves: 4

Ranchero-style steaks come in many versions. Serve these with a bowl of soupy beans on the side and soft flour tortillas for real northern Mexico fare.

1½ **pounds lean, boneless sirloin steaks, cut about ¾ inch thick**
1 **tablespoon vegetable oil**
1 **teaspoon salt**
¼ **teaspoon pepper**
4 **medium red potatoes, peeled and thickly sliced**
1 **medium onion, chopped**
3 **garlic cloves, minced**

1 **(7-ounce) can chopped green chiles**
4 **medium tomatoes, peeled and chopped, or**
1 **(15-ounce) can ready-cut tomatoes**
1 **teaspoon dried oregano**
¼ **cup loosely packed chopped cilantro**

1. Preheat oven to 350°F. Cut steak into 4 equal pieces. In a large skillet, heat oil over medium-high heat. Add steaks and cook, turning once, until lightly browned, about 2 minutes per side. Season with ½ teaspoon of salt and ⅛ teaspoon of pepper. Transfer to a medium heatproof casserole. Place potato slices on top of steaks.

2. Add onion and garlic to same skillet and cook over medium heat, stirring, until onion softens, about 3 minutes. Add chiles, tomatoes, oregano, and remaining ½ teaspoon salt and ⅛ teaspoon pepper. Bring to a boil, stirring. Pour over steak and potatoes and cover with aluminum foil.

3. Bake about 45 minutes, or until potatoes are tender when pierced with point of a sharp knife. Serve garnished with chopped cilantro.

206   PICADILLO
Prep: 25 minutes   Cook: 15 minutes   Makes: about 5 cups

Picadillo is a ground meat mixture used for filling tortillas and empanadas, or for stuffing chiles to make chiles rellenos. As a bonus, it freezes well.

2 tablespoons vegetable oil	⅓ cup raisins
1½ pounds ground beef or pork	10 pitted green olives, coarsely
1 medium onion, minced	chopped
3 garlic cloves, minced	½ teaspoon cinnamon
3 medium tomatoes, peeled,	¼ teaspoon allspice
seeded, and finely	½ teaspoon salt
chopped	⅛ teaspoon freshly ground
1 small apple, peeled and	pepper
finely chopped	
3 pickled jalapeño peppers,	
minced	

1. In a large skillet, heat oil over medium-high heat. Add meat and cook, stirring to break it up into bits, until lightly browned, about 5 minutes. Add onion and garlic. Cook, stirring, until onions are limp, about 2 minutes.

2. Add tomatoes, apple, pickled jalapeños, raisins, olives, cinnamon, allspice, salt, and pepper. Reduce heat to medium and cook, stirring frequently, until juices have evaporated and mixture is almost dry, about 8 minutes. Transfer to a bowl. If made ahead, cool to room temperature, cover, and refrigerate up to 3 days, or freeze up to 3 months.

207   CARNITAS
Prep: 15 minutes   Cook: 45 to 55 minutes   Serves: 4

Carnitas, which translates as "little meats," are small cubes of pork cooked until browned and crispy. They are used to fill tacos, burritos, and tortas and are served with rice, beans, or eggs. Some fat should remain on the meat to make them crispy. Speared on toothpicks and served with your favorite salsa or dipping sauce, these make a great appetizer. The pork cubes can be cooked ahead and reheated on a baking sheet.

2 pounds boneless pork butt	3 garlic cloves, chopped
or shoulder, cut into	½ teaspoon salt
1-inch pieces	⅛ teaspoon pepper
1 tablespoon dried oregano	1 tablespoon vegetable oil

1. In a large deep skillet or saucepan, place meat in a single layer. Add cold water to nearly cover. Add oregano, garlic, salt, and pepper. Bring to a boil, reduce heat to medium, and cook, uncovered, until liquid has evaporated, and meat begins to sizzle in its own fat, 35 to 40 minutes. Stir in vegetable oil. (Recipe can be made ahead to this point.)

2. Preheat oven to 425°F. Transfer meat to a baking sheet. Bake uncovered 10 to 15 minutes, until pork cubes are crisp and brown.

208   BEEF TONGUE WITH CILANTRO SALSA

Prep: 15 minutes   Cook: 2 hours   Stand: 1 hour
Chill: 1 hour   Serves: 6

Thanks to Gloria Bowers, Santa Rosa, California, cooking teacher, for her chilled tongue recipe to enjoy Mexican style with spicy fresh salsa. Serve it as part of a cold meat and vegetable plate with drinks.

1 beef tongue, 2½ to 3 pounds
1 small onion, quartered
1 medium carrot, cut into
    2-inch pieces
1 celery rib, cut into 2-inch
    pieces

6 garlic cloves
½ teaspoon salt
¼ teaspoon peppercorns
    Cilantro Salsa (recipe
    follows)

1. In a large saucepan or flameproof casserole, place tongue, onion, carrot, celery, garlic, salt, peppercorns, and enough cold water to cover by 1 inch. Bring to a boil over medium-high heat. Reduce heat to low and simmer until very tender, about 2 hours. Remove from heat and let meat cool to room temperature in cooking liquid, about 1 hour.

2. Remove tongue from liquid, reserving stock. Trim off all fat and gristle. Peel off tough outer skin. Skim off and discard fat from cooking stock. Return tongue to stock and refrigerate until cold, at least 1 hour.

3. To serve, slice tongue ¼ inch thick. Arrange slices on a platter. Top each slice with about 1 teaspoon salsa. Pass remaining salsa on the side.

209   CILANTRO SALSA

Prep: 15 minutes   Cook: 9 to 12 minutes   Stand: 1 hour
Makes: about ¾ cup

1 Anaheim pepper
2 medium tomatillos, husked
    and rinsed
2 garlic cloves, unpeeled
1 jalapeño pepper, stemmed
    and seeded
½ cup loosely packed fresh
    cilantro sprigs

2 tablespoons chopped white
    onion
2 tablespoons fresh lime juice
2 teaspoons frozen orange
    juice concentrate, thawed
2 tablespoons olive oil
⅛ teaspoon salt

1. In a heavy, dry medium skillet, preferably cast iron, toast Anaheim pepper over medium-high heat, turning frequently, until charred all over, 5 to 6 minutes. Place in a bag to steam until cool enough to handle, about 5 minutes. Remove skin, stem, and seeds. Rinse and place in a blender or food processor.

2. In same dry skillet, toast tomatillos and garlic over medium-high heat, turning frequently, until they begin to brown in spots, 4 to 6 minutes. Remove skins from garlic and place in blender or food processor with Anaheim pepper. Add tomatillos, jalapeño pepper, cilantro, onion, lime juice, orange juice concentrate, olive oil, and salt. Blend to a coarse puree. Transfer to a medium bowl.

3. Let salsa stand at room temperature about 1 hour before serving.

---

210 CHILE VERDE
Prep: 30 minutes   Cook: 48 minutes   Serves: 4

Chile verde, a green chile and pork stew from northern Mexico, is very popular in our American Southwest. It is commonly served with soft, warm flour tortillas. A bowl of Fresh Tomatillo Salsa (page 92) should be on the table for those who like it hotter.

3 **tablespoons vegetable oil**	2 **(7-ounce) cans diced green**
2 **pounds boneless pork butt,**	**chiles**
well trimmed and cut into	1 **(10-ounce) can tomatillos,**
½-inch cubes	**drained, rinsed, and**
1 **teaspoon salt**	**pureed in a blender**
1 **white onion, chopped**	¾ **cup chicken broth**
4 **garlic cloves, minced**	½ **teaspoon sugar**
1½ **teaspoons dried oregano**	2 **tablespoons chopped**
½ **teaspoon ground cumin**	**cilantro**
2 **bay leaves**	½ **cup sour cream**

1. In a large deep nonreactive skillet or flameproof casserole, heat 2 tablespoons of oil over medium-high heat. Season pork cubes with salt and cook in 2 batches, stirring frequently, about 5 minutes for each batch, or until lightly browned. With a slotted spoon, remove meat to a dish.

2. In same pan, heat remaining 1 tablespoon oil. Add onion and garlic and cook until softened, about 3 minutes. Return meat and accumulated juices to pan. Add oregano, cumin, bay leaves, diced chiles, tomatillos, chicken broth, and sugar. Stir to combine. Bring to a boil. Reduce heat to low, cover, and cook about 35 minutes, or until meat is tender. Serve with a sprinkling of cilantro and a dollop of sour cream.

211 DRUNKEN PORK CHOPS WITH HOMINY
Prep: 35 minutes   Cook: 51 to 59 minutes   Serves: 4

Pork chops and hominy, braised in a picante sauce spiked with tequila, give this dish its name. Serve with Fresh Pineapple Salsa (page 91).

1 (15-ounce) can white hominy	3 tablespoons corn oil
1 tablespoon flour	1 medium onion, chopped
½ teaspoon dried oregano	2 garlic cloves, minced
¼ teaspoon ground allspice	2 medium tomatoes, peeled and chopped
½ teaspoon salt	1½ tablespoons ancho or pasilla chili powder
⅛ teaspoon pepper	
4 pork chops with bone, cut about ¾ inch thick (about 2 pounds)	2 tablespoons tequila
	⅓ cup orange juice
	1½ teaspoons red wine vinegar

1. Drain and rinse hominy in hot water 2 to 3 times, to help rid it of any tinny taste. Place drained hominy in a medium bowl.

2. Preheat oven to 325°F. In a pie plate, mix flour, oregano, allspice, salt, and pepper. Dust pork chops on both sides with seasoned flour. In a large nonreactive skillet, heat oil over medium-high heat. Add pork chops and cook, turning once, until lightly browned on both sides, 3 to 5 minutes. Transfer to an 8½ x 11-inch baking dish. Spoon hominy around chops.

3. In same skillet, cook onion and garlic, stirring, until onion is translucent, 3 to 4 minutes. Add tomatoes, chili powder, tequila, orange juice, and vinegar. Bring to a boil, stirring. Spoon sauce evenly over pork chops and hominy. Cover dish tightly with aluminum foil and bake 45 to 50 minutes, or until pork is tender.

212 GRILLED LOIN OF PORK
Prep: 10 minutes   Marinate: 4 hours   Cook: 8 to 10 minutes   Serves: 6 to 8

This is a typical way to grill pork loin Mexican style. The meat is cut lengthwise, along the grain, for these pork steaks. Add black beans, salsa, guacamole, and tortillas for a Guadalajara-style combination plate.

3 to 4 pounds center-cut boneless pork loin	2 garlic cloves, minced
¼ cup unseasoned rice vinegar	¼ cup vegetable oil
1 teaspoon dried oregano	1 teaspoon salt
½ teaspoon ground cumin	¼ teaspoon freshly ground pepper

1. Trim excess fat from pork. Slice meat lengthwise into long strips about ½ inch thick. Score each piece in a diamond pattern with thin diagonal knife cuts about ⅛ inch deep. Place meat in a dish.

2. In a medium bowl, whisk together vinegar, oregano, cumin, garlic, oil, salt, and pepper. Pour marinade over meat, turning to coat. Cover and refrigerate about 4 hours, turning occasionally.

3. Prepare a hot fire in a barbecue grill. Remove meat from marinade. Pat dry with paper towels. Place on an oiled grill rack, 4 to 6 inches from heat and cook 4 to 5 minutes on each side, or until white throughout but still juicy.

---

213 PORK TENDERLOIN WITH ANCHO CITRUS SAUCE
Prep: 25 minutes   Cook: 26 to 32 minutes   Serves: 4 to 6

Pork tenderloin is simple and quick and the perfect companion for this sauce. The flavorful sauce can be made ahead, refrigerated or frozen. Try it with other roasted meats or poultry.

4 **ancho chiles, seeded and rinsed**	1 **tablespoon unseasoned rice vinegar**
2 **tablespoons vegetable oil**	2 **tablespoons tomato paste**
3 **shallots, minced**	1 **tablespoon brown sugar**
2 **garlic cloves, chopped**	1 **teaspoon salt**
¾ **cup canned chicken broth**	2 **pork tenderloins, about**
½ **cup dry red wine**	**¾ pound each, silver**
3 **tablespoons frozen orange juice concentrate, thawed**	**membrane removed**
	⅛ **teaspoon pepper**

1. Bring a small saucepan of water to a boil. Add ancho chiles, reduce heat to low, cover, and cook 3 minutes. Remove from heat and let chiles soak 20 minutes. Drain, reserving soaking liquid.

2. Meanwhile, in a medium skillet, heat 1 tablespoon of oil over medium heat. Add shallots and garlic and cook, stirring, until soft and fragrant, about 1 minute. Add broth, wine, orange juice concentrate, vinegar, tomato paste, brown sugar, and salt. Bring to a boil, reduce heat to low, and simmer, stirring, 3 minutes.

3. Scrape skillet contents into blender or food processor. Add chiles and puree until smooth. Sauce should be about as thick as ketchup. If too thick, add reserved chile soaking water 1 tablespoon at a time to achieve desired consistency. Place a wire strainer over a medium saucepan and strain sauce into pan. Press soft pulp through with a wooden spoon. Discard remaining bits of skin. Bring sauce to a boil over medium heat; cook, stirring, 1 minute. Remove sauce from heat, cover, and set aside.

4. Preheat oven to 450°F. Rub pork with remaining ½ teaspoon salt and pepper. Heat remaining 1 tablespoon oil in a large nonstick skillet over medium-high heat. Add pork and cook, turning, until lightly browned all over, 4 to 6 minutes. Transfer to a small roasting pan and roast in oven 14 to 18 minutes, or until white throughout but still juicy. Reheat reserved chile sauce. Carve pork into ¼-inch-thick slices and serve with ancho citrus sauce.

214 VILLAHERMOSA PORK ROAST WITH SPRIGHTLY BARBECUE SAUCE

Prep: 20 minutes   Marinate: 8 hours   Cook: 1 hour 20 minutes
Serves: 6

Roasted pork dishes are succulent and delicious throughout Mexico. Pineapple, Jicama, and Bell Pepper Salad (page 69) and Baked Corn Casserole (page 203) are good go-withs.

1 (3-pound) pork loin roast, bone in	¼ teaspoon dried thyme leaves
1 tablespoon ancho or pasilla chili powder	2 teaspoons brown sugar
3 garlic cloves, crushed through a press	½ teaspoon salt
1 teaspoon ground allspice	¼ cup dry sherry
½ teaspoon dried oregano	1 tablespoon red wine vinegar
	1 tablespoon olive oil
	Sprightly Barbecue Sauce (recipe follows)

1. With a metal skewer or small sharp knife, pierce meat all over. Place in a ½-gallon heavy-duty freezer bag. In a small bowl, whisk together chili powder, garlic, allspice, oregano, thyme, brown sugar, salt, sherry, vinegar, and 1 tablespoon water. Pour into bag containing meat. Close bag and turn meat several times to coat with marinade. Refrigerate 8 hours or overnight, turning several times.

2. Preheat oven to 350°F. Remove meat from marinade. Scrape off excess. Rub meat all over with olive oil. Place in a medium baking pan and roast about 1 hour 20 minutes, or until meat thermometer registers 150°F. Remove from oven. Let rest about 10 minutes before slicing. Serve with barbecue sauce.

215 SPRIGHTLY BARBECUE SAUCE

Prep: 5 minutes   Cook: 5 minutes   Makes: about 1 cup

Make this sauce at least several hours or the day before using so the flavors have a chance to mellow. The sauce keeps, covered in the refrigerator, for months.

¾ cup ketchup	½ teaspoon ground allspice
3 tablespoons fresh orange juice	½ teaspoon dried thyme leaves
1 tablespoon red wine vinegar	2 tablespoons brown sugar
1 teaspoon Worcestershire sauce	2 tablespoons red plum jam

In a small nonreactive saucepan, combine all ingredients. Bring to a boil over medium heat, stirring. Reduce heat to low and simmer 5 minutes.

216 PORK LOIN ROAST WITH QUICK RANCHERO SAUCE
Prep: 15 minutes   Cook: 1 hour 30 minutes   Serves: 6

1 (3- to 4-pound) boneless
    pork loin roast
1 teaspoon dried oregano
2 garlic cloves, minced
½ teaspoon salt
⅛ teaspoon pepper

1 tablespoon olive oil
1 medium onion, chopped
1 (14½-ounce) can ready-cut
    salsa tomatoes
¼ cup chopped cilantro

1. Preheat oven to 350°F. Trim all excess fat from roast. Rub all over with oregano, garlic, salt, and pepper. Place in a medium roasting pan and place in oven. Roast, uncovered, 1 hour 20 minutes, or until a meat thermometer registers 160°F.

2. Meanwhile, in a medium saucepan, heat olive oil over medium heat. Add onion and cook, stirring, until tender and lightly browned, about 5 minutes. Add salsa tomatoes and cook, stirring frequently, 5 minutes.

3. When pork roast is done, remove from oven and let rest 5 minutes. Reheat sauce if necessary. Slice meat and arrange on a warm platter. Spoon sauce over roast. Sprinkle with cilantro and serve.

217 CHORIZO
Prep: 20 minutes   Cook: 8 minutes   Makes: about 1 pound

Mexican chorizo is spicy fresh pork sausage used as a taco filling, with eggs, and many other delicious dishes. This is an easy recipe to make using packaged chili powder, herbs, and spices. It is much better than many of the ready-made chorizos. There is no need to pipe it into casings, since it is traditionally cooked the same as any ground meat.

1 pound fresh ground pork
2 tablespoons ground ancho
    or pasilla chile
1 teaspoon dried oregano
1 teaspoon ground cumin
½ teaspoon ground coriander
¼ teaspoon crushed hot red
    pepper

⅛ teaspoon ground allspice
½ teaspoon salt
¼ teaspoon freshly ground
    pepper
2 garlic cloves, minced
1 tablespoon unseasoned rice
    vinegar
1 ounce tequila

1. Place all ingredients in a large bowl. Mix very well by hand. Cover with plastic wrap and refrigerate up to 4 days, or freeze, if not to be used within that time.

2. To cook, crumble sausage into a medium skillet and cook over medium-low heat, stirring frequently to break up lumps, until well done, about 8 minutes. Cook chorizo slowly to avoid burning spices. If pork is very lean, add 1 to 2 tablespoons each oil and water during cooking to add moisture.

218 PORK IN ADOBO SAUCE

Prep: 20 minutes   Cook: 1 hour 3 minutes to 1 hour 14 minutes
Serves: 6 to 8

Adobo is an authentic Mexican seasoning paste of dried red chiles, herbs, and spices, originally used to help preserve and flavor meats. When broth is added, a delicious rich-tasting stew results. Serve with rice or beans and soft tortillas.

2 tablespoons vegetable oil
2½ pounds lean pork, trimmed
    of fat and cut into 1-inch
    pieces
½ medium onion, chopped
1 teaspoon dried oregano

1 bay leaf
½ teaspoon salt
⅛ teaspoon pepper
1 recipe Adobo Sauce (recipe
    follows)

1. Heat oil in a large saucepan or flameproof casserole over medium-high heat. In 2 or 3 batches without crowding, add meat and cook, turning until browned all over, 3 to 4 minutes for each batch. Transfer meat to a dish as it browns.

2. Add onion to fat in pan and cook, stirring, until softened, about 2 minutes. Return meat to pan and add oregano, bay leaf, salt, and pepper. Add 1½ cups water. Bring to a boil, stirring up brown bits from bottom of pan. Reduce heat to low, cover, and simmer until meat is tender, 40 to 45 minutes. Stain through a sieve, reserving meat and broth separately. Return meat to pan, cover, and set aside while preparing adobo sauce. Skim fat off broth and measure out ¾ cup to use in sauce in following recipe.

3. Add prepared adobo sauce to meat in pan. Cover and bring to a simmer. Reduce heat to low, cover, and cook, stirring occasionally, 15 minutes.

219 ADOBO SAUCE

Prep: 25 minutes   Cook: 21 minutes   Makes: 1½ to 2 cups

6 to 8 ancho chiles
2 tablespoons chopped onion
2 garlic cloves, chopped
½ teaspoon dried oregano
1 teaspoon ground cumin
½ teaspoon ground cinnamon
⅛ teaspoon ground allspice
1 whole clove

½ teaspoon sugar
½ teaspoon salt
2 tablespoons unseasoned rice
    vinegar
¾ cup meat stock (from
    cooking pork) or canned
    broth

1. Wipe chiles with a damp paper towel. In a large dry skillet, toast chiles over medium heat, turning, 30 seconds per side, or until aromatic; do not brown. Immediately transfer to a plate; remove stems and seeds. Place chiles in a medium saucepan of boiling water. Cover and soak until chiles are soft and plumped, about 20 minutes. Strain over a bowl, reserving soaking water.

2. In a blender or food processor, place chiles, onion, garlic, oregano, cumin, cinnamon, allspice, clove, sugar, salt, vinegar, and ½ cup of meat stock. Puree until smooth. Add remaining meat stock and as much soaking water from chiles as needed to achieve consistency of heavy cream. (Sauce can be made up to 3 days ahead. Cover and refrigerate.)

220 PORK STEW WITH FRIED PLANTAINS, SWEET POTATO, AND PINEAPPLE

Prep: 45 minutes   Cook: 1 hour 21 minutes   Serves: 6 to 8

Called *manchamanteles,* or "tablecloth stainer" in Mexico, this dish is made with pork or chicken, fruits, and vegetables all simmered together in a rich sauce. Serve with soft, warm tortillas and rice.

¼ cup vegetable oil
1 medium plantain or firm
   banana, peeled and sliced
¼ cup blanched almonds
½ medium onion, chopped
3 garlic cloves, chopped
2 medium tomatoes, peeled
   and chopped
¼ cup pasilla or ancho chili
   powder
1 teaspoon dried oregano
½ teaspoon ground cinnamon

½ teaspoon ground allspice
2 pounds boneless pork loin,
   trimmed and cut into
   1-inch pieces
1 teaspoon salt
½ teaspoon pepper
1 medium sweet potato,
   peeled and cut into
   ¾-inch pieces
1 cup pineapple chunks, fresh
   or canned

1. In a nonreactive medium skillet, heat 1 tablespoon of oil over medium heat. Add plantain and cook, turning once, until golden brown, about 1 minute on each side. Remove to a small plate. In same skillet, heat 1 tablespoon of oil. Add almonds and cook, tossing, until fragrant and lightly browned, about 2 minutes. With a slotted spoon, transfer to a blender or food processor.

2. Add onion and garlic to oil remaining in skillet and cook, stirring occasionally, until they begin to brown, about 3 minutes. Add tomatoes, chili powder, oregano, cinnamon, and allspice. Cook, stirring, 3 minutes; transfer to blender with almonds. Blend to a smooth thick puree. If sauce is too pasty, add 1 to 2 tablespoons water. Set sauce aside.

3. In a large saucepan, heat remaining 2 tablespoons oil over medium-high heat. Add meat and cook, stirring frequently, until no longer pink, about 6 minutes. Season with salt and pepper. Add 1 cup water and bring to a boil. Cover, reduce heat to medium-low, and simmer until fork-tender, about 45 minutes.

4. Add sweet potato and reserved sauce. Cook, stirring frequently, until sweet potato is tender, 18 to 20 minutes. Add pineapple and sautéed plantain. Cook until hot and bubbling, 2 to 3 minutes.

221 GRILLED BUTTERFLIED LEG OF LAMB

Prep: 15 minutes   Marinate: 8 hours   Cook: 35 to 40 minutes
Serves: 6 to 8

¼ cup olive oil
3 tablespoons fresh lime juice
3 garlic cloves, minced
2 tablespoons chili powder
1 teaspoon dried oregano
1 teaspoon salt

1 (5- to- 6-pound) leg of lamb, boned, butterflied, and trimmed of fat (about 3 pounds meat after boning and trimming)

1. In a large nonreactive bowl, mix together olive oil, lime juice, garlic, chili powder, oregano, and salt. Add lamb and turn to coat with marinade. Cover with plastic wrap and refrigerate at least 8 hours or up to 24 hours, turning occasionally. Let leg of lamb return to room temperature before grilling.

2. Prepare a hot fire in a barbecue grill. Place meat on an oiled grill rack and cook, turning several times, 35 to 40 minutes, or until lamb is browned outside and pink and juicy inside and registers 130°F. to 135°F. on an instant-reading thermometer when inserted in thickest part of meat.

3. Transfer meat to a cutting board. Let rest about 5 minutes before slicing.

222 PORK RIBS IN TOMATILLO SAUCE

Prep: 20 minutes   Cook: 1 hour 11 minutes   Serves: 6

This is a classic Mexican way to cook pork ribs. Serve with rice, beans, and soft tortillas.

1 pound fresh tomatillos, husked and rinsed
1 medium white onion, quartered
3 garlic cloves
2 serrano peppers, stemmed and halved lengthwise
1 teaspoon dried oregano

½ teaspoon ground cumin
½ teaspoon sugar
1 teaspoon salt
¼ cup packed cilantro leaves
3 pounds lean country-style pork ribs
⅛ teaspoon pepper
1 tablespoon vegetable oil

1. In a medium saucepan half-filled with boiling water, place tomatillos, onion, garlic, and serrano peppers. Cook over medium-high heat until tomatillos are barely soft, 5 to 6 minutes. Drain and transfer contents to a blender or food processor. Add oregano, cumin, sugar, ½ teaspoon of salt, and cilantro. Blend to a coarse puree.

2. Season pork ribs with remaining ½ teaspoon salt and pepper. In a large deep skillet or flameproof casserole, heat oil over medium heat. Add ribs and cook, turning, until lightly browned, about 5 minutes on each side. Add reserved tomatillo sauce and stir to combine. Cover and cook over medium-low heat, stirring occasionally, until pork is very tender, about 1 hour.

223 SHEPHERD'S LAMB STEW
Prep: 20 minutes   Cook: 39 to 47 minutes   Serves: 4 to 6

Buy meat cut from the leg for this very special lamb stew. It's company fare.

2 pounds boneless leg of lamb, trimmed and cut into 1-inch cubes
½ teaspoon salt
3 tablespoons vegetable oil
1 large onion, chopped
4 garlic cloves, chopped
1 tablespoon pure pasilla chili powder
1 teaspoon ground cumin
½ teaspoon ground allspice
½ teaspoon ground cinnamon
1 teaspoon dried oregano

2 medium red potatoes, peeled and cut into ½-inch dice
2 medium carrots, peeled and cut into ½-inch dice
1 small turnip, peeled and cut into ½-inch dice
1 cup canned ready-cut salsa tomatoes
1 (14½-ounce) can beef broth
4 scallions, chopped
2 tablespoons chopped cilantro

1. Season lamb with salt. In a large saucepan or flameproof casserole, heat oil over medium heat. Add meat and cook, stirring frequently, until it begins to brown, 6 to 8 minutes. Add onion, garlic, and salt. Cook, stirring, until onion begins to soften, 3 to 4 minutes.

2. Add pasilla chili powder, cumin, allspice, cinnamon, and oregano. Cook, stirring, 1 minute. Add potatoes, carrots, turnip, tomatoes, beef broth, and 1 cup water. Cover and cook over medium-low heat, stirring occasionally, 30 to 35 minutes, or until vegetables and meat are tender. Stir in scallions and cilantro and serve at once.

Chapter 8

Staples of the Mexican Pantry: Beans and Rice

Beans are native to Mexico, and had been harvested for centuries before the Spanish conquest. There are many varieties, sizes, and colors, and beans are certainly the most essential staple in the Mexican diet, along with corn. They are served, in some form, at almost every meal throughout the country. When the Spaniards introduced pigs, not only was the meat welcome, but lard was quickly assimilated for the richness it added to bean preparations. Beans do not need to be soaked overnight, as many cooks have the habit of doing, and since I was taught not to soak, or throw out the soaking water, most of the bean recipes in this book do not call for soaking. But beans are definitely more delicious if they are cooked the day before being eaten. The broth thickens and the beans taste richer. Exact cooking times vary quite a bit according to the kind of beans and how long they have been stored. Generally, beans will cook tender in 1½ to 2 hours. If you find they are not very tender after a couple of hours, give them a little more time. It's often necessary to add additional water during cooking. Add boiling water, and the cooking time will not be interrupted. Beans are easy to cook, very nutritious, and worth the time spent. You'll find colorful bean salads here, as well. They are terrific for buffets and parties, and for a lighter touch, can take the place of cooked beans on a plate of Mexican food.

Rice also came via the Spaniards, but much later. It, too, became a favorite dish on the Mexican table, but not as part of a combination plate, such as we know in the United States. Rice is usually served as a separate course and fits the category called *sopa secas*, or dry soups. Mexican rice dishes are delicious and easy to prepare. In our meal plan, rice fits as a side dish to accompany the main course.

The recipes in this chapter have been chosen to accompany entree dishes. Some, such as Ranch Beans with Bacon, Pinto Bean Casserole, and Rice and Corn Casserole, are rustic—just right for barbecues and informal meals. Others, such as White Bean Casserole with Roasted Garlic or Yellow Rice with Peas, are perfect side dishes to pair with roasted or grilled meats and poultry. To accompany dishes with spicy sauces, try La Palma Rice with Plantains, Refried Black Beans, or typical Mexican Rice.

These are basic dishes meant to be cooked often and served with many different foods to give variety, color, and satisfaction to Mexican menus.

224   BASIC POT BEANS
Prep: 5 minutes   Cook: 1½ to 2 hours   Serves: 8

A simmering pot of beans, called *frijoles de olla*, is basic to Mexican cooking. It's easy, but does take a watchful eye to avoid scorching the beans. The finished pot of soupy beans are delicious just as they are, or they can be used as a base for other bean dishes. Cook beans one day ahead for best flavor. Presoaking is not required.

1 pound dried beans: pinto,
    red, black, or other bean
    of your choice
	1 bay leaf
	1 teaspoon dried oregano
	2 teaspoons salt

1. Rinse beans and pick over to remove any grit. Place beans in a large saucepan or flameproof casserole. Add water to cover by about 2 inches. Bring to a boil over medium-high heat and reduce heat to medium-low. Add bay leaf and oregano. Partially cover and cook, stirring occasionally, until beans are tender and liquid thickens, 1½ to 2 hours. Check water level during cooking. There should always be about ½ inch water above surface of beans. Add hot water, when needed, about ¼ cup at a time, to avoid interrupting the cooking. Do not let beans boil dry.

2. When beans are tender, add salt. Serve hot with the bean broth. To store, let cool, then cover and refrigerate up to 3 days, or freeze up to 3 months.

225   REFRIED BLACK BEANS
Prep: 8 minutes   Cook: 9 to 11 minutes   Serves: 6

Beans can be refried in a number of ways. This recipe is easy and healthy. It can be used whenever you want thick, flavorful beans.

3 tablespoons corn oil
½ medium red onion, chopped
2 garlic cloves, minced
½ teaspoon ground cumin
½ teaspoon dried oregano
⅛ teaspoon crushed hot red
    pepper
	1 cup canned tomatoes, with
	    their juices
	2 (15-ounce) cans black beans,
	    drained but not rinsed

1. In a large skillet, heat 1 tablespoon of oil over medium-high heat. Add onion and garlic and cook, stirring, until onion is softened, about 2 minutes. Add cumin, oregano, and hot pepper. Cook 1 minute. Stir in tomatoes with their juices and drained beans. Transfer mixture to a food processor and process to a coarse puree.

2. In a large skillet, heat remaining 2 tablespoons oil over medium heat. Add bean puree and bring to a boil, stirring constantly. Reduce heat to low and cook, stirring frequently, until beans are thick enough to hold a mounded shape on a wooden spoon, 6 to 8 minutes. Serve hot.

226 BLACK BEANS WITH BACON
Prep: 25 minutes   Soak: 30 minutes   Cook: 1 hour 20 minutes
Serves: 4

½ pound dried black beans
¼ pound bacon, chopped
3 garlic cloves, minced
1 celery rib, minced
½ medium onion, minced
½ medium carrot, peeled and
    cut into ¼-inch dice
2 medium tomatoes, peeled
    and chopped

2 tablespoons ancho or pasilla
    pure chili powder
1 teaspoon dried oregano
1 teaspoon ground cumin
1 cup chicken broth
½ teaspoon salt

1. Rinse beans and pick over to remove any grit. Put beans in a medium saucepan and add cold water to cover by about 2 inches. Bring to a boil over medium heat and cook 5 minutes. Remove from heat and let soak 30 minutes to plump beans. Return to a boil over medium heat, reduce heat to medium-low, cover, and simmer, stirring frequently, 30 minutes, or until beans are almost tender.

2. Meanwhile, in a medium skillet, cook bacon over medium heat, stirring, until golden brown and crisp, about 5 minutes. Add garlic, celery, onion, carrot, and tomatoes. Cook, stirring occasionally, until vegetables are tender, about 10 minutes. Add ground chili, oregano, and cumin.

3. When beans are almost tender, stir in bacon and vegetable mixture, chicken broth, and salt. Cook over medium-low heat, partially covered and stirring occasionally, until beans are tender and broth has thickened, about 30 minutes.

227 BLACK BEAN SALAD
Prep: 10 minutes   Cook: none   Serves: 6 to 8

Black beans seem to please everyone, and this pretty salad proves it all over again. This quick version is made with canned beans.

2 (16-ounce) cans black beans
2 celery ribs, cut into ¼-inch
    dice
½ medium yellow bell pepper,
    cut into ¼-inch dice
½ medium green bell pepper,
    cut into ¼-inch dice
2 jalapeño peppers, seeded
    and minced
4 scallions, chopped

2 medium tomatoes, chopped
1 teaspoon ground cumin
½ teaspoon salt
¼ teaspoon freshly ground
    pepper
2 tablespoons red wine
    vinegar
¼ cup olive oil
2 tablespoons chopped
    cilantro or parsley

Drain and rinse beans; drain again. In a medium bowl, combine all ingredients. Toss to mix.

228   BLACK AND WHITE BEAN SALAD

Prep: 10 minutes   Cook: none   Stand: 2 hours   Serves: 6

Increased varieties of canned products really inspire today's busy cooks. You'll appreciate the excellent quality of canned black and white beans when making this striking-looking salad.

1 (15-ounce) can black beans, rinsed and drained
1 (15-ounce) can small white beans, rinsed and drained
2 scallions, white part only, minced
1 celery rib, finely chopped
1 medium tomato, seeded and chopped

1 jalapeño pepper, seeded and minced
2 tablespoons minced parsley
3 tablespoons olive oil
¼ cup unseasoned rice vinegar
Juice of 1 lime
½ teaspoon salt

In a medium nonreactive bowl, combine all ingredients. Stir to mix well. Cover and let stand at room temperature, tossing occasionally, about 2 hours for flavors to blend before serving. If made ahead, cover and refrigerate up to 1 day ahead. Let return to room temperature before serving.

229   PINTO BEAN CASSEROLE

Prep: 10 minutes   Cook: 30 minutes   Serves: 6

Need a quick bean dish for your Mexican meal? Try this no-fuss canned bean casserole. If you don't have a smaller sized flameproof casserole, cook the beans in a saucepan and then transfer to an ovenproof casserole or baking dish in step 2.

2 tablespoons vegetable oil
1 medium onion, chopped
1 medium red bell pepper, chopped
2 garlic cloves, minced
½ teaspoon dried oregano
1 (7-ounce) can chopped green chiles

1 cup thick and chunky salsa
2 (15-ounce) cans chili-seasoned pinto beans, with their sauce
1 cup shredded Cheddar cheese

1. Preheat oven to 350°F. In a 1½- to 2-quart flameproof casserole, heat oil over medium heat. Add onion, red bell pepper, garlic, and oregano and cook, stirring, until vegetables begin to soften, 4 to 5 minutes. Add chopped green chiles, salsa, and beans with their sauce. Bring to a boil, stirring.

2. Scatter cheese on top. Bake in preheated oven 25 minutes, or until beans are bubbly and cheese is melted. Serve hot.

230   MEXICAN THREE-BEAN SALAD

Prep: 15 minutes   Cook: 10 to 15 minutes   Marinate: 1 hour
Serves: 4 to 6

Bean salads are always well received. Garbanzo beans, kidney beans, and fresh green beans along with roasted Anaheim peppers give this one extra texture and flavor.

¼ pound fresh green beans, cut diagonally into 1-inch pieces
2 fresh Anaheim peppers
1 (15-ounce) can garbanzo beans (chick-peas), rinsed and drained
1 (8-ounce) can red kidney beans, rinsed and drained
2 pickled jalapeño peppers, seeded and minced

3 tablespoons minced red onion
¼ cup olive oil
3 tablespoons lime juice
2 tablespoons chopped cilantro
1 garlic clove, crushed through a press
⅛ teaspoon salt
¼ teaspoon freshly ground pepper

1. In a medium saucepan of boiling salted water, cook green beans until crisp-tender, about 5 minutes. Drain and rinse under cold running water; drain well. Place in a large bowl.

2. Preheat oven broiler. Place Anaheim peppers on a baking sheet and broil as close to heat as possible, turning, until charred all over, about 10 minutes. Place peppers in a paper bag and let steam about 10 minutes. Or roast peppers directly over gas flame, turning, until charred, about 5 minutes. Peel off blackened skin and rinse under cold running water. Cut peppers open; discard stems and seeds.

3. Cut peeled peppers into thin strips about 2 inches long. Add to bowl with green beans. Add garbanzo beans, kidney beans, jalapeño peppers, and red onion. Toss lightly to mix.

4. In a small jar, shake together olive oil, lime juice, chopped cilantro, garlic, salt, and pepper. Pour over bean salad and toss well. Marinate at least 1 hour at room temperature, tossing occasionally, or up to 2 days, covered, in refrigerator. Serve at room temperature.

231   BORDER BEANS

Prep: 8 minutes   Cook: 2 hours 4 minutes to 2 hours 36 minutes
Serves: 8

This is a great pot of beans for a party or informal outdoor meal cooked in Southwestern ranch style. Make them a day ahead for convenience and richer flavor.

1 **pound dried pinto or red kidney beans**	1½ **teaspoons ground cumin**
2 **bay leaves**	3 **tablespoons New Mexico chili powder**
1 **teaspoon dried oregano**	1 **(16-ounce) can stewed tomatoes, crushed**
1 **smoked ham hock**	**Salt**
2 **medium onions, chopped**	
2 **tablespoons vegetable oil**	

1. Pick over beans to remove any grit or debris. Place in a colander and rinse well. Place beans in a large saucepan or flameproof casserole. Add enough cold water to cover by about 3 inches. Bring to a boil over medium-high heat. Add bay leaves, oregano, and ham hock. Reduce heat to low, cover, and cook, stirring occasionally, 1½ to 2 hours, or until beans are tender.

2. While beans cook, heat oil in a medium saucepan. Add onion and cook over medium heat, stirring occasionally, until beginning to brown, 3 to 5 minutes. Add cumin and chili powder. Cook, stirring, 1 minute. Add tomatoes and cook, stirring frequently, about 10 minutes. Set tomato sauce aside.

3. When beans are tender, remove ham hock and shred meat. Discard bone and excess fat. Add ham meat and reserved tomato sauce to beans. Simmer, uncovered, over medium-low heat until slightly thickened, about 20 minutes. Season with salt to taste.

232   BLACK BEAN CAKES

Prep: 10 minutes   Cook: 12 minutes   Serves: 4 to 6

Refried beans take a new form when turned into thin pancakes and served as a separate course with fresh salsa. Canned black beans shorten preparation time and work very well for this recipe.

1 **(15-ounce) can black beans, drained and rinsed**	1 **tablespoon flour**
1 **tablespoon ancho or pasilla chili powder**	3 **to 4 tablespoons vegetable oil**
½ **teaspoon ground cumin**	**Salsa Fresca Mexicana (page 84)**
⅛ **teaspoon ground allspice**	½ **cup sour cream**
1 **egg**	**Cilantro sprigs, for garnish**

1. In a food processor, combine drained beans, chili powder, cumin, and allspice. Pulse to a dry, thick paste. There will be some texture.

2. In a medium bowl, beat egg with a fork. Stir in pureed beans and flour. Mix well.

3. In a large nonstick skillet, heat 1 tablespoon of oil over medium heat. Spoon about 1 heaping tablespoon bean mixture into pan. With back of an oiled teaspoon, spread gently into a 2- to 3-inch round pancake. Add 2 more cakes to pan. Cook 2 minutes, or until lightly browned on bottom. With a wide spatula, carefully turn bean cakes over and cook 1 minute. Place on a warm platter. Repeat until all bean cakes are cooked, adding more oil to pan as needed to facilitate browning.

4. To serve, put 2 or 3 bean cakes on each serving plate. Top each bean cake with some fresh salsa and a dollop of sour cream. Garnish with a sprig of cilantro.

233 RANCH BEANS WITH BACON
Prep: 15 minutes   Cook: 1 hour 57 minutes to 2 hours 27 minutes
Serves: 8 to 10

Typical of home-style cooking, these tasty beans go especially well with barbecued meats. On their own they make a satisfying winter meal with tortillas or Mexican Corn Bread (page 224) and Cabbage and Carrot Salsa (page 80).

1 **pound pinto beans**	1 **teaspoon ground cumin**
2 **bay leaves**	1 **(14½-ounce) can ready-cut**
1 **teaspoon dried oregano**	**tomatoes**
½ **pound sliced bacon, cut**	½ **teaspoon salt**
crossways into ½-inch	⅛ **teaspoon freshly ground**
pieces	**pepper**
1 **medium onion, finely**	
chopped	

1. Rinse beans and pick over to remove any grit. Place in a large saucepan or flameproof casserole. Add cold water to cover by 2 inches. Add bay leaves and oregano. Bring to a boil over medium-high heat, reduce heat to low, cover, and simmer, stirring occasionally, until beans are tender and broth begins to thicken, 1½ to 2 hours. Add additional hot water during cooking, if needed, to prevent beans from boiling dry.

2. Meanwhile, in a nonreactive medium saucepan, cook bacon pieces over medium heat until crisp, about 2 minutes. With a slotted spoon, add bacon to beans. Discard all but 2 tablespoons bacon fat. Add onion and cumin to pan and cook, stirring, until softened, about 2 minutes. Add tomatoes, salt, and pepper. Cook about 3 minutes.

3. Add tomato mixture to beans and cook over low heat, about 20 minutes, or until broth is thick. Taste and add salt, if needed. The amount of salt in the bacon will determine if extra salt is needed. Serve hot, or cover and refrigerate up to 3 days.

234   GREEN RICE PUEBLA STYLE

Prep: 15 minutes   Cook: 24 to 30 minutes   Serves: 4

This rice dish, from the Puebla region of Mexico, gets its green color from poblano peppers, parsley, and cilantro. The color fades a little during cooking, but the accent of yellow corn kernels adds to its visual appeal. If the large dark green poblano peppers are not available, Anaheim peppers may be substituted.

3 poblano peppers
1¾ cups canned reduced-
     sodium chicken broth
2 tablespoons vegetable oil
½ medium onion, minced
2 garlic cloves, minced
1 cup long-grain white rice

½ cup fresh or frozen corn
     kernels
¾ teaspoon salt
⅛ teaspoon pepper
1 tablespoon minced parsley
2 tablespoons chopped
     cilantro

1. Preheat oven broiler. Place peppers on a baking sheet and broil as close to heat as possible, turning, until charred all over, about 10 minutes. Or roast peppers directly over a gas flame, turning, until charred, about 5 minutes. Place peppers in a paper bag and let steam 10 minutes. Peel off blackened skin and rinse under cold running water. Cut peppers open; discard stems and seeds. Chop peppers coarsely and place in a blender or food processor. Add ½ cup of chicken broth and puree until smooth.

2. In a medium saucepan, heat oil over medium heat. Add onion and garlic and cook, stirring, until softened but not brown, about 2 minutes. Add rice and cook, stirring, until coated with oil and opaque, 2 to 3 minutes. Add remaining chicken broth and pureed chiles. Bring to a boil, reduce heat to low, cover, and simmer 15 minutes, or until rice is tender and liquid is absorbed.

3. Add corn kernels, salt, pepper, and parsley. Stir gently to combine. Cover and let stand off heat 5 minutes. Stir in cilantro and serve.

235   MEXICAN RICE

Prep: 10 minutes   Cook: 22 to 25 minutes   Serves: 8

1 medium carrot, peeled and
     cut into ¼-inch dice
2 tablespoons vegetable oil
2 cups long-grain white rice
1 medium onion, chopped
3 garlic cloves, minced

½ teaspoon ground cumin
¾ cup canned pureed tomatoes
1 (14½-ounce) can reduced-
     sodium chicken broth
½ teaspoon salt
¼ teaspoon pepper

1. In a small saucepan of boiling salted water, cook carrot until just tender, about 3 minutes. Drain and rinse under cold running water; drain well.

2. In a large saucepan, heat oil over medium heat. Add rice and cook, stirring, about 1 minute to coat with oil. Stir in onion and garlic. Cook, stirring, until onion is translucent, about 3 minutes.

3. Stir in cumin, tomatoes, chicken broth, salt, pepper, and 1 cup water. Bring to a boil. Reduce heat to low, cover, and cook 15 to 18 minutes, or until liquid is absorbed and rice is tender. Remove from heat and let stand 5 minutes. Add cooked carrot and stir gently to combine. Serve hot.

236 WHITE BEAN CASSEROLE WITH ROASTED GARLIC

Prep: 20 minutes   Cook: 2 hours 55 minutes   Serves: 6 to 8

Beans of many hues, including tiny white ones, are used in Mexican cuisine. This casserole of pureed white beans is an attractive alternative to the common dark bean dishes. Cook beans one day ahead, if possible, for more flavor and a thicker broth. Serve as a side dish with meat and chicken.

½ pound small dry white
  beans
1 bay leaf
½ teaspoon dried oregano
8 large garlic cloves
½ teaspoon olive oil
3 tablespoons unsalted butter
1 celery rib, chopped

1 medium white onion,
  chopped
½ teaspoon dried marjoram
1 teaspoon salt
½ teaspoon freshly ground
  pepper
2 tablespoons finely chopped
  parsley

1. Rinse beans and pick over to remove any grit. Place in a medium saucepan and add enough water to cover by 2 to 3 inches. Add bay leaf and oregano. Bring to a boil over medium-high heat. Reduce heat to low, cover, and simmer about 2 hours, or until very tender. Let cool to room temperature, or cover and refrigerate if cooked ahead.

2. Preheat oven to 350°F. Cut ⅛ inch tip off each garlic clove and place on a 6-inch square of aluminum foil. Drizzle olive oil over garlic. Wrap foil and put in a small baking pan. Bake 25 to 30 minutes, or until garlic is soft when pierced with tip of a knife. Remove garlic from oven. Leave oven on. Unwrap garlic and set aside to cool.

3. Drain beans, reserving cooking water as bean broth. Put beans in a food processor. Add roasted garlic by squeezing it out of skins.

4. In a large skillet, melt butter over medium-high heat. Add celery, onion, and marjoram and cook, stirring occasionally, 2 minutes. Reduce heat to medium-low, cover, and cook until onion is tender, about 3 minutes longer. Transfer to processor bowl. Puree beans and vegetables, adding enough reserved bean broth to achieve a smooth, thick mixture that holds its shape on a spoon. Season with salt and pepper. Turn mixture into an ovenproof casserole.

5. Bake in preheated oven about 20 minutes, or until piping hot. Sprinkle with parsley and serve at once.

237 WHITE BEAN SALAD WITH OLIVES AND PICKLED JALAPENO PEPPERS

Prep: 25 minutes   Cook: 1 hour   Stand: 30 minutes
Chill: 2 hours   Serves: 4 to 6

A nice change from the more usual kidney or pinto beans. In this recipe, the beans are not soaked before cooking.

½ pound small dry white beans, rinsed and picked over
1 bay leaf
1 teaspoon dried oregano
¼ medium red onion, minced
1 to 2 pickled jalapeño peppers, seeded and minced
1 medium tomato, chopped
12 pitted black olives, cut lengthwise in eighths

½ teaspoon ground cumin
2 tablespoons olive oil
2 tablespoons unseasoned rice vinegar
2 tablespoons lime juice
¾ teaspoon salt
⅛ teaspoon pepper
2 tablespoons chopped cilantro or parsley

1. Place beans in a colander and rinse under cold running water. Place rinsed beans in a large saucepan, with water to cover by about 3 inches. Bring to a boil over medium-high heat. Reduce heat to low. Add bay leaf and oregano, cover, and simmer until beans are tender, about 1 hour. Drain, but do not rinse. Transfer to a medium bowl and let cool to room temperature, about 30 minutes.

2. Add red onion, jalapeno peppers, tomato, olives, cumin, olive oil, vinegar, lime juice, salt, and pepper. Stir to combine, cover, and refrigerate until cold, about 2 hours. (Recipe can be made ahead to this point, covered, and refrigerated overnight.) Shortly before serving, stir in cilantro.

238 RICE AND CORN CASSEROLE

Prep: 15 minutes   Cook: 33 minutes   Serves: 8

2 tablespoons vegetable oil
½ medium onion, chopped
2 cups long-grain white rice
1 cup corn kernels, frozen or fresh
1 teaspoon ground cumin

2 tablespoons butter
¼ cup sour cream
1 teaspoon salt
¼ teaspoon pepper
1 cup shredded Monterey Jack cheese (about 4 ounces)

1. In a medium flameproof casserole, heat oil over medium heat. Add onion and cook, stirring, until it begins to brown, 3 minutes. Add rice and cook, stirring, until grains are coated with oil and begin to look opaque, 1 to 2 minutes. Stir in 3¾ cups water and bring to a boil. Cover, reduce heat to low, and cook 18 minutes, or until liquid is absorbed and rice is tender.

2. Preheat oven to 375°F. Remove rice from heat and let stand, covered, 5 minutes. Gently stir in corn, cumin, butter, sour cream, salt, and pepper. Top with shredded cheese.

3. Place casserole in oven and bake, uncovered, until rice is heated through and cheese is melted, about 10 minutes.

239   LA PALMA RICE WITH PLANTAINS
Prep: 8 minutes   Cook: 25 minutes   Serves: 4

La Palma restaurant in Mexico City presents a rice plate this way. The cooking banana called plantain is delicious sautéed to a golden brown, but firm barely ripe regular bananas can be substituted. Plantain skins should be almost black when ripe, but still quite firm. This recipe is a good way to serve leftover rice, too.

1   **cup long-grain white rice**
¾   **teaspoon salt**
1   **tablespoon butter**
1   **tablespoon vegetable oil**

1   **large plantain, peeled and cut crossways on an angle into ovals about ¼ inch thick**
1   **tablespoon minced flat-leaf Italian parsley**

1. In a medium saucepan, bring 1¾ cups water to a boil over medium-high heat. Stir in rice and ½ teaspoon of salt. Reduce heat to low, cover, and simmer 18 to 20 minutes, or until all liquid is absorbed.

2. Meanwhile, in a large nonstick skillet, melt butter in oil over medium heat. Add plantain slices and cook, turning, until golden on both sides, 4 to 5 minutes. Season with remaining ¼ teaspoon salt. Remove from heat and set aside.

3. When rice is cooked, remove pan from heat and let stand 5 minutes, covered. Fluff with a fork and gently mix in parsley. Pack hot rice into a round-bottomed 3-cup bowl. Invert onto center of a large warmed serving plate. Arrange cooked plantain slices around rice dome and serve hot.

240   FIESTA RICE SALAD

Prep: 20 minutes   Cook: 18 to 20 minutes   Serves: 6 to 8

A colorful salad for parties and picnics, this holds well and is easy to transport. Remember to make the rice ahead so it has time to cool.

1 cup long-grain white rice	2 pickled jalapeño peppers,
½ cup vegetable oil	seeded and minced
¼ cup fresh orange juice	½ medium red bell pepper, cut
¼ cup white wine vinegar	into ¼-inch dice
½ teaspoon ground cumin	1 cup cooked corn kernels,
½ teaspoon salt	fresh or frozen
¼ teaspoon pepper	2 tablespoons chopped
2 scallions, finely chopped	cilantro
	Cherry tomatoes

1. Cook rice according to package directions, 18 to 20 minutes. Transfer to a large bowl and let cool. Cover and refrigerate if made ahead.

2. In a small bowl, combine oil, orange juice, vinegar, cumin, salt, and pepper. Whisk until dressing is well blended.

3. Add scallions, pickled jalapeño peppers, bell pepper, corn, and cilantro to rice. Toss to mix. Add dressing and toss to coat evenly.

4. To serve, mound salad on a serving platter. Garnish with cherry tomatoes.

241   WHITE BEANS WITH PEPPERS AND MUSHROOMS

Prep: 25 minutes   Cook: 11 to 15 minutes   Serves: 6

These savory beans give good color contrast on the plate and taste wonderful with lamb and pork dishes. Everything cooks in one pan here for easy cleanup.

¼ cup olive oil	½ cup canned chicken broth
1 medium red onion, minced	⅛ teaspoon crushed hot red
3 garlic cloves, minced	pepper
½ teaspoon dried oregano	¼ teaspoon salt
½ teaspoon dried thyme leaves	⅛ teaspoon freshly ground
½ pound small fresh	pepper
mushrooms, thinly sliced	2 tablespoons chopped
2 medium tomatoes, peeled	parsley
and chopped	2 (15-ounce) cans small white
1 (4-ounce) can diced green	beans, rinsed and drained
chiles	

1. In a large saucepan, heat olive oil over medium heat. Add red onion, garlic, oregano, and thyme and cook, stirring frequently, until onion begins to soften, 3 to 5 minutes.

2. Add mushrooms, tomatoes, chiles, chicken broth, hot pepper, salt, pepper, and parsley. Bring to a boil, reduce heat to medium-low, and simmer, stirring occasionally, until thickened, 5 to 7 minutes.

3. Add beans and cook until completely heated through, about 3 minutes. Serve hot.

---

242   YELLOW RICE WITH PEAS
Prep: 10 minutes   Cook: 22 minutes   Serves: 8

Achiote, or annatto, seeds color the cooking oil to give this Mexican rice its typical yellow hue, elusive aroma, and subtle flavor. The seeds can be found in health food stores, Latin American food stores, or in the Mexican section of many supermarkets. As a boon for busy cooks, this rice reheats well in a microwave or conventional oven.

3 **tablespoons vegetable oil**
1 **tablespoon achiote seeds**
½ **medium onion, minced**
1 **garlic clove, minced**
2 **cups long-grain white rice**
3½ **cups canned reduced-
   sodium chicken broth**

½ **teaspoon salt**
¼ **teaspoon pepper**
1 **cup cooked fresh or thawed
   frozen peas**

1. In a medium saucepan, heat oil over medium heat. Add achiote seeds and cook until seeds are sizzling and oil is a rich gold color, about 1 minute. Remove from heat. With a spoon, scoop up and discard seeds, leaving oil in pan.

2. Return pan to medium heat. Add onion and garlic and cook until softened, about 2 minutes. Add rice and cook, stirring, 1 minute, or until grains begin to look opaque. Stir in chicken broth, salt, and pepper. Bring rice to a vigorous boil, then turn heat to low, cover pan, and cook about 18 minutes, or until liquid is absorbed. Remove pan from heat. Cover and let rice stand 5 minutes. Gently stir in peas.

Variation

MINTED YELLOW RICE WITH PEAS:
Prepare Yellow Rice with Peas as directed above. Stir in 2 tablespoons chopped fresh mint along with peas.

Chapter 9

Totally Tortillas

These are the dishes we often prepare when entertaining Mexican style. Most of them make economical party fare and are universally liked. Festive and spicy, they need little else as accompaniment. You'll find a variety appropriate for snacks, lunch, and supper.

The dishes based on corn are also deeply rooted in Mexican history. In ancient times, corn was worshipped and was considered the mother of human life. As corn cultivation grew and circled the globe, varieties and quality improved, but corn dough and tortillas changed little. They are still the bread of life in Mexican culture, and they form the bases for many delicious dishes. White flour tortillas, made from wheat, came along much later and contributed some newer twists to the cuisine.

There are recipes for enchiladas, chilaquiles, tacos, tostadas, burritos, and chimichangas. There are casserole dishes containing cut-up corn tortillas, or masa dough combined with meats, poultry, vegetables, and a sauce to make satisfying one-dish meals, such as Spicy Tamale Pie and Easy Chicken Tortilla Bake. Other specialties include Mushroom and Eggplant Enchiladas and Cheese Enchiladas in Red Sauce.

This chapter also offers tamales, made from a variation of the same dough corn tortillas are made from. Here it encloses savory fillings, which are then wrapped and steamed in corn husks, or sometimes in banana leaves. The basic tamale recipe is easy enough for home cooks, and there are also recipes for making your own corn and flour tortillas, as well as delicious Mexican crepes and Southwestern Corn Crepes. Any of the enchilada fillings and sauces can be used with crepes in place of corn tortillas.

Whether you want a special one-dish meal for family dinners or something fun and economical for entertaining, try one of the recipes from this chapter. Add a salad or first course from Chapter 3 and an easy dessert from Chapter 13 to complete the menu.

243 SPEEDY MICROWAVE BEAN BURRITOS
Prep: 5 minutes   Cook: 1 to 2 minutes 40 seconds   Serves: 4

All family members can use the microwave to fix super-speedy burritos whenever they feel like a snack.

4 (10-inch) flour tortillas
1 (16-ounce) can refried beans

1½ cups shredded Cheddar or Monterey Jack cheese
Pickled jalapeño slices

1. Place 4 tortillas stacked between 2 damp paper towels. Microwave on High about 40 seconds, or until warm and pliable.

2. Spread each tortilla with one fourth of refried beans. Top each evenly with shredded cheese. Add a few slices of pickled jalapeño peppers. Fold in one side and roll up tortillas into tight cylinders. Place seam side down on a greased microwave-safe platter or casserole.

3. Cover with plastic wrap and microwave on High until heated through and cheese is melted, 1 to 2 minutes. Serve at once.

244 SOFT BURRITOS
Prep: 20 minutes   Cook: 15 to 17 minutes   Serves: 6

Burritos are rolled sandwiches made with soft flour tortillas. They are intended to be eaten by hand, like a sandwich, and they should be served as soon as they are filled and rolled. Start with this basic ground meat recipe, or create your own, using any imaginative combination.

1 tablespoon vegetable oil
1 medium onion, finely chopped
2 garlic cloves, minced
1 pound ground beef, pork, or turkey
1 teaspoon chili powder
½ teaspoon ground cumin
1 teaspoon chopped fresh mint

¼ cup prepared red or green salsa
6 (7- to 8-inch) flour tortillas
1½ cups canned refried beans, heated
1 cup shredded lettuce
1 cup shredded Monterey Jack or Cheddar cheese

1. In a large skillet, heat oil over medium heat. Add onion and garlic and cook until onion is slightly softened, about 2 minutes. Add ground meat and cook, stirring and breaking up lumps, until meat is browned and cooked through, 6 to 8 minutes. Stir in chili powder, cumin, mint, and salsa. Cook 1 minute. Remove from heat and cover to keep warm.

2. In a dry medium skillet set over medium-high heat, soften and warm tortillas, 1 at a time, about 30 seconds on each side. Stack and wrap in a kitchen towel to keep warm.

3. To serve, place 1 tortilla on a flat surface. Spread with about 2 tablespoons warm refried beans to within 1 inch of edge of tortilla. Top with about 2 tablespoons each meat mixture, shredded lettuce, and cheese. Fold in one side and then roll up from bottom, enclosing filling, except for opening on one edge. (The folded "tucked in" end becomes the bottom and helps hold in the filling when eating.)

245 FLOUR TORTILLAS
Prep: 15 minutes   Stand: 45 minutes   Cook: 2 minutes
Makes: 12 (8-inch) tortillas

For a real sense of accomplishment, make your own flour tortillas. They really are easy with the aid of a food processor to do the kneading.

2 cups flour
1 teaspoon baking powder
½ teaspoon salt
¼ cup solid vegetable
    shortening

½ cup plus 1 tablespoon
    lukewarm water

1. In a food processor, combine flour, baking powder, and salt. Pulse to blend. Add shortening. Process about 10 seconds until mixture is mealy. Add water all at once by drizzling over flour mixture. Process until dough cleans sides of bowl and knead in bowl about 15 seconds. Remove dough to a lightly floured board and roll gently into a fat rope for easier cutting. Cut into 12 uniform pieces. Roll each piece into a ball, place on a plate, and cover with plastic wrap. Let dough balls rest 45 minutes to 1 hour at room temperature.

2. With a rolling pin on a lightly floured board, roll each ball into a very thin circular tortilla about 8 inches in diameter. Heat a medium ungreased cast-iron skillet over high heat. Place 1 tortilla in hot pan. If pan is hot enough, it should show spots of raising on top surface in about 2 seconds. Cook 4 to 6 seconds, or until underside has brown spots. Turn and cook about 3 seconds on second side, until barely spotted on bottom. Place hot baked tortilla between folds of a clean kitchen towel. Repeat. Stack tortillas together as they are baked and keep them wrapped. When completely cooled, place in a heavy-duty plastic bag and refrigerate.

3. Reheat to serve in a hot skillet or directly over a gas flame, turning every 3 to 4 seconds until soft and pliable. These tortillas reheat well in a microwave oven, too; follow manufacturer's instructions. Flour tortillas keep refrigerated up to 2 weeks, or they can be frozen up to 3 months.

246 TURKEY SALAD BURRITOS
Prep: 10 minutes   Cook: 1 to 4 minutes   Serves: 4

½ cup shredded lettuce
½ cup shredded carrot
1 tablespoon chopped cilantro
½ teaspoon ground cumin
¼ cup bottled red salsa
¼ cup mayonnaise

2 cups shredded or diced
  cooked turkey meat
  (about ½ pound)
4 (7- or 8-inch) flour tortillas
2 avocados, peeled and cut
  into 8 slices each

1. In a medium bowl, mix lettuce, carrot, cilantro, cumin, salsa, mayonnaise, and turkey. Stack tortillas and wrap in damp paper towels. Microwave on High 45 to 50 seconds, or until warm and pliable. (Tortillas can also be heated 1 at a time in a hot skillet, over medium heat, about 30 seconds per side.)

2. Put about ¾ cup turkey salad on each tortilla. Put 2 slices avocado over turkey and roll up. Serve at once.

247 EASY CHICKEN TORTILLA BAKE
Prep: 20 minutes   Cook: 1 hour 5 minutes to 1 hour 18 minutes   Serves: 8

6 skinless, boneless, chicken
  breast halves
12 corn tortillas, cut into 2-inch
  strips
2 tablespoons vegetable oil
1 medium onion, halved and
  thinly sliced
1 (14-ounce) can cream of
  mushroom soup
1 (14-ounce) can cream of
  chicken soup

1 cup canned chicken broth
1 (15-ounce) can chili beans,
  without meat
1 cup thick and chunky green
  chile salsa
1 (2¼-ounce) can sliced black
  olives, drained
1½ cups shredded Cheddar
  cheese (about 6 ounces)

1. Preheat oven to 350°F. Place chicken breasts in a large deep skillet or flameproof casserole. Add water to barely cover. Bring to a simmer and cook over medium heat until chicken is white throughout but still moist, 12 to 15 minutes; drain. When cool enough to handle, tear meat into strips about 1 inch wide. Layer chicken pieces in bottom of a greased 9 x 13-inch baking dish. Layer corn tortilla strips evenly over chicken.

2. In a medium skillet, heat oil over medium heat. Add onion and cook, stirring, until soft and translucent, about 3 minutes. Scatter onion over tortilla pieces in casserole. In a large bowl, mix mushroom soup, chicken soup, chicken broth, chili beans, and green salsa. Pour mixture evenly over casserole. Scatter sliced olives on top and sprinkle on shredded cheese.

3. Bake 50 minutes to 1 hour, or until casserole is bubbly and hot throughout. Serve directly from casserole.

248   SHRIMP-FILLED CHIMICHANGAS
Prep: 10 minutes   Cook: 12 to 15 minutes   Serves: 4

Chimichangas are fried burritos and are unique to the state of Sonora in northern Mexico. They are also very popular in Arizona. Most often made with large flour tortillas, chimichangas can be filled with just about anything. They are usually served with guacamole or various salsas. A well-filled chimichanga is a meal on a plate.

1 tablespoon butter
5 tablespoons vegetable oil
6 scallions, chopped
2 garlic cloves, minced
1 (4-ounce) can diced green
  chiles
1 pound cooked bay shrimp,
  rinsed and drained

3 ounces cream cheese
½ teaspoon salt
⅛ teaspoon pepper
4 (10-inch) flour tortillas
  Guacamole and fresh salsa,
  as accompaniment

1. In a large skillet, melt butter in 1 tablespoon of oil over medium heat. Add scallions and garlic, and cook, stirring, until fragrant, about 1 minute. Add diced green chiles, shrimp, cream cheese, salt, and pepper. Cook, stirring, until mixture is completely heated through and cream cheese is melted, 1 to 2 minutes. Remove from heat and set aside.

2. In a large dry skillet, warm tortillas, 1 at a time, over medium heat, until soft and pliable. Stack together and wrap in a kitchen towel to keep from drying out. Or wrap tortillas in damp paper towels and microwave on High about 1 minute, or until hot.

3. Place 1 warmed tortilla on a plate. Spoon about a quarter of shrimp filling in center, fold up bottom, fold in edges, and roll over to enclose filling, envelope style. Secure with toothpicks. Repeat until all are filled and rolled.

4. In a large nonstick skillet, heat about 2 tablespoons of oil over medium heat. Add 2 chimichangas, seam side down, and fry, turning once, until golden brown on bottom, about 2 minutes. Turn and cook until brown on second side, 1 to 2 minutes. Drain on paper towels. Repeat with remaining chimichangas in remaining oil. Serve at once, with guacamole and salsa as accompaniment.

249 CHIMICHANGAS WITH PICADILLO
Prep: 25 minutes   Cook: 41 to 43 minutes   Serves: 6

An easy spicy picadillo enfolded in flour tortillas and topped with a light tomato sauce makes a special chimichanga. Serve with rice or beans.

1 tablespoon olive oil
1 pound lean ground beef
½ small onion, minced
¾ cup spicy prepared thick and chunky salsa
1 small apple, peeled and chopped
¼ cup raisins
½ teaspoon ground cinnamon

⅛ teaspoon ground allspice
1 teaspoon Worcestershire sauce
½ teaspoon salt
6 (10-inch) flour tortillas
  Vegetable oil, for frying
  Easy Chimichanga Sauce (recipe follows)

1. In a large skillet, heat olive oil over medium heat. Add meat and cook, breaking it up as it cooks, until no longer pink, about 3 minutes. Add onion and cook, stirring, until onion is limp, about 3 minutes longer. Add salsa, apple, raisins, cinnamon, allspice, Worcestershire, and salt. Simmer, stirring occasionally, until mixture is nearly dry, 6 to 8 minutes. Remove from heat and set picadillo filling aside.

2. In a large dry skillet, soften tortillas, 1 at a time, over medium heat, turning once or twice until soft and pliable, about 1 minute total for each tortilla. Stack and cover to keep warm. Or wrap tortillas in damp paper towels and microwave on High about 1 minute, or until hot.

3. Preheat oven to 200°F. Put 1 warmed tortilla on a plate; spoon one sixth of the filling in center. Fold bottom up over filling, fold sides in, and fold top down, overlapping, envelope style. Secure with toothpicks. Repeat with all tortillas and remaining filling.

4. In a large skillet, heat 2 tablespoons oil over medium heat. Add filled tortillas 2 at a time, folded side down, and fry until golden brown on bottom, about 2 minutes. Turn and brown second side, about 1 minute. Place on a baking sheet and keep warm in oven while frying remaining chimichangas.

5. When all are cooked, transfer chimichangas to plates, ladle sauce on top, and serve at once.

250 EASY CHIMICHANGA SAUCE
Prep: 2 minutes   Cook: 5 minutes   Makes: about 2 cups

Serve this light, bright sauce over chimichangas or enchiladas.

1 (15-ounce) can Mexican-
    style stewed tomatoes
1 bay leaf

¼ teaspoon ground cinnamon
¼ teaspoon dried oregano
½ cup canned beef broth

In a food processor or blender, puree tomatoes briefly, leaving some texture. In a nonreactive saucepan, combine pureed tomatoes with bay leaf, cinnamon, oregano, and beef broth. Bring to a boil over medium heat, reduce heat to medium-low, and simmer 5 minutes.

251 CHILAQUILES WITH GROUND BEEF AND RED CHILE SAUCE
Prep: 25 minutes   Cook: 41 to 44 minutes   Serves: 6

Chilaquiles is a tortilla casserole made with crisp pieces of corn tortillas mixed with "something saucy." This feisty beef mixture goes together quickly. It needs only a salad to be a complete meal. In this version the tortilla strips are oven-toasted, so very little fat is used.

8 corn tortillas
2½ tablespoons vegetable oil
1 pound lean ground beef
1 large onion, chopped
2 garlic cloves, minced
¼ cup chili powder
1 teaspoon ground cumin
1 teaspoon dried oregano

1 (15-ounce) can ready-cut
    tomatoes, pureed
1½ cups canned reduced-
    sodium chicken broth
¾ teaspoon salt
1 cup shredded Cheddar
    cheese (about 4 ounces)

1. Preheat oven to 325°F. Brush tortillas on one side with 1 tablespoon of vegetable oil. Cut each tortilla in half, then into strips about ¾ inch wide. Place strips on a large baking sheet and toast in oven 12 to 15 minutes, or until lightly browned and crisp. Remove from oven and set aside.

2. In a large saucepan, heat remaining 1½ tablespoons oil over medium heat. Add ground beef, breaking it into bits, and cook until lightly browned and no longer pink, about 6 minutes. Add onion and garlic. Cook, stirring frequently, until onion is softened and translucent, about 3 minutes. Add chili powder, cumin, oregano, tomatoes, chicken broth, and salt. Stir thoroughly. Bring to a boil over medium heat. Reduce heat to medium-low, cover, and cook, stirring occasionally, 10 minutes. Add tortilla strips and stir to combine. Mixture will be thick. Transfer contents to a 1½- to 2-quart oven-proof casserole. Top with shredded cheese.

3. Bake until cheese is melted, about 10 minutes.

252   CHEESE ENCHILADAS IN RED SAUCE

Prep: 25 minutes   Cook: 15 to 20 minutes   Makes: 6

2½ cups Easy Red Enchilada
     Sauce (page 82)
⅓ cup vegetable oil
6 corn tortillas
8 ounces Cheddar cheese,
     shredded (about 2 cups)

½ medium onion, chopped
1 cup Crema (page 82) or sour
     cream
3 scallions, chopped

1. Prepare enchilada sauce. Transfer to a medium skillet and keep warm, covered, over low heat. Preheat oven to 350°F.

2. In another medium skillet, heat oil over medium heat. With tongs, dip tortillas, 1 at a time, in hot oil 6 to 8 seconds, or until limp. Drain on paper towels. Stack and cover with a clean kitchen towel to keep soft and warm.

3. Dip tortillas, 1 at a time, in warm enchilada sauce and lay on a plate. Put about 2 tablespoons cheese in center of tortilla and add about one sixth chopped onion. Roll up and place seam side down in a 7x11-inch baking dish. Repeat until all tortillas are filled and rolled. Pour remaining red sauce over enchiladas and sprinkle remaining cheese on top.

4. Bake 15 to 20 minutes, or until cheese is melted and enchiladas are heated through. Garnish with crema and chopped scallions. Serve at once.

253   CRAB ENCHILADAS
WITH TOMATILLO SAUCE

Prep: 25 minutes   Cook: 20 minutes   Serves: 8

Enchiladas can be folded, as well as rolled, as in this recipe. It's quicker and they look great, too. This filling is wonderful with Southwestern Corn Crepes.

2 (12-ounce) cans tomatillos,
     drained and rinsed
½ cup prepared bottled red or
     green salsa
½ cup chicken broth
½ cup loosely packed cilantro
     leaves
1 teaspoon dried oregano
½ teaspoon ground cumin
½ teaspoon sugar
½ teaspoon salt
2 tablespoons vegetable oil

1 medium onion, minced
2 cups cooked crabmeat
1 tablespoon chopped parsley
8 freshly made corn tortillas,
     or Southwestern Corn
     Crepes (recipe follows)
1 cup shredded Monterey Jack
     cheese (4 ounces)
1 large avocado, peeled and
     cut into ¼-inch dice
8 radishes, sliced

1. In a blender or food processor, place tomatillos, salsa, chicken broth, cilantro, oregano, cumin, sugar, and ¼ teaspoon of salt. Puree until smooth. In a large saucepan, cook tomatillo sauce over medium heat, stirring occasionally, 5 minutes.

2. Preheat oven to 375°F. In a medium skillet, heat oil over medium heat. Cook onion, stirring, until softened, about 3 minutes. Remove pan from heat. Stir in crab, parsley, and remaining ¼ teaspoon salt.

3. Put 1 cup warm tomatillo sauce in a shallow bowl. Dip 1 tortilla on both sides into sauce and place on a plate. Put ¼ cup crab mixture on half of tortilla. Fold over to enclose mixture; place on a large greased baking sheet. Repeat until all tortillas are filled and folded. Spoon remaining sauce over enchiladas. Scatter cheese over top.

4. Bake 12 minutes, or until enchiladas are heated through and cheese is melted. Garnish with diced avocado and sliced radishes. Serve at once.

---

254 SOUTHWESTERN CORN CREPES

Prep: 5 minutes   Stand: 2 hours   Cook: 15 minutes
Makes: about 16

Savory tender corn crepes are useful, tasty, and quite elegant as a substitute for tortillas to prepare enchiladas with a different flavor and texture. Corn crepes hold very well when sauced ahead of baking.

2 **large eggs**	½ **teaspoon salt**
1 **cup milk**	¼ **teaspoon sugar**
½ **cup flour**	2 **tablespoons butter, melted**
½ **cup yellow cornmeal**	**Vegetable oil**

1. Put all ingredients except oil, in order listed, in a blender or food processor. Blend 15 seconds. Scrape down sides of jar or bowl. Blend 20 seconds. Transfer batter to a deep medium bowl and let stand at room temperature about 2 hours before baking. (Cover and refrigerate, if holding batter longer.)

2. Lightly oil a 6- to 7-inch crepe pan or 8-inch nonstick skillet and place over medium-high heat. When oil is hot, pour about 2 tablespoons batter into pan and quickly tilt pan in all directions so batter runs over entire flat surface. Cook crepe 8 to 10 seconds, or until surface looks dry and edge is lightly browned. Run a wide spatula under edge of crepe to loosen. Lift and flip crepe over. Cook 5 to 10 seconds, until lightly speckled on second side. Flip pan over a plate to turn out crepe. Repeat, oiling pan if crepes begin to stick. Stir batter occasionally. Stack cooked crepes. Use as directed in recipe.

NOTE: *Crepes may be made ahead, cooled, wrapped in plastic wrap, and refrigerated up to 3 days, or placed in heavy-duty plastic bags and frozen for up to 1 month. Let return to room temperature before separating to prevent crepes from sticking together. Handle carefully: they are tender.*

255   SWISS ENCHILADAS
Prep: 30 minutes   Cook: 31 to 41 minutes   Makes: 12

Swiss enchiladas, or *enchiladas Suisses*—chicken-filled enchiladas baked in green tomatillo sauce and cheese and garnished with sour cream—is one of the most popular enchilada dishes in Mexico. This version comes from Sanborn's, a popular combination coffee shop and gift shop in Mexico City.

4 poblano or Anaheim	1½ teaspoons salt
peppers	¼ cup vegetable oil
2 pounds tomatillos, husked,	12 corn tortillas
rinsed, and quartered	1 Poached and Shredded
2 tablespoons chopped onion	Chicken (page 126)
½ cup cilantro sprigs,	2 cups shredded Monterey
lightly packed, plus	Jack cheese (about
2 tablespoons chopped	8 ounces)
2 serrano peppers, chopped	4 scallions, finely chopped
1 teaspoon dried oregano	½ cup sour cream
½ cup chicken broth	2 tablespoons milk
½ to 1 teaspoon sugar	

1. Preheat oven broiler. Place peppers on a baking sheet and broil as close to heat as possible, turning, until charred all over, about 10 minutes. Or roast peppers directly over a gas flame, turning, about 5 minutes. Place peppers in a paper bag and let steam 10 minutes. Peel off blackened skin and rinse under cold running water. Cut peppers open; discard stems and seeds. Coarsely cut up peppers.

2. In a blender or food processor, combine cut-up peppers, tomatillos, onion, cilantro sprigs, serrano peppers, oregano, chicken broth, ½ teaspoon sugar, and salt. Puree until smooth. Transfer to a large nonreactive saucepan. Partially cover and cook over medium-low heat, stirring often, 10 minutes. If too tart, add remaining sugar. Set green sauce aside.

3. Preheat oven to 350°F. In a medium skillet, heat oil over medium-high heat. Soften tortillas, 1 at a time, by dipping them in hot oil on both sides 2 to 3 seconds; drain between layers of paper towels to keep soft. When all are finished, place 1 tortilla on a plate. Put about 1 tablespoon green sauce and 2 tablespoons shredded chicken on lower third of tortilla and roll up. Place seam side down in a 9 x 13-inch baking dish. Continue until all are filled and rolled. Pour remaining cooked green sauce over all. Cover top with shredded cheese and scallions.

4. Bake, uncovered, 15 to 20 minutes, or until enchiladas are heated through and bubbly. In a small bowl, stir together sour cream and milk. Drizzle over casserole. Sprinkle cilantro on top and serve at once.

256   BEEF ENCHILADA PIE
Prep: 25 minutes   Cook: 1 hour 25 minutes to 1 hour 34 minutes   Serves: 4

Enchiladas can be rolled, folded, or stacked, as they are in this recipe.

½ cup vegetable oil
1½ pounds lean beef stew meat, cut into 1-inch chunks
2 garlic cloves, chopped
1 teaspoon dried oregano
½ teaspoon salt
¼ teaspoon pepper
1 medium onion, chopped
1 cup ready-cut salsa tomatoes

8 corn tortillas
2 cups canned enchilada sauce
1 cup shredded Cheddar cheese (4 ounces)
3 scallions, chopped
¼ cup sliced black olives
Sour cream and chopped cilantro

1. In a large saucepan or flameproof casserole, heat 3 tablespoons of oil over medium heat. Add meat and cook, stirring frequently, until lightly browned, 6 to 8 minutes. Add garlic, oregano, salt, and pepper. Stir to combine. Add 1 cup water and bring to a boil. Reduce heat to medium-low, cover, and cook until meat is very tender, about 1 hour. Let meat cool in broth, then tear into shreds. Place in a large bowl.

2. Preheat oven to 350°F. In a medium skillet, heat 1 tablespoon of oil. Add onion and cook, stirring, until it begins to brown, 3 to 5 minutes. Add to bowl with meat. Stir in tomatoes. Set filling aside.

3. Wipe out skillet with paper towels. Add remaining oil and heat over medium heat. Using tongs, fry tortillas, 1 at a time, until soft and pliable, about 5 seconds on each side. Drain on paper towels.

4. Spoon 2 tablespoons of enchilada sauce into each of 2 (9-inch) glass pie plates. Lay 1 tortilla on sauce in each pie plate. Spoon about ¼ cup reserved meat mixture on each tortilla. Drizzle in 2 tablespoons enchilada sauce. Lay another tortilla on sauce. Cover each with ¼ cup meat and 2 tablespoons sauce. Lay on third tortilla and repeat layers of meat and sauce. Lay fourth tortilla on each stack and pour remaining sauce over all. Top each stack with half of cheese, scallions, and olives.

5. Bake, uncovered, in preheated oven 15 to 20 minutes, or until cheese is melted and sauce is bubbly. Cut each stack into quarters and serve at once with sour cream and chopped cilantro.

257 PARTY-TIME BEEF TACOS
Prep: 20 minutes   Cook: 18 minutes   Makes: 24

Everybody likes to build their own tacos. This is an easy way to feed friends at a very informal gathering. You make the filling. They do the rest.

2 tablespoons olive oil	24 purchased crisp taco shells
1 large onion, chopped	or homemade (recipe
2 garlic cloves, minced	follows)
1½ pounds ground beef	Shredded Cheddar cheese,
1 tablespoon chili powder	shredded lettuce,
1 teaspoon dried oregano	chopped scallions, sliced
½ teaspoon ground cumin	olives, and chopped
1 cup bottled red salsa	tomatoes

1. In a large skillet, heat oil over medium heat. Add onion and garlic. Cook, stirring occasionally, until onion is softened and translucent, about 3 minutes. Add ground beef, chili powder, oregano, and cumin. Cook, breaking up lumps of meat, until beef is browned, about 10 minutes. Add salsa, reduce heat to medium-low, and simmer about 5 minutes to blend flavors.

2. Fill each taco shell with about 3 tablespoons meat mixture and arrange on a large platter. Place cheese, lettuce, scallions, olives, and tomatoes in separate bowls as accompaniment.

258 TACO SHELLS
Prep: 2 minutes   Cook: 24 to 36 minutes   Makes: 12

If you prefer to make your own taco shells, here is how. Of course, homemade are better than store-bought. These can be made 2 to 3 days ahead and still maintain their crispness and flavor.

1 cup vegetable oil	12 corn tortillas

In a medium skillet, heat oil to 360°F. over medium heat. Hold tortilla by one edge with tongs and dip in hot oil on both sides to soften the tortilla and make it pliable. Continue holding tortilla edge with tongs and fold in half, leaving an opening between the two edges. Fry 2 to 3 minutes, or until crisp and golden brown. Drain on paper towels. Fill and eat, or store at room temperature, in plastic bags or an airtight container, up to 3 days for best texture and taste.

259 AVOCADO AND CHEESE QUESADILLAS WITH CHIPOTLE MAYONNAISE

Prep: 8 minutes   Cook: 8 minutes   Serves: 4

1 large ripe avocado, peeled
1 teaspoon fresh lime juice
1 tablespoon chipotle salsa
¼ cup mayonnaise
4 (7-inch) corn or flour tortillas

1 cup shredded Monterey Jack cheese (about 4 ounces)
2 to 4 tablespoons vegetable oil

1. In a medium bowl, mash avocado with a fork. Add lime juice, chipotle salsa, and mayonnaise and mix well.

2. In a dry medium skillet, or on a griddle, over medium heat, warm a tortilla by turning it over 2 to 4 times until soft and pliable. Lay tortilla on a flat surface and spread 2 to 3 tablespoons avocado mixture over tortilla to within 1 inch of edge. Put about ¼ cup of cheese on one half and fold tortilla over to form a semicircle. Place on a plate. Cover with foil to keep soft and warm. Repeat procedure with remaining tortillas.

3. In a medium skillet, heat 1 tablespoon of oil over medium heat. Add quesadilla and cook, turning once, until lightly browned and cheese is melted, about 1 minute per side. Repeat with remaining quesadillas, adding oil as needed. Cut each turnover in half and serve hot.

260 QUICK QUESADILLAS

Prep: 5 minutes   Cook: 12 minutes   Makes: 4

Cheese-filled tortilla turnovers are a favorite quick snack. These are made with either corn or flour tortillas, and they are exceptionally easy.

4 (7-inch) corn or flour tortillas
1 cup shredded Monterey Jack or Cheddar cheese (about 4 ounces)

2 pickled jalapeño peppers, seeded and finely chopped
¼ cup vegetable oil

1. In a dry heavy skillet or on a griddle, warm each tortilla over medium heat, turning 2 or 3 times, until soft and pliable, about 30 seconds on each side. Lay heated tortilla out flat and put about ¼ cup cheese on half of surface. Add a few bits of chopped jalapeño. Fold tortilla in half to form a semicircle. Put on a plate and cover with foil to keep soft while assembling remaining turnovers.

2. In same skillet, heat 1 tablespoon of oil over medium heat. Add quesadilla and cook, turning once, until tortilla is lightly browned on both sides and cheese is melted, about 1 minute per side. Repeat with remaining quesadillas, adding oil as needed. Serve immediately. Each turnover may be cut into wedges, if desired.

261 MUSHROOM AND EGGPLANT ENCHILADAS

Prep: 25 minutes   Cook: 24 to 31 minutes   Makes: 8

3 tablespoons olive oil
½ medium onion, minced
10 ounces mushrooms, finely chopped
3 small, narrow Asian eggplant, or ½ small regular eggplant, cut into ¼-inch dice
½ red bell pepper, chopped
1 fresh jalapeño pepper, seeded and minced

½ teaspoon dried oregano
½ teaspoon dried thyme leaves
½ teaspoon salt
⅛ teaspoon pepper
3 tablespoons vegetable oil
8 corn tortillas
2 cups prepared enchilada sauce
1½ cups shredded Monterey Jack cheese (about 6 ounces)

1. In a large nonstick skillet, heat olive oil over medium heat. Add onion, mushrooms, eggplant, bell pepper, and jalapeño pepper. Cook, stirring frequently, until vegetables are soft and juices evaporate, 8 to 10 minutes. Stir in oregano, thyme, salt, and pepper. Remove filling from heat and set aside.

2. Preheat oven to 350°F. In a medium skillet, heat vegetable oil over medium heat. Using tongs, dip tortillas in hot oil, 1 at a time, until very limp, about 3 seconds on each side. Drain on paper towels and keep covered to prevent drying out.

3. Lay 1 tortilla on a plate. Put 3 to 4 tablespoons filling across lower third of tortilla. Roll up and place seam side down in a buttered 8½ x 11-inch baking dish. Repeat until all tortillas are filled and rolled. Cover completely with enchilada sauce. Sprinkle shredded cheese on top.

4. Bake 15 to 20 minutes, or until sauce is bubbling and cheese is melted. Serve at once.

262 VEGETARIAN ENCHILADAS
Prep: 20 minutes   Cook: 18 to 20 minutes   Makes: 8

2 tablespoons unsalted butter
½ medium onion, minced
8 medium mushrooms, finely chopped
3 medium zucchini (about 1 pound), shredded
1 jalapeño pepper, seeded and minced
3 scallions, chopped

½ teaspoon dried oregano
½ teaspoon salt
⅛ teaspoon pepper
3 tablespoons vegetable oil
8 corn tortillas
2 cups prepared red enchilada sauce
1 cup shredded Monterey Jack cheese (4 ounces)

1. In a large skillet, melt butter over medium heat. Add onion and mushrooms and cook, stirring, until juices evaporate, 3 to 5 minutes. Add zucchini, jalapeño pepper, scallions, oregano, salt, and pepper. Raise heat to high and cook, stirring constantly, until zucchini skin is bright green, about 3 minutes. Remove from heat and set filling aside.

2. Preheat oven to 350°F. In another medium skillet, heat vegetable oil over medium heat. Using tongs, dip tortillas into hot oil, 1 at a time, until very limp, about 6 seconds per tortilla. Drain on paper towels and keep covered to prevent drying out. Lay 1 tortilla on a plate. Put about 3 tablespoons filling across lower third of surface. Roll up and place seam side down in a buttered 8½ x 11-inch baking dish. Repeat until all tortillas are filled and rolled. Cover completely with enchilada sauce. Sprinkle shredded cheese on top.

3. Bake 12 to 15 minutes, or until sauce is bubbling and cheese is melted. Serve at once.

263 TURKEY AND BLACK BEAN TOSTADAS
Prep: 10 minutes   Cook: none   Serves: 4

Leftover turkey? Lucky you. Turkey tostadas are super for a snack or light lunch.

3 cups diced cooked turkey
2 celery ribs, chopped
¾ cup mayonnaise
1 teaspoon ground cumin
4 packaged crisp tostadas
2 cups shredded lettuce

1 (15-ounce) can black beans, rinsed and drained
1 cup shredded Monterey Jack cheese (about 4 ounces)
Salsa, sour cream, and avocado slices

1. In a large bowl, combine diced turkey, celery, mayonnaise, and cumin. Toss to mix well.

2. On each of 4 plates, place 1 crisp tostada. Top each tostada with ½ cup shredded lettuce, one fourth of beans, ¾ cup turkey salad, and ¼ cup shredded cheese.

3. Garnish tostadas with salsa, sour cream, and avocado slices. Serve slightly chilled or at room temperature.

264   HAM AND CHEESE TOSTADAS
Prep: 15 minutes   Cook: none   Serves: 4

A flavorful ham and cheese salad mounded on crisp corn tortillas makes fine tostadas. Offer these with Mexican beer to TV sports fans and earn yourself a few cheers.

1 **pound fully cooked smoked ham, cut into ½-inch dice**
½ **pound Cheddar or Swiss cheese, cut into ½-inch dice**
2 **medium tomatoes, chopped**
¼ **cup mayonnaise**

2 **pickled jalapeño peppers, seeded and minced**
1 **large avocado, cut into ½-inch dice**
4 **packaged crisp tostadas**
1 **cup shredded iceberg lettuce**
Radishes and black olives

1. In a large bowl, combine ham, cheese, tomatoes, mayonnaise, and jalapeño peppers. Toss to mix well. Add avocado and toss lightly.

2. On each of 4 plates, place 1 crisp tostada. Distribute lettuce evenly over tostadas. Mound ham salad mixture on lettuce. Garnish with radishes and black olives. Serve at once.

265   TOSTADAS WITH GROUND MEAT TOPPING
Prep: 10 minutes   Cook: 7 minutes   Makes: 6

Tostadas are crisp corn tortillas, which serve as the edible base for any number of imaginative toppings. Use convenient ready-fried tostadas, 12 to a package, or you can crisp-fry or oven-bake your own tostadas. Serve as a snack or light meal.

1 **tablespoon vegetable oil**
½ **medium onion, finely chopped**
1 **pound ground beef chuck or fresh ground pork**
1 **teaspoon dried oregano**
½ **teaspoon ground cumin**
½ **cup prepared red salsa**

1 **(16-ounce) can spicy refried beans**
6 **crisp tostadas**
2 **cups shredded lettuce**
½ **cup sour cream, thinned with 1 tablespoon milk**
3 **medium tomatoes, cut into thin wedges**

1. In a medium skillet, heat oil over medium-high heat. Add onion and cook, stirring, until softened and translucent, about 2 minutes. Add ground meat and cook until browned and cooked through, 4 to 5 minutes, breaking meat into bits with a wooden spoon. Add oregano, cumin, and red salsa. Mix well. Remove from heat. Drain off excess fat and cover meat to keep warm. In a medium saucepan over low heat, or in a microwave dish, heat beans until they are warmed through.

2. Place 1 tostada on each of 6 plates. Spread beans over tostadas, distributing them evenly. Add ⅓ cup lettuce over each tostada. Distribute meat mixture over tostadas. Drizzle each with sour cream and garnish with tomato wedges. Serve at once.

---

266 CORN TORTILLAS
Prep: 10 minutes   Cook: 24 minutes   Makes: 12 (6-inch) tortillas

Occasionally, you might want to try making your own tortillas. Corn tortillas can be made from prepared corn flour called *masa harina*, or from prepared wet dough called *masa*, which is used in tortilla factories. Fresh masa is excellent, but it is not available everywhere; so to make your own corn tortillas, you'll need a tortilla press, masa harina, and plastic sandwich bags. With a little practice, you'll soon learn to make this Mexican staple.

2 **cups masa harina**   ¼ **teaspoon salt**
1¼ **cups warm water**

1. In a large bowl, mix masa, water, and salt with a wooden spoon or your hands until completely combined. Using hands, knead dough until evenly moistened but not sticky. Cover bowl with plastic wrap and let dough rest 10 minutes.

2. Form dough into 12 equal balls. Keep covered with plastic wrap while working since masa dough dries out very quickly. If dough seems dry, moisten hands and work dough again; reworking is okay. Line a tortilla press with 2 plastic bags, one on the bottom and one draped over lid. (Do not place dough directly on metal surface of press. It will stick and make a mess!) Flatten 1 ball with palm and place on center of plastic-lined bottom. Place other bag on top. Lower hinged lid and press out to a 6-inch round tortilla. Lift lid. Leave tortilla on press.

3. Heat a heavy medium skillet, preferably cast iron, over medium-high heat. When dry pan is hot, lift tortilla onto palm of hand. Carefully peel off top plastic bag. Flip again and peel off second bag. Put tortilla in hot pan. (If it wrinkles, don't attempt to straighten or pick up, or it will stick to pan.) Cook 30 to 40 seconds, or until edges look dry. With a wide spatula, flip over and cook second side 1 minute. Turn again and cook about 20 seconds. Put between folds of barely dampened kitchen towel. Repeat, always returning plastic bag to line press, until all tortillas are cooked. Stack together as they are finished. When cool, place tortillas in a heavy-duty plastic bag and refrigerate up to 1 week. Do not freeze corn tortillas, or they will lose their texture. Reheat in a hot skillet or directly over gas flame until warm and pliable, or reheat in microwave oven following manufacturer's instructions.

267   MEAT-FILLED TAMALES
Prep: 1 hour   Cook: 2¼ hours   Serves: 6 to 8

To make tamales in a relaxed fashion, prepare the dough 1 day ahead, and be sure to allow time for the filling to cool enough to handle. Corn husks are available in Latin American markets and in some supermarkets. If you cannot obtain dried corn husks, wrap each tamale in a 4- by 6-inch piece of aluminum foil.

16 soaked corn husks	4 ancho chiles
2 pounds boneless pork shoulder or beef chuck, trimmed and cut into 1-inch cubes	1 medium tomato, peeled, seeded, and chopped
1 medium onion, chopped	1 teaspoon ground cumin
2 garlic cloves, chopped	1 teaspoon salt
1 bay leaf	¼ teaspoon pepper
1 teaspoon dried oregano	Tamale Dough (recipe follows)

1. Soak dried corn husks overnight, or at least 2 hours, until pliable.

2. In a large saucepan or flameproof casserole, combine meat, onion, garlic, bay leaf, and oregano. Add just enough cold water to cover. Bring to a boil, reduce heat to medium-low, and simmer, partially covered, until meat is fork-tender, about 1 hour. Let meat cool in broth; then remove and tear into shreds. Put meat in a medium bowl, cover, and set aside. Strain broth and reserve.

3. While meat cooks, remove stems and seeds from ancho chiles. Rinse and place in a medium saucepan with water to cover. Bring to a boil over medium-high heat. Remove from heat, cover, and soak 30 minutes. Drain peppers and place in a blender or food processor. Add tomato, oregano, cumin, and ½ cup reserved meat broth. Puree until smooth. Add to shredded meat. Season with salt and pepper. Mix well.

4. Remove corn husks from soaking water and put between layers of damp kitchen towels to keep moist. Place 1 husk on a flat surface and put about 2 tablespoons dough in center. Spread to within ½ inch of wide end and halfway toward pointed end. Put 1 heaping tablespoon meat filling in center of tamale. Fold sides of husk toward center to overlap. Fold pointed end toward filling. Repeat with remaining husks.

5. Put 2 cups water into a large steamer and line steamer rack with extra dry corn husks. Arrange tamales folded ends down. Cover with aluminum foil and a white kitchen towel, to catch dripping steam. Put lid on pan, bring water to a boil, and steam tamales 45 minutes, or until dough is firm and husk pulls away from dough.

6. To serve, peel back husk and serve with red or green cooked chile sauce. Keep wrapped and refrigerated up to 3 days, or freeze up to 3 months. Reheat directly from refrigerator or freezer, wrapped in foil for conventional oven, or covered with plastic for microwave.

268 TAMALE DOUGH
Prep: 10 minutes   Cook: none   Makes: about 2¼ cups

For good tamales, the dough must be as light as possible, so beating the mixture very thoroughly is important. First-time tamale makers will find this an easy amount of dough to handle; it makes about 16 small tamales. The special finely ground Mexican corn flour called *masa harina* is available in most supermarkets.

1½ cups masa harina	3 tablespoons butter, softened
¾ teaspoon baking powder	¾ cup plus 3 tablespoons
¾ teaspoon salt	lukewarm water
⅓ cup solid vegetable	
shortening	

1. In a medium bowl, combine masa harina, baking powder, and salt. Whisk gently to mix well.

2. In another medium bowl, with electric mixer, beat shortening and butter until creamy. Gradually beat in 3 tablespoons masa mixture, then 3 tablespoons water until light and fluffy, about 1 minute. Continue beating in masa and water alternately until dough is very smooth and of spreading consistency, about 5 minutes. Cover and refrigerate up to 3 days. Let return to room temperature before using.

269 CHICKEN TAMALE PIE
Prep: 30 minutes   Cook: 39 to 47 minutes   Serves: 6

1   tablespoon corn oil
3   skinless, boneless chicken
    breast halves (¾ to
    1 pound), cut into
    ¾-inch pieces
1½ teaspoons salt
1   medium onion, chopped
2   garlic cloves, minced
½   green bell pepper, cut into
    ¼-inch dice

¾   cup canned Mexican-style
    stewed tomatoes
½   cup chicken broth
2½ tablespoons chili powder
1½ cups yellow cornmeal
3   tablespoons butter
2   tablespoons grated
    Parmesan cheese

1. In a large nonstick skillet, heat oil over medium heat. Add chicken and cook, stirring, until lightly browned, 3 to 4 minutes. Add ½ teaspoon of salt, onion, garlic, and bell pepper. Cook, stirring frequently, until onion is softened, about 3 minutes. Add pureed tomatoes, chicken broth, chili powder, and 1 tablespoon of cornmeal. Stir to combine. Bring to a boil, stirring, until mixture thickens, about 2 minutes. Remove from heat and set chicken filling aside.

2. Preheat oven to 375°F. In a large heavy saucepan, whisk together 4 cups warm water, remaining cornmeal, and remaining 1 teaspoon salt. Bring to a boil over medium-high heat, whisking frequently, until mixture boils. Reduce heat to medium-low and cook, whisking occasionally, until thick and smooth, 6 to 8 minutes. Be careful of spattering. Remove from heat and stir in butter until melted.

3. Immediately spread about a third of hot cornmeal in bottom of a buttered 8 x 11-inch ovenproof casserole. Spoon chicken filling over cornmeal, spreading evenly. Spoon on remaining two thirds cornmeal, spreading gently to completely cover filling. Sprinkle Parmesan cheese on top.

4. Bake 25 to 30 minutes, or until filling bubbles around edges and top is lightly browned. Serve hot, directly from casserole.

270 SPICY TAMALE PIE
Prep: 20 minutes   Cook: 1 hour   Serves: 4 to 6

1 tablespoon vegetable oil
1 small onion, chopped
½ medium green bell pepper, chopped
¾ pound lean ground beef
2 tablespoons chili powder
½ teaspoon dried oregano
1 (14½-ounce) can ready-cut tomatoes

1 (16-ounce) can red kidney beans, drained and rinsed
1 cup corn kernels
¾ teaspoon salt
¾ cup yellow cornmeal
½ cup shredded Cheddar cheese

1. In a large skillet, heat oil over medium heat. Add onion and bell pepper and cook, stirring, until onion begins to brown, 3 to 5 minutes. Crumble ground beef into pan and cook, stirring to break up lumps, until meat is no longer pink, about 5 minutes. Add chili powder, oregano, tomatoes, beans, corn, and ¼ teaspoon of salt. Bring to a simmer, reduce heat to medium-low, and cook, stirring frequently, until slightly thickened, 8 to 10 minutes. Transfer to a greased 2-quart ovenproof casserole.

2. Preheat oven to 350°F. In a medium saucepan, combine cornmeal, remaining ½ teaspoon salt, and 1¼ cups cold water. Stir until blended. Bring to a simmer over medium heat, stirring. Continue to cook, stirring, until thickened, about 5 minutes.

3. Spread cornmeal batter evenly over casserole ingredients. Sprinkle cheese evenly over cornmeal topping. Bake in preheated oven 30 to 35 minutes, or until casserole is hot throughout and top is golden brown.

Chapter 10

From a Mexican Garden

Mexico has a stunning array of fresh vegetables, as a visit to a Mexican market will attest. Mexico's bounty of produce generally comes to the market fresh and full of flavor, and daily shopping is still an important cultural activity. Market stalls are piled high with artfully arranged produce, both native and a world of others now being cultivated in Mexico. Indigenous food products include corn, tomatoes, hot chiles, sweet peppers, fresh and dry beans, squash, potatoes, cactus, jicama, avocados, chocolate, vanilla, and more, all sharing space with broccoli, cabbage, cauliflower, cucumbers, radishes, turnips, beets, oranges, lemons, and an impressive number of other fruits and vegetables introduced from Europe and Asia.

With its mild climate and long growing season, just about everything is grown somewhere in Mexico. Vegetables are used in many ways, from feisty fresh salsas, pureed sauces, and stews to carefully composed salads and dressed-up side dishes. Cooked vegetables are tossed into soups and stews, and they are frequently served as separate courses, especially Chiles Rellenos with Cheese, a shining example, which are best presented alone bathed in traditional brothy tomato sauce.

Be sure to look in Chapter 3 for a wide variety of Mexican salads. Most of the vegetable dishes in this chapter are savory side dishes, some innovative and some traditional, to accompany entrees. These dishes provide bright color and healthy variety to our diets, and when prepared in the Mexican way, there's added zip and excitement with the touch of chiles, herbs, and spices. Some lesser known native Mexican vegetables, such as chayote, jicama, certain peppers, chiles, and herbs like cilantro and epazote, are becoming more available in the United States. Some exotic items, like the herb *hoja santa* and the corn fungus *huitlacoche,* are rarely found north of the border, and I have not called for them here, but keep your eyes open. Exposure creates demand, and someday the unique or unknown will be in our own markets.

271 ASPARAGUS WITH CHIPOTLE MAYONNAISE

Prep: 5 minutes   Cook: 4 to 6 minutes   Serves: 3 to 4

We may not think of asparagus as a Mexican vegetable, but excellent asparagus is grown in Mexico and it is available in markets seasonally, just like here.

1 **pound asparagus spears,**	1 **tablespoon lime juice**
thick ends broken off	½ **cup mayonnaise**
½ **teaspoon salt**	1 **tablespoon bottled chipotle**
1 **teaspoon olive oil**	**salsa**

1. In a large skillet, bring 3 cups water to a boil over medium-high heat. Add asparagus spears and cook, uncovered, until just tender, 4 to 6 minutes. Drain and return asparagus to skillet. Add salt, olive oil, and lime juice. Toss to coat. Arrange on a platter.

2. In a small bowl, stir together mayonnaise and chipotle salsa until well blended. Spoon a band of mayonnaise over centers of asparagus spears. Serve warm or at room temperature.

272 BAKED CHAYOTES RELLENOS

Prep: 10 minutes   Cook: 42 to 47 minutes   Serves: 4

The term *rellenos* refers to something prepared with a filling. Chayotes can be stuffed in advance and baked just before serving. This is an attractive, tasty side dish, and it makes a fine vegetarian entree served with rice. For ease, these can be prepared through step 3 and baked at the last minute.

2 **chayotes, cut in half**	¼ **teaspoon salt**
lengthwise	⅛ **teaspoon pepper**
3 **tablespoons butter**	8 **(¾-inch) cubes Monterey**
½ **medium onion, finely**	**Jack cheese**
chopped	¼ **cup grated Parmesan cheese**
¼ **cup bread crumbs**	

1. Preheat oven to 375°F. In a large saucepan of boiling water, cook chayotes over medium-high heat until tender, about 25 minutes. Drain and let cool. Scoop out chayote into a medium bowl, leaving shells intact. Reserve shells. Mash chayote with a fork.

2. In a large skillet, melt butter over medium heat. Add onion and cook until limp, about 2 minutes. Add mashed chayote, bread crumbs, salt, and pepper. Stir to mix well. Remove from heat.

3. Put 2 cubes of cheese into each reserved chayote shell. Divide filling among shells. Sprinkle 1 tablespoon Parmesan cheese over each. Arrange stuffed chayote in a single layer in a small baking dish.

4. Bake in middle of oven 15 to 20 minutes, or until tops are browned.

273 CAULIFLOWER WITH CARROTS AND JALAPENOS

Prep: 10 minutes   Cook: 4 minutes   Serves: 6

A simple platter of buttery cauliflower is a popular Mexican vegetable, accompanied by pickled carrots and pickled jalapeños. I improvised by including all the ingredients in the same dish. This goes particularly well with pork dishes.

1 medium head of cauliflower, separated into 1½-inch florets	1 small carrot, peeled and coarsely shredded
1 teaspoon salt	½ teaspoon ground cumin
1 tablespoon butter	2 pickled jalapeño peppers, seeded and minced
2 tablespoons olive oil	3 scallions, chopped

1. In a large saucepan of boiling water, cook cauliflower over medium heat until crisp-tender, about 3 minutes. Drain and place in a serving dish. Season with ½ teaspoon of salt.

2. In a small skillet, melt butter in olive oil over medium-high heat. Add carrot, cumin, jalapeños, scallions, and remaining ½ teaspoon salt. Cook, stirring, until carrot is limp, about 1 minute. Scrape carrot and seasoned oil from skillet over cauliflower and serve.

274 GARLIC GREEN BEANS

Prep: 10 minutes   Cook: 5 to 7 minutes   Serves: 4

Tender young green beans cook very quickly and are best for this vegetable dish.

2 tablespoons unsalted butter	1 pound small fresh green beans, stems trimmed
1 tablespoon vegetable oil	½ teaspoon salt
4 garlic cloves, minced	⅛ teaspoon freshly ground black pepper
1 fresh red serrano or jalapeño pepper, seeded and minced	

1. In a small skillet, melt butter with oil over medium-low heat. Add garlic and cook, stirring, until golden but not brown, about 2 minutes. Stir in red pepper. Cover and remove from heat.

2. In a medium saucepan of boiling salted water, cook green beans until crisp-tender, 3 to 5 minutes. Drain and return beans to pan. Add reserved garlic butter, salt, and black pepper. Toss and serve.

275 CUMIN CARROT COINS

Prep: 5 minutes   Cook: 4 to 6 minutes   Serves: 6

Their natural sweetness and bright color make carrots a perfect complement to almost any Mexican entree.

2 **tablespoons unsalted butter**	½ **teaspoon ground cumin**
1 **tablespoon olive oil**	½ **teaspoon salt**
6 **medium carrots, peeled and**	⅛ **teaspoon pepper**
cut on a slight angle into	1 **tablespoon chopped cilantro**
oval rounds ¼ inch thick	**or parsley**

1. In a large skillet, melt butter with olive oil over medium-high heat. Add carrots and cook, tossing frequently, until crisp-tender, 3 to 4 minutes.

2. Stir in cumin, salt, and pepper. Reduce heat to low, cover, and cook until tender but still firm, 1 to 2 minutes. Garnish with cilantro and serve.

276 CHAYOTES WITH TOMATO AND CHEESE TOPPING

Prep: 15 minutes   Cook: 39 to 45 minutes   Serves: 4

Related to squash, chayotes are indigenous to Mexico and are widely used in both savory and sweet dishes. Since chayote is quite bland on its own, the topping used here makes this a flavorful and appealing side dish worth trying as an introduction to this vegetable. The soft seed in the center is edible and is considered a special treat for the cook. Seeds seldom reach the table.

2 **whole chayotes**	2 **garlic cloves, minced**
2 **tablespoons vegetable oil**	½ **teaspoon dried oregano**
½ **medium onion, finely**	½ **teaspoon salt**
chopped	¼ **teaspoon black pepper**
3 **medium ripe tomatoes,**	1 **cup shredded Cheddar**
peeled, seeded, and	**cheese**
chopped	

1. Cut chayotes lengthwise in half. In a large saucepan of boiling water, cook chayotes over medium-high heat until crisp-tender, about 20 minutes. Drain and let cool; then peel off skin and cut chayotes lengthwise into ½-inch strips. Blot on paper towels to remove excess moisture.

2. In a medium skillet, heat oil over medium-high heat. Add onion and cook until limp, 2 to 3 minutes. Stir in tomatoes, garlic, oregano, salt, and pepper. Cook, stirring often, until juices have reduced and mixture is nearly dry, about 2 minutes.

3. Preheat oven to 350°F. Arrange chayote slices close together in a single layer on a greased baking sheet. Spread tomato sauce over the chayotes, allowing ends to show. Top with shredded cheese. Bake 15 to 20 minutes, or until vegetables are heated through and cheese is melted. With a wide spatula, transfer to a platter and serve.

277   CHILES RELLENOS CASSEROLE
Prep: 15 minutes   Cook: 1 hour   Serves: 4

Here's a well-known, north-of-the-border casserole that's a snap to make using ingredients from the pantry. All the flavors of chiles rellenos without the work.

3 (4-ounce) cans whole green
   chiles
1 cup milk
⅓ cup flour
2 eggs, beaten with a fork

¼ teaspoon salt
1 pound Cheddar cheese,
   shredded (about 4 cups)
1 (14½-ounce) can ready-cut
   salsa tomatoes, mashed

1. Preheat oven to 375°F. Slit open green chiles; remove seeds. Rinse chiles and lay flat on paper towels to dry.

2. In a medium bowl, whisk milk and flour with beaten eggs. Season batter with salt. Layer half of chiles in bottom of a greased 1½-quart baking dish. Top with half of cheese and pour on half of batter. Repeat with remaining chiles, cheese, and batter.

3. Place in middle of oven and bake 30 minutes. Spoon mashed tomatoes evenly over top of casserole. Bake about 30 minutes longer, or until set.

278   GREEN CHILE PEPPERS WITH TWO CHEESES
Prep: 20 minutes   Cook: 6 to 7 minutes   Serves: 4

Light and lively stuffed peppers don't require batter. A quick warming to melt the cheese makes this modern relleno a terrific treat in late summer, when peppers and tomatoes are abundant and at their best.

4 fresh Anaheim or poblano
   peppers
½ cup shredded Cheddar
   cheese
4 teaspoons fresh goat cheese
   or cream cheese

¼ teaspoon salt
1 tablespoon vegetable oil
1 cup tomato sauce

1. Roast peppers over gas flame or under oven broiler to char skin all over. Place in a paper bag to steam for about 5 minutes. Cool under running water and rub off skins. Cut off tops. Rinse and remove seeds. Pat dry. Fill each pepper with 2 tablespoons of Cheddar cheese and 1 teaspoon goat cheese. Season with salt.

2. In a medium nonreactive skillet, heat oil over medium-low heat. Add chiles and cook, turning frequently, just until cheese is melted, 1 to 2 minutes.

3. To serve, spoon ¼ cup tomato sauce onto each of 4 small plates. Put 1 pepper on each plate. Serve at once.

279 CHILES RELLENOS WITH CHEESE
Prep: 20 minutes   Cook: 21 to 26 minutes   Serves: 4

These are authentic traditional chiles rellenos, as served in many regions of Mexico. The batter is light and fluffy, and the sauce is a tomato broth seasoned with herbs and spices. It is customary to eat chiles rellenos as a separate course, with soft warm corn tortillas to dip in the delicious sauce.

4 fresh poblano or Anaheim peppers	¼ teaspoon salt ½ cup flour

4 to 6 ounces Monterey Jack
   cheese, shredded
	1 cup vegetable oil
	   Tomato Sauce for Rellenos

4 eggs, separated	(recipe follows)

1. Preheat oven broiler. Place peppers on a baking sheet and broil as close to heat as possible, turning, until charred all over, about 10 minutes. Or roast peppers directly over a gas flame, turning, about 5 minutes. Place peppers in a paper bag and let steam 10 minutes. Peel off blackened skin and rinse peppers under cold running water. With a small sharp knife, slit each peeled pepper lengthwise, keeping stems intact, to within 1 inch of bottom end. Carefully cut out seed pod and rinse under running water to remove remaining seeds. Pat peppers dry, inside and out.

2. Stuff each prepared pepper with a quarter of cheese, squeezing cheese gently with your hands to conform to shape of pepper. Reshape peppers and secure with toothpicks to keep cheese from falling out. Place filled peppers on a tray.

3. In a large bowl, with electric beater, beat egg whites with salt until soft peaks form. Beat in egg yolks, 1 at a time. Beat in 1 tablespoon of flour. Place remaining flour on a plate and dust each stuffed pepper with flour. Place floured peppers on tray.

4. Preheat oven to 200°F. In a heavy medium skillet, heat vegetable oil to 375°F. One at a time, dip peppers into batter to coat and place gently in hot oil. Cook, turning, until golden brown, about 2 minutes per side. With a slotted spoon, remove to paper towels to drain. Keep warm in oven while frying remaining peppers. Serve with heated tomato sauce.

280 TOMATO SAUCE FOR RELLENOS
Prep: 10 minutes   Cook: 13 to 18 minutes   Makes: about 3 cups

This sauce is more flavorful if made ahead and allowed to stand several hours, or covered and refrigerated overnight. Reheat before serving.

4 large ripe tomatoes, peeled
  and chopped
2 tablespoons chopped white
  onion
2 garlic cloves, chopped
2 tablespoons vegetable oil
½ teaspoon ground cinnamon
½ teaspoon dried oregano

¼ teaspoon dried thyme leaves
1 bay leaf
¾ cup canned reduced-sodium
  chicken broth
½ teaspoon salt
⅛ teaspoon freshly ground
  pepper

1. In a blender or food processor, combine tomatoes, onion, and garlic. Puree until smooth.

2. In a medium nonreactive saucepan, heat oil over medium heat. Add tomato puree and cook, stirring, 3 minutes. Add cinnamon, oregano, thyme, bay leaf, broth, salt, and pepper. Reduce heat to low and simmer, stirring occasionally, until sauce is thickened and onion no longer tastes raw, 10 to 15 minutes. Serve hot with chiles rellenos.

281 POBLANO PEPPER STRIPS
Prep: 12 minutes   Cook: 9 to 17 minutes   Serves: 4

Thin strips of dark green poblano peppers, called *rajas*, are used so often, all over Mexico, that just the word *rajas* means strips of poblano to native cooks. Other fresh peppers, such as Anaheim, red or yellow bell peppers, or fresh pimientos, also make delicious *rajas*. Roasted pepper strips add spice and visual excitement to grilled poultry, meat, and fish dishes. All the large fresh peppers are roasted and peeled the same way.

4 large poblano peppers
1 tablespoon vegetable oil

½ medium onion, halved and
  sliced ½ inch thick
½ teaspoon salt

1. Preheat oven broiler. Place peppers on a baking sheet and broil as close to heat as possible, turning, until charred all over, about 10 minutes. Or roast peppers directly over a gas flame, turning, about 5 minutes. Place peppers in a paper bag and let steam 10 minutes. Peel off blackened skin and rinse peppers under cold running water. Cut peppers open; discard stems and seeds. Cut out veins if peppers seem too hot for your taste. (Your senses let you know by smell, or try a tiny taste on tip of your tongue.) Cut peppers into thin strips (*rajas*) about ¼ inch wide and 2 inches long.

2. In a large skillet, heat oil over medium heat. Add onion and cook, stirring, until it begins to brown, 3 to 5 minutes. Add pepper strips and salt. Cook, stirring, until heated through, 1 to 2 minutes.

282 CHILES EN NOGADA
Prep: 40 minutes   Cook: 38 to 46 minutes   Serves: 4

In this classic recipe, dark green poblano peppers are stuffed with a spicy pork mixture, called *picadillo*, then topped with a creamy walnut sauce and a bright garnish of pomegranate seeds and bits of parsley. It is an elegant dish that reaches its peak of popularity during walnut harvest in August and September, especially in the city of Puebla. Chiles en Nogada can be made out of season by freezing pomegranate seeds; remove them from the thick outer skin and freeze them in zip-lock plastic bags. This version, which is my favorite, requires no batter or frying. The stuffed poblano peppers can be completely prepared in advance, then reheated in the oven and garnished at the last minute. Serve as a first course or light entree.

4 large poblano peppers	2 tablespoons finely chopped
½ pound ground pork	blanched almonds
½ medium onion, minced	¾ cup walnut pieces
1 garlic clove, minced	3 ounces cream cheese, at
1 teaspoon dried oregano	room temperature
½ teaspoon salt	1 cup Crema (page 82) or sour
¼ teaspoon pepper	cream
1 large tomato, peeled and	1 teaspoon sugar
finely chopped	¼ cup pomegranate seeds
½ small apple, peeled, cored,	(about ½ pomegranate)
and finely chopped	1½ tablespoons chopped flat-
¼ cup raisins	leaf Italian parsley

1. Preheat oven broiler. Place peppers on a baking sheet and broil as close to heat as possible, turning, until charred all over, about 10 minutes. Or roast peppers directly over a gas flame, turning, about 5 minutes. Place peppers in a paper bag and let steam 10 minutes. Peel off blackened skin and rinse peppers under cold running water. With a small sharp knife, slit each peeled pepper lengthwise, keeping stems intact, to within 1 inch of bottom end. Carefully cut out seed pod and rinse under running water to remove remaining seeds. Pat dry, inside and out. Place on a plate.

2. In a medium nonstick skillet, crumble pork into pan and cook over medium heat, stirring to break up lumps, until meat is no longer pink, about 3 minutes. Add onion, garlic, oregano, salt, and pepper. Cook, stirring frequently, until onion is softened, 4 to 5 minutes. Add tomato, apple, raisins, and almonds. Cook, stirring frequently, until mixture is nearly dry, 6 to 8 minutes. Remove from heat and let cool slightly. When meat mixture is cool enough to handle, use to stuff roasted peppers, dividing equally. If done ahead, put stuffed peppers on a baking sheet, cover, and refrigerate until 1 hour before serving.

3. In a food processor, pulse walnuts until crumbly, 3 to 4 times. Add cream cheese, crema (or sour cream), and sugar. Pulse until smooth. Transfer to a medium bowl.

4. About 30 minutes before serving, preheat oven to 350°F. Place peppers in preheated oven until heated through, about 20 minutes, or alternatively, heat in a microwave. To serve, place 1 pepper on each of 4 plates, spoon a quarter of room-temperature walnut cream sauce over each warm stuffed pepper. Scatter 1 tablespoon pomegranate seeds over each pepper and sprinkle each with ½ teaspoon chopped parsley.

283   BAKED CORN CASSEROLE
Prep: 15 minutes   Cook: 48 to 50 minutes   Serves: 6

This is a great dish to eat with spicy stews and chili dishes.

2 tablespoons vegetable oil	2 eggs, beaten with a fork
½ medium onion, minced	1 (5-ounce) can evaporated
½ medium red bell pepper, finely chopped	milk
	1 teaspoon salt
2 (10-ounce) packages frozen corn, thawed	¼ teaspoon pepper
	1 tablespoon grated Parmesan cheese
1 tablespoon yellow cornmeal	
½ teaspoon ground cumin	

1. Preheat oven to 350°F. In a large skillet, heat oil over medium heat. Add onion and bell pepper and cook, stirring occasionally, until softened, 3 to 5 minutes.

2. In a medium bowl, mix corn, cornmeal, cumin, eggs, evaporated milk, salt, and pepper. Stir in cooked onion and peppers. Transfer to a buttered 8-inch square baking dish.

3. Bake about 45 minutes, or until set and golden on top. Sprinkle with Parmesan cheese. Cut into squares and serve.

284   SKILLET CORN WITH EPAZOTE
Prep: 8 minutes   Cook: 3 to 5 minutes   Serves: 3 to 4

Fresh corn kernels cooked briefly in butter and tossed with hot peppers and epazote is called *esquites* in Mexico. Serve with grilled meats or saucy enchiladas. If you cannot find epazote in your market, cilantro or basil can be substituted, although the flavor will not be authentic.

4 large ears of fresh corn	1 tablespoon chopped epazote
3 tablespoons unsalted butter	½ teaspoon salt
1 fresh jalapeño pepper, seeded and cut into ⅛-inch strips	

Cut corn kernels from cobs. In a large skillet, melt butter over medium heat. Add corn and cook, stirring frequently, until tender, 3 to 5 minutes. Add jalapeño, epazote, and salt. Serve hot.

285   CHILI-COATED POTATOES
Prep: 10 minutes   Cook: 17 to 18 minutes   Serves: 4

These terra-cotta–hued potatoes taste great with almost any meat or chicken. They reheat successfully, so make them ahead for extra convenience.

3 tablespoons vegetable oil
1½ tablespoons chili powder
¾ teaspoon ground cumin
¼ cup tomato puree
1½ tablespoons cider vinegar

1 teaspoon salt
6 medium red or white
  potatoes
3 tablespoons unsalted butter

1. In a small skillet, heat oil over medium-low heat. Add chili powder, cumin, and tomato puree. Cook, stirring, 1 minute. Stir in vinegar and ½ teaspoon of salt. Remove from heat and set aside.

2. In a large saucepan of boiling water, cook potatoes until barely tender when pierced with tip of a sharp knife, about 10 minutes. Drain and rinse under cold running water to cool. Peel potatoes and cut into ½-inch dice.

3. In a large nonstick skillet or flameproof casserole, melt butter over medium heat. Add diced potatoes and remaining ½ teaspoon salt. Cook, stirring frequently, until potatoes are tender, about 5 minutes. Add reserved chili mixture and cook, stirring, to coat potatoes and heat through, 1 to 2 minutes.

286   HOMINY AND THREE-ONION SAUTE
Prep: 8 minutes   Cook: 7 to 10 minutes   Serves: 6

A taste-enhancing way to prepare common and often underrated hominy. The stark white variety looks great alongside rich red chile-sauced dishes. It's particularly good with mole and other saucy Mexican meat dishes.

2 tablespoons unsalted butter
½ white onion, finely chopped
3 shallots, finely chopped
2 (15-ounce) cans white
  hominy, rinsed well and
  drained

½ cup chicken broth
4 scallions, finely chopped
⅛ teaspoon pepper
  Salt (optional)

1. In a large flameproof casserole, melt butter over medium-high heat. Add onion and shallots and cook until softened, about 2 minutes.

2. Add hominy and chicken broth. Bring to a boil, reduce heat to medium, and cook until liquid is reduced to about 1 tablespoon, 5 to 8 minutes. Remove from heat. Stir in scallions and pepper. Season with salt to taste.

287 FRESH PEAS WITH CHORIZO

Prep: 5 minutes   Cook: 5 to 6 minutes   Serves: 4

Fresh peas are patiently shelled by Indian women, while sitting and chatting in the marketplace. Customers appear and buy any amount desired. The shelling, and selling, goes on until the seller's supply is gone. Barely cooked fresh peas served with spicy chorizo is a treat.

3 cups shelled fresh peas, or 2 (10-ounce) packages frozen	½ pound chorizo sausage, casings removed 2 scallions, thinly sliced

1. In a large saucepan of boiling water, cook fresh peas over medium-high heat until barely tender, 1 to 2 minutes. Thaw frozen peas but do not cook. Drain and cool under cold running water; drain well.

2. In a large skillet, cook chorizo over medium heat, breaking up lumps as it cooks, until browned and cooked through, about 3 minutes. Add peas and scallions. Stir gently to combine. Cook until heated through, about 1 minute. Serve at once.

288 HACIENDA POTATOES WITH POBLANO PEPPER STRIPS

Prep: 15 minutes   Cook: 12 to 18 minutes   Serves: 4

In Mexico, thin strips of poblano chile pepper are called *rajas*, and this rustic fried potato dish is called *papas fritas con rajas*. It's appropriate for breakfast, brunch, or barbecues. It's one of the favorites among cooks all over Mexico. Most often, the peppers are roasted and peeled, but not in this recipe.

3 tablespoons vegetable oil 1 medium white onion, halved and cut into ¼-inch slices 4 medium red potatoes (about 2 pounds), scrubbed, halved lengthwise, and sliced ¼ inch thick	½ teaspoon salt ¼ teaspoon freshly ground pepper 2 large poblano peppers, seeded, deveined, and cut into ¼-inch-wide strips

In a large nonstick skillet, heat oil over medium-high heat. Add onion and cook until softened, 2 to 3 minutes. Add potatoes, salt, and pepper. Cook, tossing, until potatoes begin to brown, 3 to 5 minutes. Add poblano pepper strips, reduce heat to medium-low, cover, and cook, stirring occasionally, until potatoes are tender and lightly browned, 7 to 10 minutes. Serve hot or at room temperature.

289 GOLDEN PLANTAINS
Prep: 10 minutes   Cook: 3 minutes   Serves: 4

Plantains are similar to bananas in looks and taste, but they are very starchy and are always cooked before eating. When ready to eat, the thick skin should be nearly black and a bit soft to the touch. Peeled, sliced, and sautéed, plantains turn a lovely golden color. They're often served with rice dishes and black beans.

2 large ripe plantains	1 tablespoon butter
2 tablespoons vegetable oil	¼ teaspoon salt

Peel plantains and cut on an angle into elongated ovals about ⅜ inch thick. In a large skillet, heat oil and butter over medium-low heat. Add plantain slices and cook, turning 2 to 3 times, until golden brown, about 3 minutes. Season with salt and serve warm.

290 POTATO PATTIES
Prep: 8 minutes   Cook: 12 minutes   Serves: 6

Oaxaca-style potato patties are easy to manage using instant mashed potatoes. Serve with Salsa Fresca Mexicana (page 84) as a first course or side dish.

½ cup milk	3 tablespoons grated
1 tablespoon butter	Parmesan or Romano
¼ teaspoon salt	cheese
1½ cups instant potato buds	⅛ teaspoon pepper
1 egg, lightly beaten	3 to 4 tablespoons corn oil

1. In a medium saucepan, combine milk, butter, salt, and 1 cup water. Heat to boiling. Remove from heat and stir in dried potatoes until evenly moistened. Transfer to a medium bowl and let stand about 2 minutes, until slightly cooled. Add beaten egg and quickly beat in with a fork until well blended. Stir in cheese and pepper.

2. In a large nonstick skillet, heat 2 tablespoons oil. Take about 2 heaping tablespoons potato mixture and form with your hands into a round patty about 2 inches across and ½ inch thick. Cook patties, in batches without crowding, turning once, until golden brown on both sides, about 2 minutes on each side. Repeat until all are cooked, adding more oil as needed. Transfer to a warm platter and serve hot.

291 POTATO CASSEROLE WITH ONIONS AND CHEESE

Prep: 20 minutes   Cook: 35 to 45 minutes   Serves: 4

3 tablespoons olive oil
½ medium onion, minced
4 large russet potatoes (about 3 pounds), peeled and cut into ¾-inch dice
1 teaspoon dried oregano
1 teaspoon ground cumin
½ teaspoon salt
¼ teaspoon freshly ground pepper

¾ cup reduced-sodium chicken broth
¾ cup heavy cream
4 scallions, cut into 1-inch pieces
1 cup shredded Monterey Jack or Cheddar cheese (4 ounces)

1. Preheat oven to 350°F. In a large saucepan, heat oil over medium heat. Add onion and cook, stirring frequently, until translucent, about 3 minutes. Add potatoes, oregano, cumin, salt, and pepper. Cook, stirring, 2 minutes. Stir in broth, cream, and scallions. Bring to a boil. Transfer contents to a 2- to 3-quart ovenproof casserole.

2. Sprinkle cheese over top of casserole. Bake, uncovered, 30 to 40 minutes, or until potatoes are tender and sauce is bubbling. Serve hot.

292 JICAMA STICKS WITH PARSLEY

Prep: 10 minutes   Cook: 3 to 5 minutes   Serves: 4 to 6

Jicama is nearly always served raw, but it takes to quick skillet cooking very well and makes a surprising accompaniment with grilled meats and poultry.

1 medium jicama (about 1½ pounds), peeled
3 tablespoons unsalted butter

½ teaspoon salt
¼ teaspoon pepper
1½ tablespoons minced parsley

1. Cut jicama into slices about ⅜ inch thick. Stack slices and cut into thin strips about ⅜ inch wide and 2 inches long, resembling thin French fries.

2. In a large skillet, melt butter over medium-high heat. Add jicama and cook, stirring frequently, until just limp, 3 to 5 minutes. Stir in salt, pepper, and parsley. Serve hot.

293   SWEET POTATO PANCAKES
Prep: 12 minutes   Cook: 15 minutes   Makes: about 12

A side dish of these yummy golden pancakes looks and tastes fabulous.

1 medium sweet potato or yam (about ¾ pound), shredded	¼ teaspoon ground cinnamon
	½ teaspoon salt
3 scallions, finely chopped	¼ teaspoon freshly ground pepper
1 jalapeño pepper, seeded and minced	2 eggs, beaten
⅓ cup flour	¼ cup vegetable oil

1. Preheat oven to 200°F. In a large bowl, combine shredded sweet potato, scallions, jalapeño pepper, flour, cinnamon, salt, and pepper. Add beaten eggs and mix well. Batter will be coarse and moist.

2. In a large cast-iron or nonstick skillet, heat 2 tablespoons of oil over medium heat. Add a scant ¼ cup batter and press out with a spoon to form a 3-inch pancake. Cook, in batches, turning once or twice, until pancakes are brown with crisp edges, about 5 minutes. Drain on paper towels and keep warm in oven while cooking remaining pancakes. Add additional oil to pan, as needed to prevent sticking.

NOTE: *Pancake batter can be made ahead, covered, and refrigerated several hours or overnight. Stir to recombine before using.*

294   YELLOW SQUASH RINGS
Prep: 8 minutes   Cook: 4½ to 5½ minutes   Serves: 4

6 medium yellow zucchini or crookneck squash	½ teaspoon dried oregano
2 tablespoons olive oil	1 scallion, thinly sliced
1 garlic clove, minced	½ teaspoon salt
	Freshly ground pepper

1. Slice squash into rounds ¼ inch thick. Cut center from each round with a circle canape cutter, melon baller, or paring knife. (Save centers for soup or toss into salad.)

2. In a large skillet, heat olive oil over medium heat. Add squash rings, garlic, and oregano. Cook, tossing frequently, until squash is crisp-tender, 4 to 5 minutes. Add scallion, salt, and pepper. Toss 30 seconds and serve.

295 STUFFED SPAGHETTI SQUASH
Prep: 25 minutes   Cook: 53 minutes   Serves: 6

American spaghetti squash goes Mexican here with great results.

1 (4-pound) spaghetti squash
3 tablespoons olive oil
1 medium onion, minced
1 teaspoon dried oregano
1 (14½-ounce) can ready-cut
   salsa tomatoes

2 tablespoons bottled picante
   sauce
½ cup sour cream
2 cups shredded jalapeño
   Monterey Jack cheese
   (8 ounces)

1. Cut squash in half lengthwise. Remove seeds. In a large flameproof casserole, bring 2 inches water to a boil. Add squash, cut side down, cover, and cook 20 minutes, or until tender. Remove squash from pan. With a fork, remove squash strands, put in a large bowl, and reserve. Save squash shells.

2. Preheat oven to 375°F. In a medium skillet, heat oil over medium heat. Add onion and cook, stirring occasionally, until softened, about 3 minutes. Add to bowl with squash strands. Add oregano, tomatoes, picante sauce, sour cream, and 1½ cups of shredded cheese. Stir to mix well. Spoon mixture into reserved squash shells. Sprinkle remaining cheese evenly over tops.

3. Bake 30 minutes, or until squash is heated through and cheese is melted. Serve hot.

296 ZUCCHINI WITH CORN AND CREAM
Prep: 8 minutes   Cook: 9 to 13 minutes   Serves: 4

Calabacitas con crema, as this mild creamy dish is called, is a frequently served vegetable side dish.

2 tablespoons unsalted butter
½ medium onion, quartered
   and sliced
4 medium zucchini (about
   1 pound), cut into ½-inch
   dice
½ teaspoon salt

¼ teaspoon pepper
1 cup corn kernels, fresh or
   thawed frozen
1 (4-ounce) can diced green
   chiles
½ cup heavy cream

1. In a large skillet, melt butter over medium heat. Add onion and cook, stirring, until it begins to brown, 3 to 5 minutes. Add zucchini, salt, and pepper. Stir to combine. Cover and cook, stirring frequently, until zucchini is barely tender, 3 to 5 minutes.

2. Add corn and diced green chiles. Cook, uncovered, stirring, until corn is tender, about 2 minutes. Stir in cream and bring to a boil, about 1 minute. Serve hot.

297   ZUCCHINI PANCAKES

Prep: 12 minutes   Cook: 4 to 6 minutes   Makes: about 8

In Mexican homes, vegetable fritters, really flat pancakes, are served often, though they're seldom seen in restaurants. Serve with grilled and roasted meats.

2 **cups shredded zucchini**	2 **eggs, beaten with a fork**
(about ½ pound)	1 **serrano pepper, minced**
½ **cup flour**	1 **tablespoon vegetable oil**
1 **teaspoon baking powder**	1 **tablespoon unsalted butter**
½ **teaspoon salt**	

1. Place shredded zucchini in a medium bowl and cover with paper towels. Press down to absorb some of moisture. In another medium bowl, mix flour, baking powder, and salt. Add eggs, serrano pepper, and shredded zucchini to flour and mix well.

2. In a large nonstick skillet, heat oil and butter over medium-high heat. For each pancake, spoon about 2 heaping tablespoons zucchini batter into pan and spread to about 3 inches in diameter. Cook in batches 2 to 3 minutes on each side, or until lightly browned. Serve hot.

298   ZUCCHINI, CORN, AND POTATOES WITH HAM

Prep: 20 minutes   Cook: 11 to 15 minutes   Serves: 6

3 **medium zucchini, cut into**	½ **cup chopped smoked ham,**
½-inch dice	**such as Black Forest**
3 **medium red potatoes,**	3 **scallions, chopped**
peeled and cut into	2 **tablespoons chopped**
½-inch dice	**cilantro or parsley**
1 **cup corn kernels, fresh or**	½ **teaspoon salt**
frozen	⅛ **teaspoon pepper**
2 **tablespoons butter**	

1. In a large pan of boiling water, cook zucchini until barely tender, 2 to 3 minutes. Scoop out with a strainer or slotted spoon, drain, and rinse under cold running water. Add potatoes to same pot of boiling water and cook until barely tender, 4 to 6 minutes. Scoop out potatoes and drain. Add corn to pot and cook 1 minute. Drain and rinse briefly under cold running water; drain well.

2. In a large skillet, melt butter over medium heat. Add ham and scallions and cook, stirring, until sizzling, about 1 minute. Add zucchini, potatoes, and corn. Cook, stirring frequently, until completely heated through, 3 to 4 minutes. Stir in cilantro, salt, and pepper. Serve hot.

299   ZESTY ZUCCHINI
Prep: 10 minutes   Cook: 4 minutes   Serves: 4

Quickly cooked zucchini is given extra zip with a slug of salsa.

2 tablespoons olive oil
4 medium zucchini, cut into
   ½-inch dice
2 scallions, cut into ½-inch
   lengths

2 garlic cloves, minced
¼ cup bottled red salsa
   Dash of salt
2 tablespoons queso fresco or
   grated Romano cheese

1. In a large skillet, heat oil over medium heat. Add zucchini, scallions, and garlic. Cook, stirring, until zucchini is crisp-tender, about 3 minutes.

2. Add salsa and salt and cook 1 minute. Transfer to a warm serving bowl. Sprinkle cheese on top and serve.

300   SAVORY ZUCCHINI PUDDING
Prep: 20 minutes   Cook: 38 to 43 minutes   Serves: 6

Vegetable puddings are often served in Mexican homes. This one is ideal as a side dish with sauced meat dishes.

¼ cup flour
¼ cup yellow cornmeal
1 teaspoon baking powder
2 tablespoons vegetable oil
½ medium onion, finely
   chopped
1 garlic clove, minced
1 pound zucchini, rinsed and
   cut into ¼-inch dice

1 jalapeño pepper, seeded and
   minced
½ teaspoon salt
2 eggs
½ cup milk
½ cup sour cream
½ cup shredded Monterey Jack
   cheese, lightly packed

1. Preheat oven to 350°F. In a small bowl, combine flour, cornmeal, and baking powder. Blend well. Set dry ingredients aside.

2. In a large skillet, heat oil over medium heat. Add onion and garlic, and cook, stirring, 1 minute. Add zucchini, jalapeño pepper, and salt. Cook, stirring, until onion is softened and zucchini skin appears bright green, about 2 minutes. Remove pan from heat.

3. In a large bowl, beat eggs until blended. Mix in milk, sour cream, and cheese. Add reserved dry ingredients and blend well. Add zucchini mixture and mix well. Scrape into a buttered 9-inch square dish.

4. Bake in middle of oven 35 to 40 minutes, or until pudding is set and a cake tester comes out clean. Cut into squares and serve hot.

Chapter 11

Eggs Are *Huevos* in Spanish

Mexican egg dishes, exceptionally interesting, are among the best egg dishes anywhere in the world, and they deserve a special place in your meal planning. Because they are so versatile, you can consider them for breakfast, brunch, lunch, or as an economical and nutritious light supper.

In Mexican cooking, eggs are generally combined with spicy sauces of tomatoes, onions, and chile peppers, and are often served with tortillas. Refried beans sprinkled with crumbly white cheese usually appear with egg dishes. This chapter contains recipes for popular and familiar dishes, such as Huevos Rancheros, and Breakfast Burritos with Scrambled Eggs and Beans, and some lesser known egg specialties like Eggs Motul Style and Scrambled Eggs with Cactus Strips. For a really fast and delicious morning surprise, try Sunrise Chilaquiles.

If your egg intake is limited, make the most of your allowance and enjoy eggs Mexican style.

---

301 BREAKFAST BURRITOS WITH SCRAMBLED EGGS AND BEANS

Prep: 15 minutes   Cook: 10 minutes   Serves: 4

1 (15-ounce) can spicy refried beans
2 tablespoons butter
6 eggs, lightly beaten
½ cup bottled green salsa
2 scallions, chopped

4 (10-inch) flour tortillas
1 cup shredded Monterey Jack cheese (4 ounces)
Sour cream or plain yogurt and salsa, as accompaniment

1. In a small saucepan, cook beans over low heat until heated through, about 5 minutes. Remove from heat and cover to keep warm.

2. In a large skillet, melt butter over medium heat. Add eggs and cook, stirring, until set, about 3 minutes. Gently stir in green salsa and scallions. Remove from heat and cover to keep warm.

3. Wrap tortillas in damp paper towels and heat in a microwave on High, about 2 minutes, or until hot. Lay 1 tortilla on a plate and spread a quarter of beans over surface. Top with a quarter of eggs and ¼ cup of cheese. Roll up to enclose filling. Repeat with remaining tortillas, beans, eggs, and cheese. Serve burritos, seam side down, garnished with sour cream and additional salsa.

302 HUEVOS RANCHEROS
Prep: 15 minutes   Cook: 18 to 20 minutes   Serves: 4

Mexico's best known egg dish and one of the world's tastiest egg preparations. The sauce can be made ahead and reheated.

¼ cup vegetable oil	⅛ teaspoon pepper
1 medium onion, chopped	4 corn tortillas
2 large tomatoes, peeled and	4 eggs
finely chopped	¼ cup crumbled queso fresco
1 serrano pepper, minced	or feta cheese
1 tablespoon chopped cilantro	2 cups refried beans, canned
½ teaspoon salt	or homemade

1. In a medium saucepan, heat 2 tablespoons of oil over medium heat. Add onion and cook until it begins to brown, 3 to 5 minutes. Add chopped tomatoes, serrano pepper, cilantro, ¼ teaspoon of salt, and pepper. Bring to a boil, reduce heat to low, cover, and simmer 10 minutes.

2. While sauce cooks, heat remaining 2 tablespoons oil in a large nonstick skillet over medium heat. Add tortillas 1 at a time and cook about 20 seconds on each side, or until soft and hot. Drain on paper towels.

3. In same skillet, cook eggs sunny-side up. Season with remaining ¼ teaspoon salt. Place 1 tortilla on each of 4 plates. Top each tortilla with 1 cooked egg. Spoon hot tomato sauce over each serving. Sprinkle crumbled cheese on top. Add hot refried beans to each plate and serve.

303 MEXICAN SCRAMBLED EGGS
Prep: 10 minutes   Cook: 3 to 4 minutes   Serves: 4

Traditional Mexican scrambled eggs, with tomatoes and chiles, are served up for breakfast all over Mexico. Refried beans of any color are usually served on the side.

8 eggs	2 tablespoons chopped green
2 tablespoons butter or	bell pepper
vegetable oil	½ medium onion, chopped
2 small tomatoes, seeded and	1 tablespoon chopped cilantro
cut into ¼-inch dice	½ teaspoon salt
2 serrano peppers, minced	⅛ teaspoon pepper

1. In a medium bowl, beat eggs with a fork until blended.

2. In a large nonstick skillet, heat butter or oil over medium heat. Add beaten eggs and cook, stirring to scramble, until almost set but still moist, about 1 minute.

3. Working quickly, add tomatoes, serrano peppers, bell pepper, onion, cilantro, salt, and pepper. Cook, stirring gently, until eggs are set and ingredients are heated through, 1 to 2 minutes. Serve at once.

304 BAKED EGGS WITH BLACK BEANS AND TOMATO SAUCE

Prep: 10 minutes   Cook: 11 to 13 minutes   Serves: 4

Don't wait for breakfast or brunch to enjoy this great egg dish. It fits any meal of the day and is easy enough to make for solitary dining.

1 cup cooked black beans, canned or homemade, drained but not rinsed
2 cups canned chopped tomatoes with juices
½ teaspoon ground cumin
½ teaspoon dried oregano

1 tablespoon bottled picante salsa
4 scallions, chopped
4 eggs
¼ teaspoon salt
2 tablespoons chopped cilantro or parsley

1. Preheat oven to 375°F. Grease 4 individual ovenproof ramekins or a 9-inch square baking dish. In a medium saucepan, cook beans, tomatoes, cumin, oregano, and salsa over medium heat, 3 minutes, stirring occasionally. Stir in scallions.

2. Divide tomato-bean mixture evenly among 4 ramekins or casserole. With back of a tablespoon make a shallow depression in sauce for eggs. Gently break eggs, 1 at a time, and drop into depressions. Season with salt. Cover pans with aluminum foil.

3. Bake 8 to 10 minutes, until white of eggs is set. Sprinkle with chopped cilantro and serve.

305 SUNRISE CHILAQUILES

Prep: 10 minutes   Cook: 9 to 12 minutes   Serves: 4

4 corn tortillas
3 tablespoons vegetable oil
1 small green bell pepper, cut into ¼-inch dice
3 scallions, chopped
6 eggs, lightly beaten

½ teaspoon salt
¾ cup thick and chunky bottled salsa
1 cup shredded Monterey Jack cheese (4 ounces)

1. Cut tortillas into 1-inch pieces. In a large nonstick skillet, heat oil over medium-high heat. Add tortilla pieces and fry until lightly browned and almost crisp, 3 to 4 minutes.

2. Add bell pepper and scallions. Cook, stirring, until pepper is softened, 2 to 3 minutes. Stir in beaten eggs and salt. Cook, stirring to scramble, until set, 2 to 3 minutes.

3. Stir in salsa. Cook 2 minutes. Remove from heat. Divide among 4 serving plates. Top each serving of chilaquiles with ¼ cup shredded cheese and serve at once.

306   EGGS WITH CHORIZO JALISCO STYLE
Prep: 10 minutes   Cook: 9 to 11 minutes   Serves: 4

¾ pound chorizo sausage,
  removed from casings
4 corn tortillas
2 tablespoons vegetable oil
4 eggs
½ cup shredded Monterey Jack
  cheese

1 avocado, peeled and cut into
  8 slices
Salsa Fresca Mexicana
  (page 84)

1. In a medium skillet, cook chorizo over medium heat, breaking meat up as it cooks, until browned and completely done, about 5 minutes. Set aside.

2. In a dry large nonstick skillet, warm tortillas over medium heat, 1 at a time, turning, 15 to 20 seconds, or until soft and warm. Wrap in a kitchen towel to keep warm and prevent drying out.

3. In same nonstick skillet, heat oil over medium heat. Gently crack eggs into skillet and cook sunny-side up or over easy, 2 to 3 minutes. Place 1 tortilla on each of 4 plates. Divide chorizo evenly over tortillas. Place 1 egg on each tortilla. Sprinkle each with a quarter of cheese. Garnish with avocado slices. Serve with fresh salsa.

307   SCRAMBLED EGGS WITH CACTUS STRIPS
Prep: 5 minutes   Cook: 5 to 6 minutes   Serves: 2 to 3

Cactus strips, called *nopalitos*, are available in the Mexican section of most supermarkets. They combine well with soft scrambled eggs.

2 tablespoons butter or
  margarine
¾ cup nopalitos, drained and
  rinsed
2 tablespoons minced onion

4 eggs, lightly beaten
¼ teaspoon salt
Dash of pepper
½ cup prepared red salsa

1. In a medium skillet, melt butter over medium heat. Add cactus and onion and cook, stirring, until onion is softened and translucent, about 3 minutes.

2. Add beaten eggs, salt, and pepper. Mix gently to combine. Cook, lifting and turning mixture, until eggs are cooked through but still moist, 2 to 3 minutes.

3. Divide eggs among 4 plates and top each with 2 tablespoons salsa. Serve at once.

308   MEXICAN OMELET
Prep: 8 minutes   Cook: 3 minutes   Serves: 1

2 extra-large eggs
2 tablespoons milk
⅛ teaspoon salt
1 tablespoon butter or
  margarine
1 tablespoon minced green
  bell pepper

1 scallion, minced
¼ cup shredded Cheddar or
  Monterey Jack cheese
Prepared salsa, sour cream,
  and chopped cilantro

1. In a small bowl, beat eggs, milk, and salt with a fork until blended. In an 8-inch nonstick skillet, heat butter over medium-high heat. Pour in eggs and spread evenly over bottom of skillet. Cook 1 minute. Tilt pan and lift edges of omelet to let uncooked egg run underneath. Cook 1 minute longer, or until top is almost set.

2. Top omelet with green pepper, scallion, and cheese. Fold omelet in half and cook until cheese is melted, about 1 minute. Slide omelet onto a warm plate. Top with salsa, sour cream, and cilantro. Serve.

309   SCRAMBLED EGGS WITH GREEN SAUCE
Prep: 15 minutes   Cook: 7 to 8 minutes   Serves: 4

Mexicans have a way with eggs, and this dish is one of my favorites. Serve with crisp tortilla chips.

1 (12-ounce) can tomatillos,
  drained and rinsed
¼ cup prepared spicy green
  salsa
¾ cup canned reduced-sodium
  chicken broth
¼ cup loosely packed cilantro
  leaves

½ teaspoon ground cumin
½ teaspoon dried oregano
½ teaspoon sugar
1 tablespoon vegetable oil
1 tablespoon butter
6 eggs, lightly beaten
¼ teaspoon salt
  Pinch of black pepper

1. In a blender or food processor, place tomatillos, salsa, chicken broth, cilantro, cumin, oregano, and sugar. Puree until smooth. Transfer to a nonreactive medium saucepan and cook, over medium heat, stirring frequently, until slightly thickened, about 5 minutes. Remove from heat and set green sauce aside.

2. In a large nonstick skillet, heat oil and butter over medium heat. Add eggs, salt, and pepper. Scramble eggs, pushing them into clumps as they cook, until just set, 1 to 2 minutes. With a large spoon, remove curds of eggs from skillet and place on a plate.

3. Pour reserved green sauce into same skillet and bring to a boil over medium heat. Reduce heat to low, spoon eggs back into sauce, and cook until heated through, 45 seconds to 1 minute. Serve at once.

310   SCRAMBLED EGGS WITH CHORIZO
Prep: 5 minutes   Cook: 5 minutes   Serves: 4

Purchase a good-quality Mexican chorizo or other spicy sausage to prepare this authentic egg dish. Serve with pan-browned potatoes and guacamole for an easy, hearty, and memorable meal.

½ pound chorizo sausage
8 eggs, lightly beaten

3 scallions, chopped
1 tablespoon chopped cilantro

1. Remove casing from chorizo. In a large nonstick skillet, cook chorizo over medium-low heat, breaking meat into bits as it cooks, until browned, about 3 minutes. Pour off excess fat, leaving about 1 tablespoon in skillet.

2. Add beaten eggs and scallions. Cook, stirring to scramble, until eggs are cooked as desired, about 2 minutes. Sprinkle with cilantro and serve at once.

311   EGGS MOTUL STYLE
Prep: 5 minutes   Cook: 7 to 9 minutes   Serves: 4

This is an easy version of a popular Yucatán egg dish that appears on restaurant menus all over the region. It's a satisfying meal of beans, eggs, ham, and peas served on a crisp tortilla and topped with a spicy tomato sauce. It's a wonderful dish for a brunch or late breakfast. I like to accompany it with Golden Plantains (page 206).

1 (16-ounce) can black beans, drained and rinsed
1 cup canned ready-cut salsa tomatoes
8 prepared crisp tostadas
3 tablespoons vegetable oil
8 eggs

Salt and freshly ground pepper
Roasted Tomato Sauce (page 95)
1 cup finely diced cooked ham, about 4 ounces
1 cup frozen peas, thawed and at room temperature

1. In a food processor, place black beans and tomatoes. Pulse to a coarse puree, 6 to 8 times. Transfer to a medium nonreactive saucepan and heat over medium heat, stirring, until heated through, about 3 minutes.

2. On each of 4 plates, lay 2 crisp tostadas, side by side, overlapping slightly.

3. In a large nonstick skillet, heat 1½ tablespoons oil over medium-high heat. Cook 4 eggs, sunny-side up, to desired doneness, 2 to 3 minutes. Season to taste with salt and pepper. Repeat with remaining oil and eggs.

4. Spread about ¼ cup bean and tomato puree on each tostada. Spoon 2 to 3 tablespoons tomato sauce on top of the beans. Place a cooked egg in center of each tostada. Drizzle another 2 tablespoons tomato sauce over each serving and garnish with ham and peas. Serve at once.

Chapter 12

From a Mexican Oven

In Mexico, every village and city neighborhood has a bakery, called a *panadería*, with a professional baker whose skills are highly respected. The bakery supplies the daily breads, rolls, and sweets for virtually all the households, since very little baking takes place in the home. Fresh hot breads and other baked sweets are turned out several times each day, and people time their buying carefully to ensure the freshness of their purchase.

This chapter gives recipes for a few delicious baked goods, both sweet and savory, that fit perfectly into Mexican meal planning. The recipes are easy and will add another special touch to your Mexican table.

Delicious French rolls, called *bolillos*, introduced by the French, are found all over the country, and they are undoubtedly among the best rolls baked anywhere in the world. The bolillo recipe in this book is a quick interpretation of the real thing, and it works very well when making tasty Mexican sandwiches, called *tortas*, or open-face bean sandwiches, called *molletes*. They are also split, buttered, and toasted for breakfast, and frequently served in baskets to eat with a meal.

Biscuits are popular morning food, and there are two recipes for the kinds of biscuits I've encountered in Mexico. Muffins and quick breads are not common, except in our American Southwest, where they're often served. They are a great addition to Mexican breakfasts and brunches. The ones in this chapter feature native ingredients.

Mexican cookies are wonderful. They can be enjoyed with a cup of coffee or hot chocolate for a morning or afternoon break, just as the Mexicans do. These cookies can also be served with fresh fruit or ice cream for dessert.

If there is an opportunity to visit a Mexican bakery, you'll find a huge array of tempting sweets and aromatic breads fresh from the oven. It's traditional to serve yourself. Pick up a tray and a pair of tongs from the counter and make your selections as you stroll by the displays. The custom of shopping for the daily bread in Mexico is a joy. No wonder this work is happily left to the professional baker and seldom done at home.

312   TROPICAL BANANA BREAD

Prep: 20 minutes   Cook: 1 hour   Makes: 2 loaves

Several varieties of bananas grow in tropical Mexico. For best flavor, select well-ripened but still yellow-skinned bananas for this bread. Serve it for breakfast or brunch, or as a snack with coffee.

2 cups mashed ripe bananas (about 3 large)	Pinch of grated nutmeg
1 cup sugar	¼ teaspoon salt
2 eggs, lightly beaten	2 tablespoons frozen orange
1 stick (4 ounces) butter, melted and cooled	juice concentrate, thawed
2 cups flour	1 tablespoon milk
1 teaspoon baking powder	½ teaspoon vanilla extract
1 teaspoon baking soda	1 cup chopped pecans (about 4 ounces)

1. Preheat oven to 350°F. Grease 2 loaf pans 9 x 5 x 3 inches. In a large bowl, combine mashed bananas, sugar, and eggs. Gradually add butter, mixing well. In a medium bowl, mix flour, baking powder, baking soda, nutmeg, and salt. Add to banana mixture and mix until well blended and creamy. Stir in orange juice concentrate, milk, and vanilla. Fold in pecans.

2. Spoon half of batter into each greased loaf pan. Bake 15 minutes. Reduce oven temperature to 325°F. and bake 45 minutes, or until top of bread is well browned and a skewer comes out clean when tested in center of loaves. Remove from oven to a rack and let stand 5 minutes. Turn out and let cool completely. Cut into thin slices and serve, or store in heavy-duty plastic bags up to 3 days or freeze up to 3 months.

313   QUICK-RISE BOLILLOS

Prep: 25 minutes   Rest: 45 minutes   Cook: 20 to 25 minutes
Makes: 12 rolls

Here is a no-fat, one-rise interpretation of Mexico's football-shaped rolls called *bolillos*. Because these rolls contain no fat, they turn stale quickly and are best the day baked. To store them, freeze in heavy-duty plastic bags.

1 cup lukewarm water (95°F. to 100°F.)	2 teaspoons sugar
1 package dry rapid-rise yeast	3 cups flour
	½ teaspoon salt

1. In a small bowl, combine ⅓ cup of warm water, yeast, and 1 teaspoon of sugar. Let stand about 5 minutes, or until foamy. In a food processor, place flour, salt, and remaining 1 teaspoon sugar. Pulse to blend. Add foamy yeast mixture. Put lid on processor and, with machine on, slowly pour remaining ⅔ cup lukewarm water through feed tube. Process 20 to 30 seconds, or until dough cleans side of bowl, with a few separate pieces whirling around bottom. Dough should be soft and sticky.

2. Turn dough out onto a lightly floured board and knead 10 to 12 turns. Divide into 12 equal pieces. Form each piece into a flattened football shape and pull ends to taper. Place about 2 inches apart on a large greased baking sheet. With a sharp thin-bladed knife, make a lengthwise cut about ½ inch deep on top of each roll. Cover and let rise until doubled in size, about 45 minutes.

3. While rolls are rising, preheat oven to 375°F. Bake rolls 20 to 25 minutes, or until they are golden brown and sound hollow when tapped. Let cool on a wire rack before serving.

314 MEXICAN SHORTCAKE BISCUITS
Prep: 12 minutes   Cook: 12 minutes
Makes: about 16 (3-inch) biscuits

Team these exceptionally light biscuits with fresh summer fruits for an impressive shortcake dessert, or serve them piping hot from the oven for breakfast. The biscuits served at the Marquis Reforma Hotel in Mexico City inspired this recipe.

1¾ cups flour	1 stick (4 ounces) cold
⅓ cup cornstarch	unsalted butter, cut into
1 tablespoon baking powder	pieces
¼ teaspoon baking soda	1 egg white
½ teaspoon salt	¾ cup heavy cream
Zest of 1 lime	1 teaspoon vanilla extract
2 tablespoons sugar	1 egg yolk beaten with
	1 tablespoon milk

1. Preheat oven to 425°F. In a food processor, place flour, cornstarch, baking powder, baking soda, salt, lime zest, and sugar. Pulse to combine. Add butter pieces. Process to a mealy texture. Remove contents to a large mixing bowl.

2. In a small bowl, beat egg white with a fork, then beat in cream and vanilla. Add to dough and stir until mixture clumps together. With hands, gather dough into a ball.

3. On a well-floured board, pat or roll dough into a circle about ¾ inch thick. Cut out biscuits with a 3-inch round cutter. Gather scraps and roll again. When all biscuits are cut, brush tops with egg yolk mixture. Sprinkle a pinch of additional sugar over top of each biscuit. Place biscuits on a greased baking sheet.

4. Bake about 12 minutes, or until biscuits are golden brown. Remove to a rack. Serve hot for breakfast or let cool and use for shortcakes.

315 JALAPENO CORN BREAD

Prep: 20 minutes   Cook: 25 to 30 minutes   Serves: 6

Corn bread studded with bits of fresh green jalapeño peppers is the perfect companion for soupy beans and stews.

1 cup yellow cornmeal	2 fresh jalapeño peppers,
½ cup flour	seeded and minced
2 teaspoons baking powder	2 extra-large eggs
½ teaspoon baking soda	1 cup buttermilk
½ teaspoon salt	¼ cup corn oil
1 cup shredded Cheddar	
cheese (4 ounces)	

1. Preheat oven to 350°F. Grease an 8-inch square baking pan. In a medium bowl, combine cornmeal, flour, baking powder, baking soda, and salt. Whisk gently or stir to mix very well. Stir in cheese and jalapeño peppers, tossing to mix thoroughly.

2. In another medium bowl, beat eggs with a fork until blended. Beat in buttermilk and oil. Add egg mixture to cornmeal mixture and stir to combine. Pour batter into prepared baking pan.

3. Bake in middle of oven 25 to 30 minutes, or until corn bread is golden brown around edges and a skewer inserted in center comes out clean. Let cool in pan on a rack about 5 minutes. Serve hot.

316 BLUE CORN MUFFINS

Prep: 12 minutes   Bake: 15 minutes   Makes: 12

Blue corn has been a staple in New Mexico and many regions of Mexico for centuries and is enjoying a current revival of popularity. It has an intriguing blue-gray color that gives a very interesting end product. Blue corn muffins are a wonderful change-of-pace breakfast treat and a good addition to any fiesta buffet. Purchase blue cornmeal in specialty shops and in some supermarkets.

1 egg, lightly beaten	¾ cup flour
1 cup milk	¼ cup sugar
2 tablespoons vegetable oil	1½ teaspoons baking powder
½ cup blue cornmeal	½ teaspoon salt

1. Butter 12 (2¾-inch) muffin forms or line with paper liners. Preheat oven to 400°F.

2. In a medium bowl, combine egg, milk, oil, and blue cornmeal. Mix well. Let stand 8 to 10 minutes to soften cornmeal. In another medium bowl, mix flour, sugar, baking powder, and salt. After cornmeal mixture has rested, stir well to remix and add to flour mixture. Stir thoroughly but gently to combine. Fill each muffin cup two-thirds full with batter.

3. Bake about 15 minutes, or until muffins are lightly browned and a cake tester inserted in center comes out clean. Remove from oven and let cool in pan 3 minutes. Invert onto a rack. Turn muffins right side up and serve immediately, or cool and freeze in heavy-duty plastic bags. (Reheat in a microwave or wrap in aluminum foil and reheat in a 325°F. oven about 20 minutes.)

---

317 COYOTE GINGERBREAD COOKIES

Prep: 20 minutes   Cook: 12 to 15 minutes   Makes: about 36 to 40

Dottye Rinefort, one of my recipe testers, contributed this delightful howling coyote cookie. Our cookies were cut with a 4½-inch-tall coyote cookie cutter, which can be purchased in specialty cookware shops. They're fun to serve as dessert with ice cream for a Mexican or Southwestern menu.

1 **cup molasses**	1 **teaspoon baking soda**
½ **cup packed dark brown sugar**	2 **sticks (8 ounces) unsalted butter, at room temperature**
½ **cup granulated sugar**	
4 **teaspoons ground ginger**	2 **eggs, lightly beaten**
4 **teaspoons ground cinnamon**	6 **cups flour**

1. Preheat oven to 325°F. Line a heavy baking sheet with parchment paper or aluminum foil.

2. In a 2-quart microwavable bowl, stir together molasses, brown sugar, granulated sugar, ginger, and cinnamon. Microwave on High 2 to 3 minutes, or until sugar is melted. Add baking soda and stir until mixture is light and foamy.

3. Place butter in a large mixing bowl. Add hot molasses mixture and stir well to combine. Let mixture cool slightly. Stir in beaten eggs. Using an electric mixer, add flour gradually, beating on low speed, until dough is well blended. Divide dough in half. Roll half the dough at a time ¼ inch thick. Cut with coyote cookie cutter. Repeat with remaining dough. Place cookies on lined baking sheet and bake 12 to 15 minutes, or until firm to the touch. Transfer to a rack and cool completely. Decorate as desired.

318   MEXICAN ALMOND COOKIES
Prep: 8 minutes   Chill: 2 hours   Cook: 10 to 12 minutes
Makes: about 36

This is a typical Mexican sweet to have with coffee or hot chocolate. For dessert, serve next to sorbet or with fresh fruit.

½ cup slivered blanched almonds
¾ cup sugar
1 stick (4 ounces) unsalted butter, at room temperature

1 egg
½ teaspoon grated lime or lemon zest
½ teaspoon vanilla extract
¼ teaspoon almond extract
1¼ cups flour

1. In a food processor, combine almonds and 2 tablespoons of sugar. Process until almonds are finely ground. Transfer to a bowl. Place butter and remaining sugar in processor. Process 15 seconds, or until creamy. Add egg. Process 15 seconds. Add ground almonds, lime zest, vanilla, and almond extract. Process 10 seconds. Add flour and pulse until blended, about 6 pulses. Transfer dough to a bowl, cover, and refrigerate 2 hours, until firm and cold.

2. Preheat oven to 375°F. Remove dough from refrigerator and roll into walnut-size balls, or smaller for petite cookies. Place about 1 inch apart on a large buttered baking sheet.

3. Bake 10 to 12 minutes, or until cookies are lightly browned around edges and tops are slightly rounded and still white.

319   MEXICAN CORN BREAD
Prep: 10 minutes   Cook: 30 to 35 minutes   Serves: 6

1 cup yellow cornmeal
2 teaspoons baking powder
½ teaspoon salt
1 (8½-ounce) can cream-style corn
1 (4-ounce) can chopped green chiles

1 jalapeño pepper, seeded and minced
½ cup sour cream
¼ cup vegetable oil
2 eggs, lightly beaten
1½ cups shredded Cheddar cheese (about 6 ounces)

1. Preheat oven to 350°F. Grease an 8-inch square baking pan. In a large bowl, combine cornmeal, baking powder, and salt. Stir to mix well.

2. Add corn, chiles, jalapeño pepper, sour cream, oil, eggs, and 1 cup of cheese. Stir to mix evenly. Pour into prepared pan. Sprinkle remaining ½ cup cheese on top.

3. Bake 30 to 35 minutes, or until corn bread is set in center and golden brown on top. Cut into squares and serve hot or at room temperature.

320   SOFT PUMPKIN SPICE COOKIES
Prep: 15 minutes   Cook: 15 minutes   Makes: 24

1 cup flour
1 teaspoon baking soda
½ teaspoon salt
½ teaspoon ground cinnamon
⅛ teaspoon grated nutmeg
½ teaspoon grated orange zest
⅔ cup parked dark brown
   sugar

6 tablespoons butter, softened
½ cup canned unsweetened
   solid-pack pumpkin
1 egg
1 teaspoon vanilla extract
¼ cup currants or raisins

1. Preheat oven to 375°F. In a medium bowl, combine flour, baking soda, salt, cinnamon, nutmeg, and orange zest. Mix well.

2. In a food processor, place brown sugar, butter, pumpkin, egg, and vanilla. Process 15 seconds, or until very smooth. Add flour mixture and process 5 seconds, or until combined. Transfer to a medium bowl and stir in currants. Drop dough by heaping tablespoons about 2 inches apart onto a large greased cookie sheet.

3. Bake 15 minutes, or until cookies are lightly browned and springy to the touch. Transfer to a rack and let cool completely.

321   MEXICAN WEDDING COOKIES
Prep: 15 minutes   Cook: 15 minutes   Makes: 24

It is traditional to wrap these rich buttery cookies individually in colored tissue paper with fringed edges. However you present them, they are easy to make and delicious to eat. The food processor simplifies the preparation even more.

1 stick (4 ounces) unsalted
   butter, at room
   temperature
½ cup sifted powdered sugar
   Pinch of salt

1 teaspoon vanilla extract
1 cup flour
1 cup finely chopped pecans
   (about 4 ounces)

1. Preheat oven to 375°F. In a food processor, combine butter, 3 tablespoons of powdered sugar, salt, and vanilla. Process about 10 seconds, or until creamy. Add flour and pecans. Process until well blended, about 5 seconds.

2. Transfer dough to a small bowl, and with hands, form into walnut-size balls. Place 1 inch apart on an ungreased cookie sheet.

3. Bake 15 minutes, or until cookies are lightly browned. Transfer to a wire rack. While cookies are still a bit warm, roll gently in remaining powdered sugar. Return cookies to rack to cool completely. Store in an airtight container up to 5 days, or freeze in heavy-duty plastic bags up to 3 months.

322   MERINGUES

Prep: 10 minutes   Cook: 40 to 45 minutes   Serves: 8

Every Mexican bakery offers crisp European-style meringues. They are very easy to make and are pretty filled with fruits and ice cream.

2 **egg whites**	½ **cup sugar**
⅛ **teaspoon salt**	½ **teaspoon vanilla extract**
¼ **teaspoon cream of tartar**	

1. Preheat oven to 250°F. In a medium bowl, using an electric hand mixer, beat egg whites until foamy. Add salt and cream of tartar. Beat until whites form soft peaks. Gradually beat in sugar until whites hold very stiff peaks. Beat in vanilla.

2. Drop meringue by heaping tablespoons onto a greased baking sheet to make 8 rounds 3 to 3½ inches in diameter. Wet spoon and use back to indent meringue centers to make a nest, swirling excess mixture around outer edges.

3. Bake in center of oven 40 to 45 minutes, or until meringues are dry, crisp, and very lightly colored. Let cool before using. If made ahead, store in an airtight container. If they soften, heat in a 250°F. oven about 5 minutes, or until crisp.

323   CHOCOLATE MERINGUES

Prep: 10 minutes   Bake: 3 minutes   Stand: 3 hours   Makes: 16 to 20

Light as a sigh, just as their Spanish name *suspiros* suggests, these were introduced into Mexican cuisine by Catholic nuns in Colonial times. These tiny meringues are delightful with coffee and fresh strawberries.

2 **egg whites**	½ **teaspoon ground cinnamon**
Dash of cream of tartar	½ **teaspoon vanilla extract**
⅛ **teaspoon salt**	2½ **tablespoons grated**
½ **cup sugar**	**bittersweet chocolate**

1. Heat oven to 350°F. In a medium bowl, beat egg whites until foamy. Add cream of tartar and salt. Beat to soft peaks. Beat in sugar, cinnamon, and vanilla until egg whites form stiff, shiny peaks. Fold in grated chocolate.

2. Drop heaping teaspoons of meringue from a spoon onto an ungreased cookie sheet, swirling in a circular fashion to end with a little peak in the center. Repeat until all meringues are formed. Bake 3 minutes. Turn oven off and leave meringues in oven for 3 hours. Do not open oven door.

3. Remove from oven and, with a spatula, gently remove meringues. They are very tender and break easily. Store in an airtight container.

324 CINNAMON REFRIGERATOR COOKIES
Prep: 12 minutes   Chill: 3 hours   Cook: 7 to 10 minutes
Makes: about 72

Patty Olson, of South Lake Tahoe, California, serves these crisp little cookies with fresh fruit or ice cream following a meal of spicy Mexican food.

½ cup pecan pieces
1¾ cups flour
½ teaspoon baking soda
1½ teaspoons ground cinnamon
⅛ teaspoon salt
1 stick (4 ounces) butter, softened

½ cup lightly packed dark brown sugar
½ cup granulated sugar
1 egg
½ teaspoon vanilla extract

1. In a food processor, coarsely chop pecans. Add flour, baking soda, cinnamon, and salt. Process until nuts are finely ground.

2. In a medium bowl, combine butter, brown sugar, and granulated sugar. With an electric mixer, beat about 1 minute, or until well blended. Add egg and mix until light and creamy, about 1 minute. Add flour-nut mixture and mix with a wooden spoon to make a stiff dough. Mix in vanilla. Cover and refrigerate about 30 minutes, or until firm enough to handle. Divide dough in half. Roll into cylinders about 1 inch in diameter and wrap tightly in plastic wrap. Refrigerate until very firm, at least 3 hours or overnight.

3. Preheat oven to 350°F. Slice dough into very thin cookies about ⅛ inch thick. Place on baking sheet about 1 inch apart and bake 7 to 10 minutes, or until crisp and golden brown.

325   GOLDEN CORNMEAL BISCUITS

Prep: 10 minutes   Bake: 12 minutes   Makes: about 14

Hotel Playa Mazatlán, in the resort region on the Pacific Coast of Mexico, serves terrific cornmeal biscuits every morning. These are my version of them, without the fabulous ocean view from the dining terrace. They are best served piping hot, right out of the oven.

1¾ cups flour	½ teaspoon salt
¾ cup yellow cornmeal	1 stick (4 ounces) cold butter,
1 tablespoon baking powder	cut into pieces
2 tablespoons sugar	⅔ cup milk

1. Preheat oven to 450°F. In a food processor, place flour, cornmeal, baking powder, sugar, and salt. Pulse 6 to 8 times to blend. Add butter pieces and process until mealy, about 8 seconds. With machine on, pour milk through feed tube until mixture begins to form a ball. Dough will be a bit sticky.

2. Transfer dough to a lightly floured board and form into a disk. Pat out flat, dusting both sides lightly with flour, and roll to a thickness of ½ inch. Cut with a 2½-inch round biscuit cutter. Gather scraps, roll again, and cut remaining dough into biscuits. Arrange about 1 inch apart on a large greased baking sheet.

3. Bake biscuits 12 minutes, or until golden brown. Serve hot.

Chapter 13

Desserts with a Spanish Accent

Desserts flowered in Mexico after the Spanish came with their sugar, butter, eggs, cream, and wheat flour. Before that time, fresh fruits, honey, and sweet tamales were served. Spanish nuns created many of the popular desserts of today, followed by the French, who later introduced most of the fashionable pastries.

Mexicans love sweets, and in modern Mexico there are many choices. It is quite traditional to enjoy the richest sweets with coffee, for *marienda*, which is equivalent to teatime in the late afternoon, and to eat lighter desserts following a meal. The agreeable and relaxing *marienda* custom takes place in private homes, certain cafes, and special sweet shops called *salons de té*.

This chapter is filled with a mix of delicious fruit desserts, cakes, and puddings to provide just the right finish to your Mexican menus. Some are traditional; others are more modern creations. Among the traditional desserts are puddings, such as Coffee Flan, Natillas, and Mexican Bread Pudding with Apples, Raisins, and Cheese.

Cakes are always welcome desserts, and you can't miss with Mexican Drunk Cake, Yucatán Almond Cake, or Pumpkin Pecan Torta.

For something more updated and elaborate, try Mango Soufflé or Mexican Chocolate Mousse. If the event calls for a touch of whimsy, consider Banana Burritos. Light refreshing desserts include Oranges with Tequila, Chilled Melon Balls with Wine and Fresh Mint, and Mangoes with Strawberry Sauce.

Whatever your occasion or mood, you'll find something among these traditional Mexican desserts to satisfy every sweet tooth.

326 BANANA BURRITOS
Prep: 8 minutes   Cook: 8 minutes   Serves: 4

These modernized burritos are amusing for dessert or as part of a brunch. They require some last-minute preparation, but are well worth it.

2 medium-ripe but firm bananas	½ teaspoon ground cinnamon
1 tablespoon lime juice	3 tablespoons vegetable oil
4 (7-inch) flour tortillas	1 tablespoon unsalted butter
¼ cup apricot preserves	Whipped cream and toasted pecans or fresh berries

1. Peel bananas and cut in half lengthwise. Brush with lime juice and set aside.

2. In a dry medium skillet, soften tortillas one at a time over medium heat by turning them over 2 to 3 times, until warm and limp, about 15 seconds. Place between folds of clean kitchen towel to keep warm and soft as you cook others.

3. Spread 1 tablespoon apricot preserves over each tortilla. Place a banana half across lower third of each tortilla, sprinkle with cinnamon, and roll up. Lay seam side down on a plate.

4. In a large heavy skillet, heat oil and butter over medium heat. Place rolled tortillas in hot oil, seam sides down. Brown lightly on both sides, about 1 minute per side. Transfer to individual serving plates. Serve with a dollop of whipped cream and nuts or berries.

327 MANGOES WITH STRAWBERRY SAUCE
Prep: 10 minutes   Cook: none   Serves: 4

All the goodness of fresh mangoes shines in this simple dessert. The tricky part is peeling the mangoes, as the peeled fruit is very slick to hold. Peel half of mango at a time for easier control.

2 large fresh mangoes	Whole fresh strawberries and fresh mint sprigs
1 (10-ounce) package frozen sweetened strawberries, thawed	

1. Peel half of each mango and cut fruit away from pit, cutting as close to seed as possible. Repeat with remaining mango halves. Cut each mango half into slices about ⅜ inch thick. Cover and refrigerate until shortly before serving, though no longer than 6 hours for freshest taste.

2. Puree strawberries in a blender or food processor. Strain to remove seeds, if desired. Spoon strawberry sauce equally over 4 serving plates. Arrange reserved mango slices evenly among the plates. Garnish each serving with 2 to 3 fresh strawberries and a sprig of mint.

328 CREMA DE MANGO
Prep: 15 minutes   Cook: none   Serves: 6

Eaten like a mousse, this mango cream can also be used as a topping for cakes, ice cream, or other fruits.

2 large ripe mangoes	1 tablespoon powdered sugar
1 teaspoon lemon juice	½ teaspoon vanilla extract
1 cup heavy cream	½ cup toasted pecan bits

1. Peel mangoes and cut fruit away from pit. Place in a food processor. Add lemon juice and puree until smooth.

2. In a medium bowl, whip cream until thickened. Add sugar and vanilla. Beat until stiff. Fold mango puree into whipped cream. Divide among 6 dessert bowls or stemmed glasses. Garnish with pecans. Serve at once or refrigerate up to 2 hours.

329 CHILLED MELON BALLS WITH WINE AND FRESH MINT
Prep: 15 minutes   Cook: none   Chill: 2 hours   Serves: 6

Sweet and juicy melons abound in Mexico. They are served as part of a meal or are purchased as a refreshing snack from street vendors.

1 ripe cantaloupe	1 cup seedless red grapes
½ ripe honeydew	3 tablespoons finely slivered
1 cup semidry white wine, such as Riesling or Chenin Blanc	fresh mint

1. Cut cantaloupe in half. Scrape out seeds from cantaloupe and honeydew. With a melon baller, scoop out melons and place balls in a large bowl. Save shells for presentation by scraping out remaining bits of melon. Reserve shells.

2. Add wine, grapes, and mint to melon balls. Toss, cover, and refrigerate at least 2 hours, or overnight.

3. To serve, fill reserved shells with fruit mixture and place on a large decorative platter.

330   ORANGES WITH TEQUILA

Prep: 15 minutes   Chill: 4 to 6 hours   Cook: none   Serves: 4

Bright juicy oranges make a delicious dessert following a rich meal, or serve as a starter for a festive breakfast or brunch. Fresh strawberries are a perfect garnish when in season, and a sprig of fresh mint will add just the right touch.

4 large navel oranges	1 ounce tequila
1 tablespoon superfine sugar	½ ounce Triple Sec

1. Peel oranges and remove as much white pith as possible. Cut into slices. Place sliced oranges in a medium bowl. Add sugar, tequila, and Triple Sec. Toss gently.

2. Cover with plastic wrap and refrigerate 4 to 6 hours, stirring occasionally to distribute juices. Serve cold in individual bowls with juices spooned over orange slices.

331   GLAZED PINEAPPLE WITH ORANGE-RUM SAUCE

Prep: 8 minutes   Cook: 5 to 7 minutes   Serves: 4

Fresh pineapple is abundant in Mexico and is enjoyed in some form around the clock. Serve this appealing dessert alone or topped with a scoop of ice cream.

1 cup fresh orange juice	¼ cup sugar
2 tablespoons dark rum	8 rings of fresh pineapple, cut
1 tablespoon honey	about ½ inch thick

1. In a small bowl, combine orange juice, rum, and honey. Stir to mix well. Sprinkle 1 tablespoon sugar on 1 side of each pineapple slice.

2. Heat a large cast-iron skillet over high heat until hot but not smoking, about 2 minutes. Place pineapple slices, sugared side down, in pan. Cook until sugar caramelizes to a golden brown color, 2 to 3 minutes, sliding pineapple with a fork for more even browning. Turn over and pour orange juice mixture into skillet. Bring to a rolling boil, then transfer pineapple slices to individual dessert plates.

3. Boil liquid in skillet until reduced to a shiny syrup, 1 to 2 minutes. Spoon hot glaze equally over pineapple slices. Serve warm.

332 FRESH MINTED PINEAPPLE
Prep: 10 minutes   Chill: 6 hours   Cook: none   Serves: 6

A thick slice of gleaming pineapple fairly bursts with flavor after macerating overnight in a sugary mint bath. This preparation works equally well for breakfast, brunch, or dessert. Add sprigs of fresh mint and top with a berry or cherry for a very pretty presentation.

1 whole fresh pineapple	6 red maraschino cherries or
½ cup sugar	strawberries
¾ cup coarsely chopped fresh	6 sprigs of fresh mint
mint leaves	

1. Cut off top and bottom of pineapple and slice into 6 rounds about 1 inch thick, leaving husk on. Sprinkle sugar over tops of pineapple slices. Sprinkle mint evenly over slices. Stack sugared fruit to reform its shape, with mint in between slices, and place in a plastic bag. Set upright in a medium bowl and refrigerate about 6 hours, or overnight.

2. To serve, remove pineapple from plastic bag and scrape off chopped mint. Place each slice on an individual serving plate and top with a cherry or strawberry and a sprig of fresh mint. Serve with a knife and fork.

333 PLANTAINS IN CARAMEL RUM SAUCE WITH WHIPPED CREAM AND WALNUTS
Prep: 10 minutes   Cook: 4 minutes   Serves: 4

Choose ripe plantains with nearly black skin that are barely soft to the touch. They become golden when sautéed in butter and make a delicious dessert. Regular firm bananas can be substituted.

2 ripe medium plantains	¼ teaspoon ground cinnamon
4 tablespoons unsalted butter	Whipped cream and
¼ cup dark rum	chopped walnuts
3 tablespoons sugar	

1. Peel plantains and slice, on the diagonal, into ovals, about ¼ inch thick. Reserve. In a medium skillet, melt butter over medium heat and cook plantain slices until golden brown on both sides, about 3 minutes total. Transfer to a warm plate and reserve.

2. In same skillet, over medium heat, cook rum, sugar, and cinnamon about 1 minute. Spoon a quarter of sauce over each of 4 serving plates. Arrange plantains over the sauce. Garnish with whipped cream and chopped walnuts.

334   BLACKBERRY-CASSIS DESSERT SAUCE

Prep: 5 minutes   Cook: none   Stand: overnight
Makes: about 2 cups

Beautiful blackberries are grown in Mexico, and this sauce was inspired by the fresh berries I saw in January during a recent winter trip. Use whole frozen blackberries to enjoy this delicious juicy sauce any time of the year. Serve it with ice cream, sliced mangoes or peaches, or with meringues.

1 (16-ounce) bag whole frozen unsweetened blackberries	1 cup sugar ½ teaspoon vanilla extract ½ cup crème de cassis

In a large bowl, toss whole frozen blackberries with sugar, vanilla, and cassis. Cover and let thaw overnight in refrigerator. Serve cold.

335   MANGO SOUFFLE

Prep: 20 minutes   Cook: 35 to 40 minutes   Serves: 6 to 8

4 ripe mangoes ¾ cup sugar 2 tablespoons cornstarch 2 tablespoons lime juice	6 egg whites ⅛ teaspoon salt Powdered sugar

1. Preheat oven to 375°F. Generously butter a 2-quart soufflé dish and dust with sugar. Place prepared dish in refrigerator. Peel mangoes. Cut fruit from pits and place fruit in a food processor. In a small bowl, mix ½ cup of sugar with cornstarch. Add to processor along with lime juice. Puree until very smooth, 10 to 15 seconds. Transfer to a large bowl. Set mango puree aside.

2. In another large bowl, beat egg whites with salt until soft peaks form. Gradually beat in remaining ¼ cup sugar. Continue beating until stiff, shiny peaks form. Stir about 1 cup beaten egg whites into reserved mango puree to lighten. Then gently fold in remaining egg whites. Transfer to prepared soufflé dish. With your index finger, make a 1-inch deep groove all around soufflé mixture about 1 inch from rim of dish. (The soufflé can be covered and refrigerated at this point up to 1 hour before baking.)

3. Place a roasting pan on center shelf of preheated oven and add hot water to reach about a third of way up on side of soufflé dish. Put soufflé dish in hot water bath and bake 35 to 40 minutes, or until soufflé is puffed and golden brown. Serve warm or at room temperature. Soufflé will sink only a little. Dust top with sifted powdered sugar just before serving.

336 MEXICAN BREAD PUDDING WITH APPLES, RAISINS, AND CHEESE

Prep: 25 minutes   Cook: 33 to 38 minutes   Serves: 6

This classic bread pudding, called *capirotada,* is a delicious homey dessert.

1 egg
¼ cup milk
1 stick (4 ounces) butter, melted
4 cups (¾-inch) stale French bread cubes
3 ounces Cheddar cheese, cut into ¼-inch dice (about ⅔ cup)
½ cup chopped walnuts
1 teaspoon ground cinnamon

¾ cup packed dark brown sugar
½ cup raisins
1 medium apple, peeled, cored, and cut into ⅜-inch dice
½ teaspoon vanilla extract
Poor Man's Rum and Butter Sauce (recipe follows), whipped cream, or vanilla ice cream

1. Preheat oven to 350°F. In a large bowl, beat together egg, milk, and melted butter. Add bread cubes and toss to moisten evenly. Add cheese and nuts and sprinkle on cinnamon. Stir gently to combine.

2. In a medium saucepan, combine brown sugar, raisins, apple, and 1 cup water. Cook over medium heat until apple is just softened, about 3 minutes. Remove from heat and stir in vanilla.

3. Place half of bread mixture in bottom of a buttered 1½-quart casserole. Spread evenly. With a slotted spoon, lift raisins and apples from syrup and distribute over bread. Cover with remaining bread mixture. Pour syrup evenly over surface. With back of a wooden spoon, press bread mixture to soak with syrup.

4. Bake 30 to 35 minutes, or until top is lightly browned and pudding is set. Serve warm with rum sauce, whipped cream, or vanilla ice cream.

POOR MAN'S RUM AND BUTTER SAUCE

Prep: 3 minutes   Cook: 3 minutes   Makes: about 1½ cups

If a good dessert sauce is needed in a hurry, this is it. Serve it warm over bread pudding or simple cakes.

1 cup sugar
1½ tablespoons cornstarch
¼ cup dark rum

½ teaspoon vanilla extract
2 tablespoons butter

1. In a small saucepan, mix sugar, cornstarch, and 1 cup water. Bring to a boil over medium heat, stirring constantly, until thick and clear, about 3 minutes. Remove from heat.

2. Stir rum and vanilla into syrup. Whisk in butter. Serve sauce hot or warm. (This keeps about a week, covered and refrigerated. Reheat over medium heat or in a microwave oven.)

337 MEXICAN CHOCOLATE MOUSSE
Prep: 15 minutes   Cook: none   Chill: 2 hours   Serves: 6 to 8

6 ounces semisweet or
   bittersweet chocolate
½ cup sugar
1 teaspoon ground cinnamon
½ cup boiling water

2 extra-large eggs, separated
1 teaspoon vanilla extract
   Dash of salt
1 cup heavy cream

1. Cut chocolate into chunks and place in a food processor. Add sugar and cinnamon and process until chocolate is pulverized. With machine on, pour boiling water through feed tube. Process until chocolate is melted. With machine still on, add egg yolks and vanilla through feed tube. Process about 30 seconds, or until mixture is very smooth. Reserve in processor bowl.

2. In a medium bowl, beat egg whites with a dash of salt until stiff peaks form. In another bowl, with same beaters, beat cream until stiff. Fold chocolate mixture into beaten egg whites. Then fold in about three quarters of whipped cream. (Cover and refrigerate remaining cream for topping.) Spoon chocolate mousse into 6 to 8 dessert dishes. Cover and refrigerate until chilled and set, at least 2 hours, or up to overnight. Serve topped with remaining whipped cream.

338 PUMPKIN FLAN
*Prep: 15 minutes   Cook: 30 to 40 minutes   Chill: 6 hours
Serves: 10*

Because flan should be made one day ahead for best results, it is a great party dessert.

¾ cup sugar
1 (14-ounce) can sweetened
   condensed milk
1½ cups milk
1 cup solid-pack canned
   pumpkin
6 eggs

½ teaspoon salt
1 teaspoon ground cinnamon
¼ teaspoon ground allspice
⅛ teaspoon grated nutmeg
¼ cup dark rum
1 teaspoon vanilla extract

1. In a heavy medium skillet, cook sugar over medium heat, stirring constantly, until it melts and becomes golden brown and syrupy. Using potholders, pour syrup into a warmed 9-inch round cake pan and tilt pan around to coat bottom and about 1 inch up sides with caramel.

2. Preheat oven to 325°F. Prepare hot water bath by placing a pan large enough to hold flan baking dish on middle shelf of oven. Pour in enough hot water to reach about one third way up outside of cake pan.

3. In a large bowl, combine all remaining ingredients. Beat with an electric mixer on low speed about 1 minute until very smooth. Pour custard through a wire strainer into reserved caramelized cake pan. Set pan in prepared hot water bath in preheated oven.

4. Bake 30 to 40 minutes, or until custard is set and a thin knife comes out clean when inserted into custard center. Let cool on a rack, then refrigerate at least 6 hours, or overnight.

5. To serve, run a knife between flan and pan rim. Invert onto a serving plate to unmold. Remove pan carefully, allowing syrup to run over top of flan. Cut into wedges and serve.

---

339 COFFEE FLAN

Prep: 10 minutes   Cook: 35 to 43 minutes   Chill: 6 hours   Serves: 8

Flan is probably the best known of all Mexican desserts. The creamy custard with its distinctive caramelized sugar sauce is found throughout the country and is universally liked. *Flan de café,* or coffee-flavored flan, is one of the more popular versions. This one comes from León, in central Mexico. Its silky smooth texture and rich flavor bring a smile with the first spoonful.

1 **cup sugar**	1 **egg yolk**
1 **(14-ounce) can evaporated milk**	1 **teaspoon vanilla extract**
1 **(14-ounce) can condensed milk**	1 **teaspoon instant coffee dissolved in 1 teaspoon boiling water**
1 **cup whole milk**	2 **tablespoons brandy or rum**
5 **whole eggs**	

1. In a heavy medium saucepan, cook sugar over medium heat, stirring, until melted and golden brown, 5 to 8 minutes. Quickly pour caramelized sugar into a warm 9-inch round cake pan. Using potholders to protect hands, tip pan around to coat bottom and about 1 inch up sides with caramel. Set aside.

2. Preheat oven to 325°F. In a blender, place evaporated milk, condensed milk, whole milk, whole eggs, egg yolk, vanilla, coffee, and brandy. Mix on low speed for 1 minute. (The beating can also be done in a large bowl with a hand-held electric mixer on low speed.) Pour custard into caramel-lined cake pan. Set in a larger pan and place on middle rack of oven. Carefully pour boiling water into larger pan to a depth of 1 inch.

3. Bake, uncovered, 30 to 35 minutes, or until custard is set and a cake tester inserted in center comes out clean. Let cool on a rack, then refrigerate at least 6 hours, or overnight.

4. To serve, run a thin knife around edge of pan between custard and pan. Place a deep serving plate over pan and invert to unmold flan. Carefully lift up pan and allow golden caramelized syrup to run over top of flan. Cut into wedges to serve.

340   NATILLAS

Prep: 10 minutes   Stand: 30 minutes   Cook: 1 to 2 minutes
Serves: 6

Natillas is a creamy vanilla pudding with a Spanish background. It's a classic Mexican dessert that is found all over the country.

⅓ cup raisins	3 cups milk
¼ cup medium-dry sherry	1 teaspoon vanilla extract
¾ cup sugar	½ teaspoon ground cinnamon
3½ tablespoons cornstarch	2 eggs, separated
⅛ teaspoon salt	

1. Soften raisins in 2 tablespoons of warmed sherry for 30 minutes to 1 hour.

2. In heavy medium nonreactive pan, mix ½ cup of sugar with cornstarch, salt, egg yolks, and milk. Bring to a boil over medium heat, whisking, and continue to cook, whisking, until thickened, 1 to 2 minutes. Remove from heat and stir in remaining 2 tablespoons sherry and vanilla. Transfer to a medium bowl, cover with plastic wrap, pressing it directly on pudding surface, and put in a larger bowl of ice to hasten cooling.

3. In a medium bowl, beat egg whites to soft peaks. Add remaining ¼ cup sugar and beat until stiff and shiny. Gently fold beaten egg whites into cooled pudding. Divide pudding among dessert bowls. Drain raisins. Garnish pudding with raisins and sprinkle with a very light dusting of cinnamon. Serve at room temperature or chilled.

341   MEXICAN PINEAPPLE RICE PUDDING

Prep: 5 minutes   Cook: 35 to 42 minutes   Serves: 8 to 10

1 cup long-grain white rice	1 teaspoon vanilla extract
2 cinnamon sticks	1 (8-ounce) can crushed
3 cups milk	unsweetened pineapple
¾ cup sugar	½ cup sliced almonds, toasted
¼ teaspoon salt	if desired
3 egg yolks	

1. In a medium saucepan, bring 2 cups water to a boil over high heat. Add rice and cinnamon sticks. Reduce heat to low, cover, and simmer 18 to 20 minutes, or until rice is tender and liquid is all absorbed.

2. Stir in milk, sugar, and salt. Raise heat to medium-low and simmer, uncovered, stirring frequently, until thickened and creamy, 15 to 20 minutes. Remove cinnamon sticks.

3. In a small bowl, beat egg yolks and vanilla until blended. Beat 3 tablespoons of hot rice pudding into yolks. Then quickly stir egg yolk mixture into hot rice pudding, mixing well. Set over low heat and cook, stirring, 2 minutes. Stir in pineapple and transfer pudding to a serving bowl. Top with toasted almonds. Serve warm or cold. To serve cold, cover and refrigerate until shortly before serving.

342 MARK MILLER'S TAPIOCA TEQUILA LIME PUDDING

Prep: 10 minutes   Cook: 10 to 15 minutes   Serves: 6 to 8

A special thanks to Mark Miller, chef of Coyote Cafe, Santa Fe, New Mexico, and Red Sage Restaurant, Washington, D.C., for permission to use this recipe.

¼ cup quick tapioca	¼ cup tequila
¾ cup sugar	2 tablespoons fresh lime juice
¼ teaspoon salt	1 teaspoon grated lime zest
3 eggs, separated	Fresh mint sprigs or
2½ cups milk	strawberries

1. In a double boiler, whisk together tapioca, sugar, salt, egg yolks, and milk. Set over boiling water and cook, stirring often, until tapioca thickens, 10 to 15 minutes.

2. Remove top of double boiler and place it over a large bowl of ice cubes and water. Stir frequently, until pudding is cool, about 15 minutes. Stir in tequila, lime juice, and lime zest.

3. In a large bowl, beat reserved egg whites to soft peaks; fold into cooled tapioca. Cover and refrigerate until shortly before serving. Serve in small glass bowls, garnished with a sprig of mint or a berry or two.

343 YUCATAN ALMOND CAKE

Prep: 20 minutes   Cook: 25 to 30 minutes   Serves: 10

This flavorful cake, known as *torta de cielo,* has a lovely texture. It's not frosted and is meant to be served with fresh sliced or pureed fruit and whipped cream.

6 ounces blanched almonds	½ teaspoon salt
1 cup sugar	5 extra-large eggs, separated
½ cup flour	2 tablespoons dark rum
½ teaspoon baking powder	1 teaspoon vanilla extract

1. Preheat oven to 350°F. Butter a 9-inch springform pan. Dust with flour; tap out excess. In a food processor, finely grind almonds with sugar to a mealy consistency, about 15 seconds. Add flour, baking powder, and ¼ teaspoon salt. Pulse about 6 times until mixed.

2. In a large bowl, beat egg whites until foamy. Add remaining ¼ teaspoon salt and continue beating to stiff peaks. Add egg yolks, 1 at a time, beating on low, until yellow is incorporated. Fold in almond mixture. Gently stir in rum and vanilla. Pour batter into prepared pan.

3. Bake in center of oven 25 to 30 minutes, or until a cake tester inserted in center comes out clean. Let cool in pan on a rack about 5 minutes. Remove cake from pan and transfer to a serving plate.

344   MEXICAN CHOCOLATE CAKE WITH TOASTED ALMONDS

Prep: 25 minutes   Cook: 30 to 35 minutes   Serves: 10 to 12

Mexico gave chocolate to the world, but even today, typical native desserts do not contain chocolate. It's mainly enjoyed as a hot beverage. I developed this recipe using the tablets of Mexican chocolate that contain cinnamon, vanilla, and ground almonds. If they are not available in your market, see mail-order source on page 9.

¾ **cup flour**	3 **eggs**
1 **teaspoon baking powder**	4 **tablespoons unsalted butter,**
½ **teaspoon baking soda**	**at room temperature**
¼ **teaspoon salt**	⅓ **cup sour cream**
½ **teaspoon ground cinnamon**	1 **teaspoon vanilla extract**
4 **ounces Mexican chocolate,**	**Chocolate Icing (recipe**
chopped into pieces	**follows)**
¾ **cup sugar**	½ **cup sliced almonds**
⅓ **cup boiling water**	

1. Preheat oven to 350°F. Cut a circle of parchment or wax paper to fit bottom of a 9-inch round cake pan. Butter sides and bottom of pan. Press in paper and smooth over bottom of pan. Butter surface of paper. In a small bowl, mix flour, baking powder, baking soda, salt, and cinnamon; set aside.

2. Place chocolate pieces and sugar in a food processor. Process until chocolate is finely chopped. With machine on, pour boiling water through feed tube and process until chocolate is melted. Add eggs. Process 20 seconds. Scrape down sides of bowl. Add butter, sour cream, and vanilla. Process 20 seconds. Add reserved flour mixture and pulse 6 to 8 times, or until just mixed. Do not overprocess. Turn batter into prepared cake pan.

3. Bake in middle of oven 30 to 35 minutes, or until toothpick inserted in center comes out clean. Remove cake from oven. Let cool on rack in pan 5 minutes. Invert cake from pan onto rack to unmold. When cake is completely cool, frost with Chocolate Icing and decorate with sliced almonds.

CHOCOLATE ICING
Makes: icing for a 9-inch cake

3 **ounces semisweet or**	½ **cup sifted powdered sugar**
bittersweet chocolate, cut	3 **tablespoons unsalted butter**
into pieces	½ **teaspoon vanilla extract**

In a double boiler, combine chocolate, powdered sugar, butter, and 1 tablespoon of water. Set over—not in—simmering water and cook, stirring, until melted and smooth, about 5 minutes. Stir in vanilla. Scrape into a bowl and let cool until thickened to spreading consistency.

345 MEXICAN DRUNK CAKE
Prep: 20 minutes   Bake: 25 to 30 minutes   Serves: 12

Torta borracha, as this cake is called in Mexico, is perfect for festive occasions. Aptly named, it is liberally soused with rum syrup. Serve it with any kind of fresh berries, fruits, whipped cream, or ice cream.

1½ cups flour	1 stick (4 ounces) unsalted
1 teaspoon baking powder	butter, melted
¼ teaspoon salt	1 teaspoon vanilla extract
6 eggs, separated	Rum Syrup (recipe follows)
¾ cup sugar	

1. Preheat oven to 350°F. Butter and flour a 10-inch round cake pan. In a medium bowl, combine flour, baking powder, and salt. Stir or whisk gently until well blended.

2. In a large bowl with electric hand mixer, beat egg whites until foamy and white. Add ¼ cup of sugar and beat until soft, shiny peaks form. In a medium bowl with same beaters, beat egg yolks with remaining ½ cup sugar until thick and fluffy. Add egg yolks to beaten whites and beat on low speed just until blended, about 5 seconds. Using a rubber spatula, in 3 additions, fold flour mixture carefully into egg mixture. Drizzle melted butter and vanilla over batter and gently stir to blend ingredients into a smooth batter. Pour batter into prepared cake pan.

3. Bake 25 to 30 minutes, or until cake is very lightly browned on top and a cake tester inserted in center comes out clean.

4. Remove cake from oven and set in pan on a wire rack 5 minutes. Gradually spoon hot rum syrup over hot cake until it is all absorbed. Let cake cool to room temperature before serving.

RUM SYRUP
Makes: about 3½ cups

2 cups sugar	½ cup dark rum

In a medium saucepan, stir together sugar and 1½ cups water. Bring to a boil over medium heat, stirring to dissolve sugar. Reduce heat to medium-low and simmer 3 minutes. Remove from heat. Stir rum into hot syrup just before spooning onto cake.

346   PUMPKIN PECAN TORTA
Prep: 20 minutes   Bake: 40 to 45 minutes   Serves: 8 to 10

This light dessert comes from my good friend Peggy Ellis.

6 tablespoons flour	1 cup solid-pack canned
1 teaspoon baking powder	pumpkin
1 teaspoon ground cinnamon	½ teaspoon vanilla extract
¼ teaspoon ground allspice	½ cup ground pecans
4 eggs, separated	Sweetened whipped cream,
⅔ cup sugar	as accompaniment

1. Preheat oven to 325°F. Butter and flour a 9-inch pan with removable bottom, or a springform pan with removable rim. In a small bowl, combine flour, baking powder, cinnamon, and allspice.

2. In a medium bowl, beat egg whites until foamy. Gradually beat in 3 tablespoons of sugar; beat until stiff peaks form. In a large bowl, beat egg yolks with remaining sugar until pale, about 1 minute. Add pumpkin and vanilla and beat until well blended. Stir in flour mixture. Fold in beaten egg whites and ground pecans. Pour batter into prepared baking pan.

3. Bake 40 to 45 minutes, or until a cake tester inserted in center comes out clean. Let cake cool in pan on rack 10 minutes. Remove bottom or rim of pan. Serve with sweetened whipped cream.

---

347   SOPAIPILLAS WITH HONEY BUTTER
Prep: 10 minutes   Stand: 30 minutes   Cook: 3 minutes   Makes: 24

Almost every country has its own fried pastry. This is Mexico's version.

2 cups flour	2 cups vegetable oil, for deep-
2 teaspoons baking powder	frying
½ teaspoon salt	3 tablespoons unsalted butter,
2 tablespoons solid vegetable	melted
shortening	6 tablespoons honey
¾ cup lukewarm water	

1. In a food processor, place flour, baking powder, and salt. Pulse 3 to 4 times to mix. Add shortening and process about 10 seconds, or to a cornmeal consistency. With machine on, pour warm water through feed tube and process about 15 seconds. Mixture should form a ball. Remove dough and place in a medium bowl. Cover and let rest about 30 minutes.

2. In a large heavy saucepan or deep-fryer, heat oil over medium-high heat to 375°F. Meanwhile, on a lightly floured board, roll out dough ⅛ inch thick. Cut into 3-inch triangles. In batches without crowding, cook dough triangles, turning once, until puffed and golden brown, about 10 seconds per side. Drain on paper towels.

3. Place pastries in a napkin-lined basket. In a small pitcher, stir together melted butter and honey. Serve with sopaipillas. To eat, cut a small slit in sopaipilla and pour in warm honey butter.

348 SPICE CAKE WITH BANANA SAUCE
Prep: 10 minutes   Cook: 25 to 30 minutes   Serves: 8 to 10

1¼ cups plus 1 tablespoon flour
2 teaspoons baking powder
¼ teaspoon baking soda
¼ teaspoon salt
2 teaspoons ground cinnamon
¼ teaspoon ground allspice
⅛ teaspoon grated nutmeg
½ cup lightly packed dark
  brown sugar

½ cup granulated sugar
3 eggs, at room temperature
1 stick (4 ounces) unsalted
  butter, at room
  temperature
½ cup vanilla yogurt
1 teaspoon vanilla extract
  Banana Sauce (recipe
  follows)

1. Preheat oven to 350°F. Butter a 6½-cup ring mold very well. Dust with flour; tap out excess.

2. In a small bowl, combine flour, baking powder, baking soda, salt, cinnamon, allspice, and nutmeg. Mix well to blend.

3. In a food processor, combine brown sugar, granulated sugar, and eggs. Process 30 seconds; scrape down sides of bowl. Add butter and process 15 seconds; scrape down bowl. Add yogurt and vanilla. Process 10 seconds. Add flour mixture. Pulse 4 to 6 times, or until flour is mixed in. Transfer batter to prepared baking pan. Spread evenly.

4. Bake 25 to 30 minutes, or until a cake tester comes out clean. Place cake in pan on a rack and let cool 5 minutes. Invert onto rack to unmold. Let cake cool. Serve with warm banana sauce.

349 BANANA SAUCE
Prep: 10 minutes   Cook: 3 minutes   Makes: about 3 cups

Use this warm buttery banana sauce spooned over cake or ice cream. It makes any everyday dessert special.

½ cup packed dark brown
  sugar
4 tablespoons butter
¾ cup fresh orange juice
2 tablespoons fresh lemon
  juice

¼ cup dark rum or brandy
¼ teaspoon ground cinnamon
¼ teaspoon ground allspice
½ teaspoon vanilla extract
3 firm ripe bananas, peeled
  and cut into ¼-inch dice

1. In a medium nonreactive saucepan, place sugar and butter. Cook over medium heat, stirring, until melted together. Add orange juice and lemon juice. Bring to a boil, stirring.

2. Reduce heat to low. Stir in rum, cinnamon, allspice, and vanilla. Add bananas and stir gently to combine. Cook until heated through, about 1 minute. Serve warm.

350 MEXICAN CARAMEL CREPES
Prep: 20 minutes   Cook: 8 minutes   Serves: 6

Just about every restaurant in the country offers *crepas de cajeta* for dessert. *Cajeta*, Mexico's caramel sauce, is available in 16-ounce jars in the Mexican section of most supermarkets. This popular dessert is very sweet. Serve with a scoop of vanilla ice cream next to the crepes.

4 tablespoons unsalted butter	2 cups cajeta or caramel sauce
½ teaspoon cinnamon	½ cup heavy cream
12 Crepes (recipe follows)	1 cup chopped pecans (about 4 ounces)

1. In a large skillet, melt 2 tablespoons butter over low heat. Sprinkle with cinnamon. Warm crepes, 1 at a time, in cinnamon butter about 30 seconds, or until limp. (Add additional butter when needed.) Fold in quarters and place on a platter, overlapping as necessary, and cover with foil to keep warm.

2. Add cajeta and cream to same skillet. Cook over medium heat, stirring, until it boils, about 2 minutes. Reduce heat to low.

3. Spoon about ¼ cup warm caramel cream onto each of 6 dessert plates. Place 2 crepes in center. Drizzle remaining caramel cream over crepes. Sprinkle chopped pecans on top. Serve at once.

351 CREPES
Prep: 2 minutes   Stand: 40 minutes   Cook: 30 to 45 seconds per crepe   Makes: 12

These crepes are used often in both sweet and savory Mexican dishes.

1 cup milk	¼ teaspoon salt
¾ cup flour	1½ tablespoons butter, melted
2 eggs	About ½ teaspoon corn oil

1. In a blender or food processor, combine milk, flour, eggs, and salt. Blend on high speed until completely smooth, about 10 seconds. Add melted butter and blend 8 seconds. Let batter rest at room temperature 40 minutes to 1 hour.

2. Brush a 6- to 7-inch crepe pan or small nonstick skillet with a little oil. Heat over medium heat. Stir batter. Pour a scant ¼ cup batter into pan, grasp handle with a potholder, and immediately tilt and rotate pan so a thin coating of batter covers bottom of pan. Cook until underside is light brown, 20 to 30 seconds. Run a spatula around edge to loosen and turn crepe over. Cook second side 10 to 15 seconds and turn out onto a plate. Repeat baking and stacking crepes between pieces of wax paper as they are cooked. Oil pan again if batter begins to stick. When completely cool, place crepes in a heavy-duty plastic bag and refrigerate up to 3 days or freeze up to 3 months. Let return to room temperature before separating, or the delicate crepes will stick together.

Chapter 14

Tropical Drinks and Coolers

     Huge glass jars containing rainbow-colored drinks are a common sight throughout Mexico. On the streets and in the market they beckon to thirsty customers. The hot, sunny climate, with its vast array of sweet fruits, has resulted in wonderful cool, refreshing drinks called *aguas frescas,* or cool waters —mixtures of blended fruits, water, and ice—and also, *liquados,* which blend fruits with milk, ice, and sugar. Mexicans love their delightful cold sweet beverages and create them in a multitude of flavors. Recipes in this chapter describe how to make these simple drinks.

     Coffee and cocoa beans grow in Mexico, too; so coffee drinks and hot chocolate are very popular beverages. This chapter also contains recipes for a few of the popular spirited drinks, such as margaritas and Planter's Punch, made with tequila and wine, that have become so popular north of the border as well.

352 JAMAICA BLOSSOM COOLER
Prep: 2 minutes   Cook: 3 minutes   Chill: 4 hours   Serves: 4

Jamaica (pronounced *hah-mý-kah*) is a dried reddish-purple hibiscus blossom. The dried flowers are steeped and sweetened to make a traditional cool drink with a bright cranberry color. Jamaica can be purchased in cellophane containers in Mexican markets.

½ cup loose jamaica flowers   ¼ to ½ cup sugar
1 cup boiling water   4 cups cold water

1. In a medium nonreactive saucepan, cook jamaica flowers in 1 cup boiling water 3 minutes. Pour mixture into a large heatproof container. Stir in ¼ cup sugar and 4 cups cold water. Cover and let steep in refrigerator 4 hours.

2. Pour punch through a fine-mesh strainer into a glass pitcher. Add additional sugar, if desired. Serve over ice in tall glasses. Keeps about 4 days refrigerated.

353 BANANA MANGO LIQUADO
Prep: 20 minutes   Cook: none   Chill: 2 hours   Serves: 4 to 6

Fresh fruits blended with milk are often called *liquados* in Mexico. This delicious combination is especially good for breakfast or brunch. Some folks add a jigger of rum to each drink, and that's good, too.

2 large mangoes, peeled and cut into chunks	1½ cups pineapple juice
	1 cup milk
2 ripe bananas, peeled and cut into chunks	1 tablespoon fresh lime juice

In a blender or food processor, combine mangoes, bananas, pineapple juice, milk, and lime juice. Puree until smooth. Transfer to a large glass pitcher or container. Refrigerate until very cold, about 2 hours. Pour into stemmed glasses and serve at once.

354 CANTALOUPE COOLER
Prep: 5 minutes   Cook: none   Chill: 1 hour   Serves: 4

Ripe juicy cantaloupe makes a delightfully refreshing cooler. It is one of the favorites among the array of fresh Mexican fruit drinks.

1 medium cantaloupe	4 sprigs of fresh mint
1 tablespoon lime juice	

1. Peel and seed cantaloupe. Cut into chunks about 2 inches square. Put about half of cantaloupe chunks into a blender or food processor. Add ⅓ cup water and puree until smooth. Pour into a pitcher. Repeat with remaining cantaloupe.

2. Stir in lime juice. Cover and refrigerate until cold, at least 1 hour. Serve in stemmed glasses with a sprig of mint.

355 SPARKLING LIMEADE
Prep: 10 minutes   Cook: none   Serves: 4

Tangy refreshing juices provide a quick lift on a hot afternoon.

5 large limes	⅓ to ½ cup sugar
1 quart club soda	

Squeeze juice from 4 limes. Put juice into a glass pitcher. Cut remaining lime into very thin slices and add to pitcher. Add club soda and sweeten with sugar to taste. Serve in tall glasses with ice cubes.

356 FRESH PINEAPPLE COOLER
Prep: 15 minutes   Cook: none   Chill: 1 hour   Serves: 6

1 ripe pineapple, peeled and cut into chunks	½ cup sugar, or to taste 4 cups water

1. In a blender or food processor, place half of pineapple, sugar, and water. Blend until smooth. Pour into a pitcher. Repeat with remaining ingredients.

2. Refrigerate 1 hour, or until cold. Strain, if desired. Serve in tall glasses.

357 STRAWBERRY COOLER
Prep: 5 minutes   Cook: none   Chill: 1 hour   Serves: 6

4 cups fresh strawberries 2 cups water	½ to ⅔ cup sugar

1. Remove stems and hulls from strawberries. Rinse well.

2. Place 2 cups berries in a blender or food processor. Add 1 cup water and ¼ cup sugar. Puree until smooth. Pour into a pitcher. Repeat with remaining berries, another cup of water, and ¼ cup sugar. Sweeten with additional sugar if needed.

3. Refrigerate 1 hour, or until cold, and serve.

358 SANGRITA
Prep: 15 minutes   Cook: none   Chill: 1 hour   Serves: 4

Sangrita is a nonalcoholic Mexican beverage traditionally served along with straight tequila. Each person has a 1-ounce shot of tequila and a 3- to 4-ounce glass of sangrita to sip alternately, or "pop" the tequila and chase with sangrita.

1 cup freshly squeezed orange juice 2 tablespoons grenadine syrup	½ cup canned tomato juice ½ cup fresh lime juice 4 to 6 dashes of Tabasco, to taste

In a pitcher, mix all ingredients. Cover and refrigerate 1 to 4 hours. Serve alone in small glasses, or with tequila. Keeps a week, covered and refrigerated.

359   MEXICAN HOT CHOCOLATE
Prep: 2 minutes   Cook: 5 minutes   Serves: 4

Thanks to Mexico's gift of chocolate to the world, we can enjoy this special treat often. Just about everyone loves it. Authentic Mexican chocolate tablets contain sugar, cinnamon, and vanilla and can be found in Mexican markets and in the Mexican food section of some supermarkets. They can also be purchased through mail order (see page 9). Each round tablet weighs about 3 ounces.

1½ circular tablets Mexican   4 cups milk
    chocolate, chopped or
    broken up

1. Place chopped chocolate and milk in a medium saucepan. Bring to a boil over medium heat, stirring constantly, until chocolate is melted, about 5 minutes.

2. Beat until frothy with a rotary beater, or a *molinillo* (a Mexican wooden chocolate beater). Pour into mugs and serve immediately.

360   MEXICAN COFFEE
*Prep: 5 minutes   Cook: 3 to 4 minutes   Stand: 5 to 6 minutes
Serves: 4*

Authentic Mexican coffee, *cafe de olla*, is brewed in an earthenware pot with cinnamon, cloves, and the hard, cone-shaped brown sugar called *piloncillo*. The delicious sweet brew is served in clay cups. This slightly simplified version tastes almost the same.

½ cup packed dark brown   1 to 3 whole cloves
    sugar   ¾ cup dark roast coffee,
2 cinnamon sticks   coarsely ground

1. In a medium nonreactive pan, combine brown sugar, cinnamon sticks, and cloves. Add 4 cups water and bring to a boil over medium heat, stirring, until sugar is melted, 3 to 4 minutes.

2. Stir in ground coffee, remove pan from heat, cover, and let steep 5 to 6 minutes.

3. Strain coffee through a coffee filter or fine-mesh sieve into a heatproof coffee server. Serve at once.

361   PLANTER'S PUNCH
Prep: 10 minutes   Cook: none   Serves: 4

Planter's Punch is a popular poolside drink at Mexican resorts. This is an especially tasty version. Serve it icy cold in tall glasses, with straws to sip through. Guava nectar or juice comes in cans or as a frozen concentrate.

2 cups guava juice
½ cup limeade

1 cup dark rum
Mint sprigs

In a glass pitcher or container, mix guava juice, limeade, and rum. Fill each of 4 tall glasses halfway with ice cubes or crushed ice. Pour punch over ice. Add 2 straws to each glass. Garnish each with a sprig of mint. Serve at once.

362   SANGRIA
Prep: 7 minutes   Cook: none   Serves: 6 to 8

The classic red wine punch is great for parties or a warm evening refresher.

1 (750-ml) bottle dry red wine,
    cold
½ cup brandy
3 tablespoons frozen
    lemonade concentrate

½ cup fresh orange juice
1 medium orange, sliced
1 lime, sliced
1 cup club soda

1. In a glass pitcher, mix wine, brandy, lemonade concentrate, and orange juice. Add orange and lime slices. Cover and refrigerate until ready to serve.

2. Just before serving, add club soda and pour into glasses over ice cubes. Garnish each serving with a slice of orange or lime.

363   WHITE SANGRIA
Prep: 15 minutes   Cook: none   Serves: 6

4 cups dry white wine, such as
    Chablis
¾ cup Triple Sec or Cointreau
½ cup sugar
1 orange, sliced

1 lime, sliced
1 lemon, sliced
1½ cups club soda, cold
Sprigs of fresh mint

1. In a large pitcher, mix together wine, Triple Sec, sugar, orange, lime, and lemon slices. Refrigerate until ready to serve, or up to about 6 hours.

2. Before serving, stir in club soda. Pour over ice cubes in 6 stemmed glasses. Garnish with mint.

364   MARGARITAS IN A PITCHER
Prep: 8 minutes   Cook: none   Serves: 6

A frothy pitcher of icy margaritas can really get a party rolling. The beguiling froth on top is achieved with egg white and powdered sugar.

2 cups finely crushed ice	1 tablespoon egg white (about
1 cup tequila	½ an egg white)
½ cup fresh lime juice	1½ tablespoons Triple Sec
¼ cup powdered sugar	6 lime slices

1. To prepare salt-rimmed glasses, rub rims of cocktail glasses with lime juice and invert onto a saucer of coarse salt. Set glasses on a tray in freezer until they are frosty and salt rim sets, about 20 minutes.

2. Shortly before serving, in blender, place crushed ice, tequila, lime juice, powdered sugar, egg white, and Triple Sec. Blend until well mixed and frothy. Transfer to a glass pitcher. Pour prepared margaritas into each glass, garnish with a lime slice, and serve.

365   TEQUILA SUNRISE
Prep: 5 minutes   Cook: none   Serves: 1

Make Tequila Sunrises directly in 8-ounce stemmed glasses for pretty color separation.

2 teaspoons grenadine	2 teaspoons lime juice
1½ ounces tequila	¼ cup strained orange juice,
(3 tablespoons)	fresh or frozen

Fill glass one-third full with crushed ice or ice cubes. Pour grenadine over ice. Without stirring, add tequila, lime juice, and orange juice. Serve at once.

Index

Acknowledgments

To Donna Nordin, a gifted cook, chef, and special friend, who started me on the culinary path by teaching me French basics, and who gave me my first opportunity to teach in her San Francisco cooking school.

To Susan Wyler, my editor, for her guidance and constructive help all through the book project, and for the happy coincidence that caused our paths to cross in the first place.

To Dottye Rinefort and Helen Prince, my recipe testing team, who gave so generously and cheerfully of their time to cook with me, and to Barbara Miller and Sandi Torrey, who stepped in to help when extra hands were needed.

To my husband, Bill, who gives me support, encouragement, and plenty of rope to achieve my personal goals.

To order any of the
365 Ways Cookbooks

visit your local bookseller or call 1-800-321-6890

Our bestselling **365 Ways Cookbooks** are wire-bound to lie flat and have colorful, wipe-clean Kivar® covers.

Each **365 Ways Cookbook** is $17.95 plus $3.50 per copy shipping and handling. Applicable sales tax will be billed to your account. No CODs. Please allow 4–6 weeks for delivery.

> **Please have your VISA, MASTERCARD, or AMERICAN EXPRESS card at hand when calling.**

◆ 365 ◆

Easy Italian Recipes 0-06-016310-0
Easy Low-Calorie Recipes 0-06-016309-7
Easy Mexican Recipes 0-06-016963-X
Easy One-Dish Meals 0-06-016311-9
Great Barbecue & Grilling Recipes 0-06-016224-4
Great Chocolate Desserts 0-06-016537-5
Great Cookies and Brownies 0-06-016840-4
Quick & Easy Microwave Recipes 0-06-016026-8
Snacks, Hors D'Oeuvres & Appetizers 0-06-016536-7
Ways to Cook Chicken 0-06-015539-6
Ways to Cook Fish and Shellfish 0-06-016841-2
Ways to Cook Hamburger & Other Ground Meats
0-06-016535-9
Ways to Cook Pasta 0-06-015865-4
Ways to Prepare for Christmas 0-06-017048-4
Ways to Wok 0-06-016643-6

FORTHCOMING TITLES

Ways to Cook Vegetarian 0-06-016958-3
Easy Chinese Recipes 0-06-016961-3
Great Cakes and Pies 0-06-016959-1
20-Minute Menus 0-06-016962-1
Soups and Stews 0-06-016960-5
Low-Fat Recipes 0-06-017137-5
Household Hints 0-06-017136-7
Ways to Cook Eggs 0-06-017138-3
More Ways to Cook Chicken 0-06-017139-1